T H E

SOUL

S E A R C H

A Spiritual Journey to
Authentic Intimacy
with God

GARY R. COLLINS

OLIVER
NELSON

THOMAS NELSON PUBLISHERS
Nashville

Published in Nashville, Tennessee, by Thomas Nelson, Inc.

Scripture quotations noted NIV are from the HOLY BIBLE: NEW INTERNATIONAL VERSION®. Copyright © 1973, 1978, 1984 by International Bible Society. Used by permission of Zondervan Publishing House. All rights reserved.

Scripture quotations noted NKJV are from THE NEW KING JAMES VERSION. Copyright © 1979, 1980, 1982, Thomas Nelson, Inc., Publishers.

Scripture quotations noted NLT are from the *Holy Bible*, New Living Translation, copyright © 1996. Used by permission of Tyndale House Publishers, Inc., Wheaton, Illinois 60189. All rights reserved.

The material in the "Spiritual Disciplines" table on page 211 is taken from *Disciplines of the Holy Spirit by* Siang-Yang Tan and Douglas H. Gregg. Copyright © 1997 by Siang-Yang Tan and Douglas H. Gregg. Used by permission of Zondervan Publishing House. Available at your local bookstore or by calling 800-727-3480.

Library of Congress Cataloging-in Publication Data

Collins, Gary R.
    The soul search : a spiritual journey to authentic intimacy with God / Gary R. Collins.
        p.   cm.
    Includes bibliographical references and index.
    ISBN 0-7852-7411-1
    1. Spirituality. I. Title.
BV4501.2.C6434   1998
248—dc21   97-49569
                                                                          CIP

Printed in the United States of America.

1 2 3 4 5 6 BVG 03 02 01 00 99 98

To

Kenneth S. Kantzer
scholar, spiritual leader, educator, visionary

who
encouraged me
inspired me
believed in me
mentored me and
was an example to me
when I was a young professor

Contents

Acknowledgments

I can't remember when I first got hooked on books. Long before my teenage years I became an avid reader, and nothing has changed since. I can lose all track of time browsing through the megabookstores near my home, and nothing relaxes me more than to turn on some music, light a log in the fireplace, and curl up with a book.

Over the years, I must have read thousands, but I've noticed that books almost always start in the same way. Someplace, usually near the beginning, each book has a page of acknowledgments, listing the names of people who have helped the author and contributed in some way to the book's production. Even when I don't recognize any of the names, I usually read the acknowledgments. Clearly you do the same. It is good to be reminded that almost no book is written or published alone. Usually a team is involved that includes supporters, encouragers, manuscript evaluators, friends of the author, family members, editors, and other publishing professionals.

I am reluctant to name my team lest I forget someone. Nevertheless, a few people deserve special mention. Victor Oliver read an article about spirituality that I had written and urged me to write this book. I resisted for months but finally relented and got into a massive project that turned out to be exhilarating. After I completed the manuscript, five very busy, knowledgeable, and wonderful friends agreed to read what I had written and give their suggestions for improvements. I knew they wouldn't hesitate to make constructive criticisms or suggestions for improvement, but they all did so in a supportive spirit of gentleness and encouragement. Steve Sandage, Gary Moon, Garry Poole, Steve Erickson, and Jeff Benner have my deepest gratitude for their insights, suggestions, observations and, most of all, their friendship. Lynn McAlister gave her help at the end by preparing the index. Then, as always, there is Julie. She has stood next to me through countless books including this one, has listened with understanding when I have announced (at least once a month during the past thirty years) that I will never write another book, and has been a constant helpmate and encourager. Without her, most of my books would never have been written.

Without you, this book would never be read. Thank you for picking up the volume that you hold in your hands. I hope you find the following pages to be interesting, enlightening, and stimulating as you make your way with me through the maze of modern spirituality.

PART 1

New Spirituality: Looking for God

For most of my life, I have been on a spiritual journey. So have you. So has everyone who lives in this confused and broken world—even those who have no interest in religion or spiritual issues. It is part of the human condition to be restless, aware that something or someone greater than we are exists. Long ago, Augustine observed that we human beings are created for communion with God and are restless until we find rest in him. There is a God-shaped vacuum in every heart, Pascal wrote, a vacuum that we can't fill on our own.

For centuries, people traveled together on their spiritual journeys, most often in the company of others who also were seeking and growing together. Today, especially in the West, more and more people are journeying alone, looking away from organized religion, and seeking to satisfy their deep spiritual hunger by searching for God within themselves. Unlike earlier times, when most spiritual voices pointed us in the same or similar directions, now we have a tidal wave of spiritual guides and gurus, each leading in a different way, each claiming to have answers for the questions about life that reside deep within our souls.

1

In Part 1 of this book we will walk through the spiritual maze that has descended on our land within the past couple of decades. Like a tour guide who directs tourists through unfamiliar country and points out the highlights, I will skim the world of the new spirituality and look at the trends that are exciting spiritual seekers at the start of the twenty-first century. There won't always be time to linger and savor the rich diversity of the current spirituality landscape, but the overview will show what is out there. You can decide whether or not to return later, with other author-guides, for more in-depth experiences.

Like any good tour guide, I must be honest in introducing myself and telling you where we are going. I have not arrived spiritually—nobody has. I am not free of spiritual struggles and uncertainties. Without struggles, nobody grows. I don't have all the answers to spiritual questions, and neither do I have the arrogance to claim that I know the details of what is best for you. Even so, I have been on this earth for more than six decades. I have read hundreds of books relating to spirituality. I have matured spiritually—at least I hope this is true—and I am convinced that I have conclusions to share and things to say that can be helpful. I don't have any need to surprise you with my perspective, so here it is, up front:

I write as a psychologist and counselor. I agree with those who argue that the current interest in spirituality is not a religious or theological interest; it is an outgrowth of psychology, similar to what I have studied all of my adult life.

I write as a respecter of persons. When you reach the last page, I hope this book will have persuaded you to find intimacy with the God described in the later chapters. I want to be convincing, but I am not into manipulating, stimulating guilt, or trying to force anybody to think as I think.

I write as a Christian. If you are not a Christian, my perspective should not be a reason for you to lay aside this book. I am saddened by the many spirituality seekers who genuinely claim to be tolerant and who want to be tolerant, but who are intolerant of anything Christian. This book is written with nonbelievers in mind even as it is intended to be helpful to followers of Christ.

This book is about spiritual growth and formation, including yours. To start, we need to get the lay of the land—seeking to make sense of what has become a giant spirituality puzzle. That is where we start in Chapter 1.

— 1 —

The Soul of the Spirituality Puzzle:
Why Are We So Fascinated with Spirituality and the Soul?

A new spirituality is engulfing the world and invading our lives with lightning speed. It attracts teenagers and business executives, physicians and psychologists, academics and homemakers, feminists and worshipers in traditional churches. It impacts the publishing industry, challenges traditional medicine, glides over the Internet, shapes the productions of Hollywood, influences big business, molds the work of therapists, dances across the screens of our television sets, and seeps into the lives of people in every size community and at every level of society. It has been called a new awakening unprecedented in modern times, a spiritual flowering that has overtaken the land. It is an unconventional and revolutionary movement that is changing psychiatry, education, government, health care, and thousands of churches. It touches almost everybody, even those who have no awareness that the new spirituality exists. Without doubt it has affected you.

The new spirituality, like the New Age movement from which it arose, has no central organization, no dominant leader, no commonly accepted creed. There is no evidence that it arises from a universal conspiracy, masterminded by demon-controlled manipulators, intent on deceiving innocent people and destroying the world. Instead, the new spirituality is a popular, grass-roots movement of epic proportions. It is strong and growing stronger, grabbing the attention of thousands with its recognition of individual needs, its focus on personal experiences, and its willingness to let people go on their own spiritual journeys without having to worry about religious rituals, rules, or creeds.

Rita McClain is a new spirituality seeker. According to *Newsweek,* where her story first appeared, McClain grew up in a pentecostal church, and she remembers tent meetings with fiery preachers who made her feel guilty.[1] Reaching adulthood, she moved to more traditional Protestant churches, but they, too, left her empty and dissatisfied. In time, she rejected the church altogether and spent almost twenty years seeking inner peace through nature, mountain climbing, and hiking in the desert.

An emotionally draining divorce brought McClain back to more organized religion. She started with Unity, a metaphysical church that she found to be "light years away from 'the Old Testament kind of thing I knew very well from my childhood.'" Next she experienced Native American spiritual practices, and then moved on to Buddhism at the Spirit Rock Meditation Center near her home. All of that merged eventually into a personal religion that centers on an ever-changing altar that McClain—now in her fifties—has created in her home. At last report, the altar consisted of an angel statue, a small bottle of "sacred water" blessed at a women's vigil, a crystal ball, a brass image of Buddha sitting on a leaf, a candle, a pyramid, a Hebrew prayer, a tiny Native American basket, and a picture of her "most sacred place," a madrona tree near her home.

Newsweek acknowledged that McClain's spiritual journey is unusual and "extreme," but she represents a generation of seekers. They fit no particular profile, the magazine asserted: "They include Wall Street investment bankers who spend their lunch hours in Bible-study groups, artists rediscovering religious themes, fitness addicts who've traded aerobics classes for meditation and other spiritual exercises. No matter what path they take the seekers are united by a sincere desire to find answers to profound questions, to understand their place in the cosmos." We are a nation searching for spiritual meaning, according to *Newsweek. "Millions of Americans are embarking on a search for the sacred in their lives."*[2] Millions are talking about the soul and thinking about their spiritual pilgrimages.

SOUL JOURNEY

Looking back, I can see that my life has been a spiritual journey—a soul journey with ups and downs, with periods of intense religious fervor mixed with times of spiritual lethargy. On some of the journey I have felt God walking with me like an intimate friend, seemingly close enough to touch. And I have passed through long wilderness experiences of spiritual dryness, afraid that I had been forgotten, wondering if God had turned from me, shut his ears to my impassioned pleas, left me to journey on my own.

During this life pilgrimage, it's been comforting to discover that I'm not traveling alone. Every other member of the human race is on a spiritual journey with me. I'd expected to find Billy Graham on the journey. We all know that Mother Teresa was there, as are the archbishop of Canterbury, the latest ayatollah in Iran, and even some of those much-maligned television evangelists. But you are on a spiritual journey as well. You may be part of the rare group whose journeys have been smooth and without much challenge or frustration. More likely, you have struggled with the journey all of your life. Or maybe you have reached this page of the book and recognized that until now, you haven't given five minutes of thought to the journey. Even so, you have been journeying, sometimes oblivious to matters of the soul, at other times engulfed in a search for the sacred. This book is about the spiritual journeys that we all take. It is about your spiritual journey, and sometimes about mine.

More than a century ago, in 1858 to be exact, a Scottish preacher wrote a fanciful novel for adults titled *Phantases*. The author, George MacDonald, eventually achieved some success as a writer, but his *Phantases* book fell flat. It attracted so little interest that the publisher was reluctant to issue any more of the novelist's works.

Seventy years later, a teenager purchased a used copy of *Phantases* in an English railroad station. The teenager's family had attended an Anglican church that lacked passion or zeal, and when his mother died, the young man began to doubt the goodness and even the existence of God. He crossed the line into atheism with the help of an influential schoolteacher who taught students to think logically and question everything rationally. Later, as a young adult, the Englishman decided to apply the same rigorous logic to the various spiritual alternatives that he encountered. After concluding that theism made the best sense, he became a dedicated follower of Christ. Looking back on that part of his spiritual journey, the Englishman—whose name was C. S. Lewis—concluded that a major influence on his conversion had been the impact of that used copy of *Phantases,* the novel written by a Scottish minister who must have thought his book was a failure when it didn't sell.

It is well known that Lewis also became a writer. A respected teacher at Oxford and later at Cambridge, he wrote a number of novels and several Christian works. One of the best known followed his marriage to an American poet named Joy Davidson. Lewis was a confirmed bachelor who surprised everyone when he married, but the marriage didn't last long. After four intensely happy years, Lewis watched helplessly as his beloved wife died of cancer. To cope with his grief and defend against a loss of faith in God, he wrote a journal that later was published as a short book with the title *A Grief Observed*.[3]

In the midst of his grief, Lewis wondered what had happened to God. "This is one of the most disquieting symptoms," he wrote.

> When you are happy, so happy that you have no sense of need-ing Him, so happy that you are tempted to feel His claims upon you as an interruption, if you remember yourself and turn to Him with gratitude and praise, you will be—or so it feels—welcomed with open arms. But go to Him when your need is desperate, when all other help is vain, and what do you find? A door slammed in your face, and a sound of bolting and double bolting inside. After that, silence. . . . Why is He so present a commander in our time of prosperity and so very absent a help in time of trouble?[4]

A more recent writer had a similar question. An effective speaker and motivator, Alan Nelson earned degrees in commu-nication and psychology and spent hundreds of hours develop-ing a personal growth seminar. It began with a bang but faded quickly. Speaking engagements were canceled, and the young man, a visionary with a master's degree, found himself folding sweaters in the men's section of a department store. He felt alone in a wilderness, abandoned by God. It was the worst year of his life, but after a lot of prayerful reflection, he and his wife decided to start a church in southern California. Nelson concluded that his congregation would be one of the hottest new churches in Orange County. Everything started gloriously. Attendance went up quickly, the people in the infant church were enthusiastic, and the pastor gave the project everything he had. Then he burned out in exhaustion and depression.

We are a people who value productivity, Nelson wrote later. We go to seminars, read books, and strive to achieve, produce, and accomplish goals: "The common result is that we are human thinkings and human doings, but God has called us to be human beings. . . . Some of the highest-paid people in the world are those who can hit, run, pass, catch, and throw better than anyone else. . . .

But unlike past societies, which emphasized the development of the soul, we keep soul expansion to a minimum."[5]

I can see myself in all of these stories, and so perhaps can you. It is easy to work on a project, as MacDonald worked on his book, and feel like a failure. All of us, at times, are like C. S. Lewis, who in his grief wondered if he had been cut off from God. Who among us has not striven to reach a goal only to feel as if we have been abandoned by God and left to fend for ourselves in a wilderness? But in this hyperactive, achievement-oriented society, we don't cope well with failure or wilderness experiences. We struggle to keep everything in life under control. We scurry incessantly to get things done. We fill our days with so many things to do that we have little time to think about God, to reflect on our spiritual journeys, or to ponder how we have neglected the soul.

SOUL GURU

This kind of thinking must have been in the mind of Thomas Moore when he wrote *Care of the Soul*.[6] The book spent eight months on the *New York Times* hardcover best-seller list and was acclaimed for several years as a popular paperback. Across the country and around the world, readers were grabbed by the first sentence in Moore's book: "The greatest malady of the twentieth century, implicated in all of our troubles and affecting us individually and socially, is 'loss of soul.'" When the soul is neglected, Moore wrote, we experience obsessions, addictions, violence, loss of meaning, and emotional pain. By caring for the soul, we can find relief from our distress and discover deep satisfaction and pleasure in life.[7]

Thomas Moore "struck a national nerve" with his book, suggested the *Dallas Morning News*. One reviewer wrote that Moore's book could "help you give up the futile quest for salvation and get down to the possible task of taking care of your soul." Another wrote that the "book's got strength and class and soul, and I suspect may last longer than psychology itself." Moore is vague about what he means by *soul*, but his message to readers is clear:

learn to accept yourself, realize that you are not perfect, give up struggling to rid your existence of all its problems, stop trying to improve yourself, and quit worrying about whether things will turn out right. Moore calls himself an "anti-self-help advocate" and tries to separate his views from pop psychology, but his perspectives on "soulful living" deal with the same needs and spiritual hunger that other popular writers address.

Raised as a Catholic and trained as a psychotherapist, Moore concluded that many people hunger for some kind of spiritual life. They are frustrated with traditional religion and don't like being told how to live and what to do: "So they're turning away from institutions and looking, yearning, for anything—gurus, experts, the latest book."[8] Aware that something is missing in their lives and marriages, many turn to writers like Thomas Moore who, more than anyone else, has made the soul a part of the new search for the sacred.

Moore is convinced that widespread preoccupation with reason and material progress has robbed our lives of excitement and taken away our appreciation for fantasy. In place of this, he believes that our spiritual lives should be richer in imagination and based on our personal preferences, visions, and tastes. This is a build-your-own spirituality that overlooks the problems that come to people who live lives of fantasy and refuse to face reality. It is a self-focused spirituality that bypasses troubling subjects such as sin, evil, and confession and has little emphasis on resisting injustice or serving the needs of others. Moore advocates a nontraditional, nondemanding spirituality that attracts thousands of adherents but is challenged by critics who call it "misguided," "artificial," and "spirituality lite."[9]

When I first worked in a counseling clinic, nobody had heard of Thomas Moore, and nobody talked about the soul. Later, when I was teaching seminary students, they thought *soul* was an old-fashioned term, not easy to define and of limited use in helping people with their problems. The word was never mentioned at professional conferences, and I don't remember hearing much about it in sermons. Then almost overnight the soul became a hot topic in the media, bookstores, campus classrooms, seminars, and counseling rooms. One recent convention for therapists held seminars entitled "Shapes of the Soul" and "Nourishing the Soul Through Exceptional Physical Healing." People everywhere seem to be enamored with soul talk.

I struggled with all of this when the magazine I edit published an entire issue on soul care.[10] Could this soul fascination be dismissed as another therapeutic fad or floundering New Age craze? I wondered. In an era of managed care, galloping change, and people with pressing problems, few of us have been inclined to give much attention to the soul—at least until Moore's books appeared. But *soul* is a biblical term used by Jesus and long assumed to be part of the Christian faith. Has the word now been hijacked by contemporary humanistic thinkers, stripped of its biblical and historical significance, redefined in therapeutic terminology, and dished up like chicken soup to replace the quick-fix, self-help remedies that have prevailed in recent years? To answer these questions, to understand why there is new interest in the soul, to focus more clearly on our spiritual journeys and our lives, we need to take a brief digression to look at what we know about worldviews.

LIVING IN FOUR WORLDS

A worldview is a set of often unquestioned assumptions that each of us holds and that help us make sense of life. A person's worldview determines how he or she thinks about human nature, marriage, emotional problems, right and wrong, religion, spirituality, or the validity of any political philosophy. We live in the midst of four worldviews.

The oldest of these, at least in the West, is the *Judeo-Christian* worldview. It assumes that a sovereign and all-powerful God exists, is alive, and knows about the affairs of individual human beings. This God created us and the universe in which we live. He reveals himself to us through his Son, his Word, and the guidance of the Holy Spirit. He has given us moral attributes, made us aware of the conflict between good and evil, and provided a way of forgiveness, salvation, and abundant living. This is a worldview on which churches are built, a worldview at the basis of innumerable spiritual journeys. It's also a worldview that many—probably most—spiritual seekers have chosen to leave behind.

The *secular-humanistic-enlightenment* worldview elevates human reason above divine revelation. Human beings replace God as the controllers of events, the determiners of morality, and the sources of truth. Science and human achievement are revered; worship and obedience to God are assumed to be irrelevant. Demons, angels, or other supernatural beings are dismissed as historical fictions. Biblical miracles are explained away scientifically and rationally. At least until recently, this worldview has formed the basis of education, science, technology, and health care. It is the worldview of modernism.

The *New Age–postmodern* worldview is a more recent addition to the West, although as we will see, it builds on centuries of Eastern philosophy. This worldview has been described as "an alternative religious paradigm that is rooted in Eastern mysticism, eclectic in its practices and beliefs, tolerant (or undiscerning, depending upon one's perspective) of nontraditional practices and beliefs, and optimistic about humanity's capacity to bring about a great evolutionary leap in consciousness."[11] This worldview tends to be pantheistic, to see god within, and to give each person the freedom to determine his or her beliefs, views of truth, ethical standards, and moral practices. Rational thought is shunned, and people are free to find fulfillment and enlightenment by looking inside. Most of the new spirituality is built on this foundation.

As international communication becomes easier, travel is more common, and networks like CNN continue to make their impact, we can see more clearly that every one of us also has a *cultural* worldview. This fourth worldview overlaps the others. In growing up, each person learns the rituals, customs, values, standards, holiday traditions, and other ways of thinking and doing things that are viewed as common sense. If we grow up, live, and work in a community surrounded by people who pretty much are all alike, we might not notice how culture has shaped our views of marriage, religion, funerals, sports, business practices, politicians, sickness, success, Christmas celebrations, patriotism, or a host of other issues. These cultural values differ from country to country and often from one community or part of a country to another.

Worldviews are not tightly organized and carefully defined ways of thinking. Each is diverse. Consider the different theological perspectives and denominations within the Judeo-Christian-biblical worldview as an example. Each worldview can be critical of the others. Each influences our lifestyles and views of life and death. Each has general perspectives on mental illness, behavior change, interpersonal relations, values, and ways to deal with guilt or bring wholeness. And each has views of the soul that can have practical implications for the way we live.

If you participate in a church worship service or listen to a sermon, you are in the midst of Judeo-Christian-biblical thinking. We might call this worldview one. Some people leave this behind when they leave the church on a Sunday morning, but others carry this perspective into their daily activities during the week. Depending on the level of commitment, knowledge, and devotion, many followers of Jesus Christ seek to live their lives and make their decisions in ways that are consistent with the truths of biblical Christianity. The word *soul* might not be used often in worldview one, but Christians know that it's a biblical term having something to do with who we are as individuals created by God.

When you went to school, probably you were taught in accordance with worldview two: the secular-humanistic-enlightenment view of life. To survive and get our diplomas, some of us who are Christians had to push our Judeo-Christian worldview to the back of our minds while we learned about secular theories and thinking. Religion was mentioned rarely (if at all) in these classrooms, and nobody talked about the soul.

Now we are faced with the increasing popularity of worldview three, New Age–new spirituality perspectives. As a counselor, I have gone to conferences and listened to discussions where people with secular-humanistic (worldview two) training struggle to understand or communicate with proponents of therapy based on worldview three. The same lack of understanding comes when people who live according to worldview one or two try to understand why anybody would seriously embrace the new spirituality of worldview three. And all of this is more complex when we try to communicate across cultures, bringing us into contact with worldview four.

People with worldviews one and two also have difficulty understanding a worldview three author like Thomas Moore, who writes a best-seller about the soul but refuses to define the soul and claims that nobody else can define it, either. We "all know intuitively that the soul has to do with genuineness and depth, as when we say certain music has soul or a remarkable person is soulful,"[12] Moore writes. He states that soul is "not specifically Christian" and adds that soul is revealed in attachment, love, and community. Moore has made the words *soul* and *soul care* very popular, but he defines them so broadly and vaguely that they mean almost nothing apart from one's intuition.

WHAT, THEN, IS THE SOUL?

Obviously the soul is not something tangible like a foot or an arm that can be seen and felt. It cannot be weighed, held in the hands, seen on a computer screen, or analyzed chemically. The soul is mentioned in Scripture, but the biblical writers didn't worry about giving concise, technical definitions of words like *heart, mind,* and *soul.* Even so, despite its many connotations, the word *soul* appears to have two distinct meanings in the Bible. *Soul* refers to one's life and to one's personality.[13]

In the Old Testament, we read that the soul (life) of a dying person departed at death (Gen. 35:18), and when a dead child was revived, his or her soul (life) returned (1 Kings 17:19–23). In Mark 8:35–37, the Greek word for *soul* is translated "life." Jesus stated, "For whoever wants to save his life [soul] will lose it, but whoever loses his life [soul] for me and for the gospel will save it. What good is it for a man to gain the whole world, yet forfeit his soul?" (NIV).

The word *soul* also refers to the inner self or personality. When God created Adam, he became a living soul (Gen. 2:7)—a personality distinct from all the animals. In Luke 1:46, Mary sang about her soul (inner self) magnifying the Lord, and in Matthew 26:38, Jesus indicated that his soul was sorrowful.

Think of your soul, then, as the core of your inner life and personality. The whole new spirituality movement is about the soul. So, too, is the nature of the spiritual journey that is a part of your life, whether or not you give it much thought.

THINGS THAT WE DON'T WANT AND THINGS THAT WE WANT

I can understand people whose spiritual journeys have taken them away from the church and into speculations about the soul. I didn't go their route—I have stayed in the church—but I see things in some of my fellow Christians that I don't want in my life. I don't want a spirituality that is rigid, dominated by rules, narrow-minded, intolerant, and irrelevant. I don't want a religion that is sour, lacking in joy, and dowdy. I'm willing and often eager to make commitments and to change my lifestyle so that I can be more like Christ, but I don't want to feel as if my faith is so confining that I can't be creative and able to blossom. I don't want a spirituality that makes me turn off my mind, stifle my desire to ask questions, and become like a zombie with no firm beliefs and no encouragement to think. I like religious experiences and appreciate spiritual enthusiasm, but I'm uncomfortable with out-of-control emotionalism and I shun any spirituality that seems to have no grounding in divine revelation, community belonging, or rational thought. I don't want a spirituality that lets somebody else manipulate me or that encourages me to manipulate others. And to be honest, I know my weaknesses well enough that I don't want a spirituality that depends solely on me, on my preferences or fantasies, and on my ability to find enlightenment within.

Like other Christians, I get concerned about immorality, insincerity, hypocrisy, and dishonesty in the church, and I am especially distressed when I see any of these elements in church leaders. I believe in high standards of morality and behavior, but I am deeply troubled when I see bitterness in the church and an unwillingness to forgive when somebody falls. I am enough of a psychologist to know that some churches and other religious bodies are pathological, sometimes led by insecure and domineering leaders, entrenched in the unhealthy attitudes and behaviors that have been called *toxic faith*.[14] I believe the Christian life is meant to be better than that.

Often it is better. I have looked at fellow believers who have consistent joyfulness and healthy enthusiasm about their walks with God. I have seen people who have a deep appreciation for their churches, who remain serene in the face of pain and disappointment, who never seem to struggle with doubt or encounter the temptations that I face. I don't know what goes on in their minds and souls, of course, but they seem to have serenity and apparent maturity that I would like to have.

Sometimes when I think about this, I wonder if these spiritual giants are real. Are they out of contact with reality? Are they putting on a mask? This may be true of some, but I know many who have genuine joy in their spiritual journeys. Most of these people are older—older than I am, but when I look at myself, I see encouraging tendencies that lead me to think that I, too, am moving toward a better spirituality.

When we see others who are spiritually alive, it is easy to blame ourselves for not being like them, to wonder if the church or some spiritual leader has failed us, to think that God has let us down. But true spirituality comes as the result of a slow and sometimes uneven maturing. It isn't a fast-track experience. It doesn't come with consumer-driven seminars and repetitious revival meetings. Almost always it has periods of discouragement—like those George MacDonald must have felt when *Phantases* didn't sell as his publisher had hoped. True spirituality and soul development sometimes grow through periods of grief like what C. S. Lewis experienced. At times there are failures like that of the man in California whose seminar program collapsed and whose energy evaporated in the midst of his hyperactivity before he could write a book about the soul.

The Bible is filled with other examples. Moses waited in the wilderness for years before he met God at a burning bush and began a spiritual ministry. Joseph spent a long time in prison and even longer away from his family before he clearly saw God working in his life. David was anointed king but then spent years running from Saul without any opportunity to ascend the throne that had been promised. Paul waited three years after his conversion before he had a ministry, and some of his most productive times were interrupted by arrests and lonely confinements to prison. All of those people were molded through adversity and times in the spiritual wilderness. At times, probably each of them felt cut off from God.

CUT OFF FROM GOD

Several of my friends feel as if they are in the wilderness. One has been there for several years. He wants to grow spiritually, to serve God faithfully, to have an impact nationally, but every one of his creative efforts seems to have hit a dead end. He has training, ability, determination, and enthusiasm, but nothing seems to be going his way. He is a Christian who understands when I remind him about Moses and Joseph and David and Paul, who spent years waiting. But my friend is impatient and anxious to get growing, spiritually and professionally.

I can appreciate his struggles and frustrations. I have been there and probably will be there again. There were years, at the prime of my life and energy, when I felt as if my career had come grinding to a halt. I still had a job but wasn't enthusiastic about what I was doing. I continued writing and even finished some books, but like MacDonald's *Phantases,* they didn't make much of an impact, at least in terms of prominence or sales. I went to church and spent a little time every day in prayer and Bible study, but I was bored in the worship services and didn't feel that much was happening in my life spiritually. After a while I began to wonder if God had forgotten me. I knew in my heart that wasn't true, but I felt cut off from God.

One day I pulled out a piece of paper and started listing times and situations when people like me *feel* cut off from God. We might believe that he still is aware of our struggles and circumstances, but haven't we all felt spiritually empty and cut off when we face disruptive circumstances, unexpected crises, or difficult people? At other times our own attitudes, values, actions, goals, or self-centered passions get in the way of a spiritual closeness with God. If you are like me, you feel cut off from God and spiritually flat when one or more of the following hurdles impede your spiritual journey.

We feel cut off from God when there are self-created, self-centered obstacles that hinder our spiritual progress. Sometimes when I feel cut off from God, I know that I'm the one to blame. It is hard to feel close to God if we have deliberately done something wrong. Do you remember the story of Jonah? He deliberately refused to do what God wanted, and his attempt to escape by way of the sea led to a Mediterranean cruise in the belly of a giant fish.

King David wrote some of the most moving psalms in the Old Testament after his adulterous relationship with Bathsheba and his attempts to hide the affair by arranging for the murder of Bathsheba's husband, Uriah.[15] The king felt a lot of guilt and knew that he had disobeyed and disappointed God. In the midst of his sinfulness, David felt cut off from God.

David's predecessor, King Saul, had a similar experience. He started his reign with supernatural power, but he got self-centered and cut off from God. King Solomon, who came to the throne after David, also started strong, but his self-indulgence and self-sufficiency ruined his relationship with God. Things haven't changed over the centuries. Immorality, actions that harm others, self-centered attitudes, self-indulgence, and self-sufficiency all get in the way of genuine spirituality. To use some old language, sin separates us from God.

As the new spirituality reminds us, *we feel cut off from God when we are involved in unhealthy and unbalanced religion.* In the New Testament book of James, the writer described the hypocrisy and emptiness of a spirituality that is self-centered and based on words, but doesn't show itself in compassionate action. In Jesus' day the Pharisees were like that. They loved to walk about looking pious, hoping that other people would notice. Jesus called them "whitewashed tombs" who looked lily-white on the outside but were corrupt and empty within.[16] We all know people who are overly committed to their churches or religions but whose lives are out of balance and spiritually empty.

When I began teaching in a seminary, I expected to encounter young spiritual giants who were growing by leaps and bounds in their spiritual journeys. More often I found dedicated people who were theologically overfed and inclined toward spiritual lethargy. The students were driven by their push for grades and so concerned about the next test or term paper that they had little time for personal spirituality. Those men and women were sincere in their desire to study about God, but there didn't seem to be much growth toward God. They were tadpole Christians—all head and not much else. Their theology might have been valid, but their lives were out of balance. I struggle with these issues more than I care to admit. It can be stimulating to read and talk about spiritual things without much substance getting into our lives. Soon we recognize that our spirituality is lopsided, and we feel cut off from closeness with God.

We feel cut off from God when we are uninformed or ignorant. The Bible tells the story about an official from Ethiopia who was very devout but lacked clear knowledge of spiritual things. One day he was riding in his chariot, reading the words of the prophet Isaiah but with no understanding of what the words meant because nobody had explained their meaning.[17] Most of us can relate to this man. I don't understand many things in the Bible and in life.

Sometimes my lack of knowledge leaves me feeling confused, isolated, and wondering if God has left me in the dark.

We feel cut off from God when we're too busy or caught up in our work and other activities. Several years ago I wrote a little booklet titled *Relax and Live Longer.* My friends laugh whenever somebody finds one of these publications today because nobody sees me as being very relaxed. I'm working to change this, but often I feel like Martha who apparently was a very busy woman. When Jesus came for a visit, Martha was distracted by all the preparations that had to be made, but her sister sat listening to what the visitor said. Martha was annoyed about being left with all the work, but when she mentioned that to Jesus, he gently rebuked her. "Martha, Martha," he said, "you are worried and troubled about many things." Because of her busy activities, she was also cut off from the theological seminar in her living room and from closeness to the Lord, who was teaching.[18]

Christians may disagree with some practices of the new spirituality, but the dedication of these seekers can be admirable even as it is unsettling. Each of us can have a genuine interest in spiritual things but be too busy to pray, to reflect, to worship, to take the time to seek God. People in busy jobs—including homemakers, individuals who care for little children or sick loved ones, and people in leadership, including spiritual leadership—encounter this problem repeatedly. We even can be focused on our families or church activities, doing things that are admirable and good. But in the midst of the rush, God gets left out of our lives, and eventually we feel that he is far away. I have a friend who joined the pastoral staff of a large church and began his ministry by asking one of the spiritual leaders for advice. The answer was concise and profound, stated in only six words: "Ruthlessly eliminate hurry from your life."[19]

One of my favorite spirituality writers has been a priest-psychologist named Henri Nouwen. At one point in his life Nouwen retreated from all of his busy activity, went to a monastery for several months, and reflected on his life. "How can I really develop a deep prayer life when I am back again at my busy work?" he asked his spiritual adviser one day. "As long as I remain surrounded by unfinished tasks, my prayer is nearly impossible since I use the time for prayer to wonder about the many things I still have to do. It always seems that there is something more urgent and more important than prayer." At another time he decided to read about prayer and got so involved in his study that he almost stopped praying. When he did pray, he couldn't concentrate because he felt drawn to the ideas that he had been discovering.[20] Busy minds and lives have difficulty really connecting with God and not feeling cut off.

Sometimes, *we feel cut off from God when our emotions are especially strong*. Everybody knows about Adam and Eve. After they had been disobedient in the garden, they hid from God because they were afraid and ashamed. Years later, Elijah felt cut off when he was burned out and depressed. Peter must have felt rejected and expected to be cut off after he denied Jesus, then plunged into guilt and remorse. C. S. Lewis felt alone in his sadness and grief after Joy died. I can feel cut off from God if I am lonely, criticized unfairly, or inclined to be critical of others.

Experiences like these can push any of us to look more carefully at our spiritual journeys and resources. It may be fun and exhilarating to explore the new spirituality landscapes when life is free of crises, but what happens when a parent dies? What happens if we are faced with a life-threatening illness? Where do we find inner strength when a marriage collapses? How does the new spirituality hold up when we look for something to provide comfort, give reassurance, or instill solid hope? Will the crises and emotional turmoil in our lives draw us closer to God, or will they nudge us to withdraw in anger or bitterness? After he was vomited up on the beach by the big fish, Jonah sulked in disgust because God showed compassion to the people of Nineveh. Does your spirituality, or mine, lead to sulking, self-pity, or anger?

Other life experiences also leave us feeling cut off from God. Get involved in occult activities and you are sure to feel alienated from God.[21] Merge with the culture so that your lifestyle is indistinguishable from people with no spiritual interests, and eventually you will feel isolated from your Creator. The same is true if you allow yourself to be distracted by materialism or the pursuit of pleasure, get addicted to drugs or alcohol, or become isolated from others who could give you spiritual encouragement.

If we look at these obstacles, it is easy to see why so many people feel that God is far away and that something is missing from the core of their lives, from their souls.

ROOTLESS AND WITHOUT RELIGION

After opening our presents one Christmas morning, I wandered down the driveway to pick up the newspaper. The front page barely mentioned the holiday. It had articles about football and politics, but most of the space was devoted to the headline story titled "America, the Rootless."[22] When the much-quoted French historian Alexis de Tocqueville wrote about America in its early days, he described it as a country of joiners who banded together to build communities and strengthen each other's lives. Today, said the newspaper, we are becoming a nation of strangers who are characterized by isolation and disconnection. We shop and work miles from where we live. We drive from place to place on crowded roadways, cocoon in our houses at night, and build one-way emotional attachments with the faces on our television screens. We hardly know any of our neighbors but build sometimes-intimate relationships with strangers on the Internet whom we will never meet face-to-face.

This increasing isolation has been linked with a century-long withdrawal from religion. There are notable exceptions, of course. Some of us are involved with churches where the worship is contagious and the people are connected and friendly, even with strangers. But beyond the sanctuary walls, out in our communities, many people don't know about these religious places, and most would feel uncomfortable entering unfamiliar church buildings. More are familiar with the half-empty, seemingly irrelevant, tired churches scattered on street corners across the land, ministering to the faithful but having little impact on their neighborhoods or on the generations that now dominate our society. The people of Generation X and the baby boomers are assuming major roles and responsibilities throughout the society, but they have brought along their lifelong commitment to a "religionless age." Slowly God has been shunted aside, cynicism and distrust of others have emerged as part of their lifestyles, and morals have become relative, leaving vulgarity and violence to run rampant. Many of our lives have no secure anchors and our souls have become rootless. The result is a nation of lonely people described best by one word: *empty*.[23]

"The empty self is soothed . . . by becoming 'filled up' with food, consumer products, and celebrities," suggests a California psychologist.[24] Two professions cater to this emptiness, advertising and psychotherapy. Both embrace a lifestyle solution, encouraging people to fill the empty self with things, gossip, idealized public figures, and promises of security. Too often the sincere advertisers and professional helpers are joined by exploitative therapists, politicians, marketers, and spirituality leaders offering products and solutions that cause harm and lead many astray.

Having rejected God and traditional religion, too many people search for a new connectedness and fulfillment. Science, technology, and rationalism are assumed to hold no hope, so millions of empty people try to get beyond their separateness by looking to new spiritualities and gurus who offer encouragement and enlightenment in vague tales about the soul. By trying to connect with a cosmic whole, with angels or aliens, with nature, or with all other creatures and things, people gain a feeling of oneness that gets them beyond their feelings of rootlessness—at least for a while. Even in the church, many people feel cut off from God so they, too, dabble in the promises of new spirituality and innocently bring these soul cures in through the doors of the church.

It would be easy perhaps for a Christian like me to ignore all of this searching, to rest secure in my spirituality, and to huddle with fellow believers isolated from "the world." But Jesus never hid from his culture; neither did Paul and the apostles, the Old Testament prophets, or most other spiritually sensitive people in the Bible or in history. I might strongly disagree with many of the spiritual directions taken by people in the world where I live, but these people are not my enemies. I am not in a culture war with them; I don't want to fight with people who are searching. But I do want to understand why so many take the journeys they do. When we have this understanding, we can move more freely to find a spirituality that genuinely fills the soul. We can make our way through the myriad of spirituality alternatives and find a spiritual pathway that is fulfilling, genuinely satisfying, and anchored in something or someone bigger than ourselves.

— 2 —

The Pieces of the Spirituality Puzzle:

What Are We Searching For?

When I was a young psychologist, taking classes at the university and getting started in my profession, almost nobody talked about religion. Words like *spirituality* and *soul* were never mentioned, religious experience was ignored, and we were not encouraged to ask our clients about the impact of religion in their lives. One time when I talked with a psychiatric patient about sin, my supervisor reprimanded me. "If a patient talks about sin, never take it seriously," I was told in no uncertain terms. "Sin is an outdated idea that contributes to pathology and has no place in treatment."

I struggled with this thinking in the early stages of my career. Spirituality had been at the core of my upbringing and had never left me as I made my way through the teenage years, the challenges of young adulthood, and the mazes of higher education. I don't know if my parents took me to church when I was a baby and left me in the church nursery with the other kids, but I started attending Sunday school at a very early age. When I reached ado-lescence, I slammed into the most emotionally wrenching time of my life and got through only because a church youth group gave me acceptance and stability without anyone knowing the des-peration that I felt inside. Entrance into the university gave me a new lease on life, let me meet new friends, and led to needed heal-ing. I joined a reserve navy program and learned that I could succeed very well in a male environment despite the athletic incompetence that had alienated me from so many of my peers in high school.

Life in the navy also forced me to make important decisions about my spirituality. Far away from home where there were no parents and church people watching, would I skip church, drink with the guys, and use their gutter language? Or would I stay true to my religious convictions and lifestyle, determined to shine as a light in the darkness of military life? I chose to take the higher road, to grow as a believer, to resist the debaucheries surround-ing me, to be as competent as possible in my military career, and to get along as best I could with my colleagues in uniform. The spiritual struggles and emotional insecurities of my teenage years gave way to one of the most fulfilling times of my life.

In graduate school I encountered the criticisms of religion that came from the books in our psychology library and the lips of our psychology professors. I tried to understand the antispirituality sentiments and sought to analyze and refute them, at least in my mind. Along with my busy life as a student, I kept active in a lit-tle campus church and led a weekly Bible class for undergradu-ates. Later, with my degree in hand, I taught psychology at a Christian college, began to build a Christian marriage, and joined my wife in providing a Christian home for our two little girls. In all of this, I never bought into the arguments of Freud that religion was only an illusion to pacify and support weak-kneed people who would abandon their spiritual crutches as they matured and grew stronger. I thought then, as I am convinced now, that healthy religion can be a powerful source of strength in life; that one's spiritual perspective can be the basis for effective counseling and permanent "soul healing."[1]

CAFETERIA-STYLE RELIGION

Today, some psychologists, psychiatrists, and other therapists ignore, dismiss, or resist religion and other spiritual issues. They still don't like to talk about sin. Others—their numbers are increasing—enthusiastically embrace the emerging trends in spirituality. I see this in the magazines and conference brochures that appear in my mailbox, bringing promises of spiritual enlightenment through therapy. One announces a conference on nourishing the body, soul, and mind. I am told that by attending, I can be refreshed with music, shared ritual, and play. I read that conference participants will be stimulated by the thoughts and actions of leading edge visionaries conducting seminars with titles like "Therapeutic Use of Light and Color as a Window to the Soul," "Self-Healing Through Bioenergetics," and a workshop on "Sacred Earth, Sacred Body, Sacred Sex." A different advertisement, this from the Institute for Narrative Therapy, tries to get my attention by asking questions: Whatever happened to the creative project that was your life? Are you stuck in a story you don't want to be in? For those who answer yes, a spirituality program is offered to stimulate rediscovery, renewal, recommitment, and opportunities to "recapture a deep sense of purpose in your life." By attending another workshop, I could learn that it is possible to discover the gateway to health, wellness, and immortal age through my "thinking body and a dancing mind."

Few of us ever attend, or want to attend, workshops like these, but we live in the midst of a flourishing hodgepodge of spiritual methodologies, philosophies, experiences, and self-help psychologies. Many are chosen, cafeteria style, from the growing abundance of spiritual alternatives. Some are combined. For example, the worship in a California church includes Tibetan prayer bells, Buddhist chants, Eastern meditation, and readings from Scripture. Most spiritual alternatives are accepted as valid and potentially helpful, especially by the often-tolerant baby boomers and members of Generation X who lead this march to new spiritual awareness.

This current fascination with the spiritual is a "complex amalgamation of thought and practice that unites Western and Eastern religious beliefs and practices," writes John A. Saliba in *Understanding New Religious Movements*.[2] The new spiritual awareness draws from philosophies with names like spiritualism, Theosophy, neopaganism, and Eastern mysticism. It often includes traditional Christian doctrines, such as the authority of the Bible as the Word of God, or the need for a new birth. But it draws as well from occult beliefs and practices, witchcraft, ESP, clairvoyance, contact with the dead, shamanism, herbal medicines, magic, drug-induced ecstasies, Native American rituals, Eastern religions, and even Satan worship. In its practices, the new spirituality might, for example, blend a reading and exposition of the Bible with unorthodox healing techniques, therapeutic dance, and exercises in something known as psychokinesis. According to Saliba, the movement draws insights from groups as diverse as the Rosicrucians, the Association for Research and Enlightenment (founded by Edgar Cayce), the Society for the Teaching of the Inner Christ, UFO religions like the Aetherius Society, and "various Spiritualist churches and New Age communities."[3]

LOOKING FOR SOMETHING NEW

For several years, starting long before I had any thoughts about writing this book, my mind has been trying to absorb and make sense of this myriad of New Age–new spirituality ideas and practices. I have tried to understand the motives of people who are leaving the church in droves, especially the mainline denominations.[4] I have watched the thriving of self-directed religions, do-it-yourself rituals, morality based on feelings, and doctrines floating on shifting subjectivity. All of us have seen spirituality become such a hot topic that it is studied by psychological researchers, discussed at professional conventions, and analyzed in scholarly journals. Popular magazines have articles and advertisements on subliminal tapes, brain machines, Zygon, mind power, global awakening, universal transformation, inward harmony, destressing, high-tech meditation, and opportunities to earn doctorates in metaphysics or synchronicity.

It is easy to be confused by the terminology, overwhelmed by the diversity, surprised by some of the reported experiences, and amazed at irrational conclusions accepted enthusiastically and sometimes without question by intelligent, often well-educated people. Searchers for the sacred often reach conclusions and engage in practices that many of us might consider strange, inconsistent, and faddish. From my perspective, and maybe from yours, many are deceived or misinformed, but they are spiritually hungry people, looking for answers wherever they can be found. I may disagree with their conclusions or practices and desperately want their spirituality to be like mine. But I also want to respect them as people, recognize their intelligence, and understand their struggles.

Philip John Neimark is an example. *Psychology Today* devoted an entire page to picture him dressed in a conservative business suit.[5] The recipient of several honorary doctorates, he was described as one of the country's most successful commodities traders; he manages $40 million of other people's money and gives them a return of about 20 percent every year.

But Philip John Neimark is also a babalawo, or high priest, in the ancient African religion of Ifa. In a dark shrine of a room in the garage of his home, Neimark replaces his business suit with embroidered robes and conducts ancient religious ceremonies. Worship includes prayers to a nature deity, submission to "Orunmila, the orisa [deity] of knowledge," and blood sacrifices of baby goats and sheep. To show this part of the businessman's life, the magazine included another photograph of Neimark the babalawo, dressed in a white robe, flooded in red light, and holding one of the knives with which he sacrifices animals.

The magazine writer used Neimark as an example of the widespread spiritual hunger among Americans and the quest for meaning that is taking people in many unorthodox directions. The businessman-babalawo is no weak-minded simpleton. He is a well-educated, competent professional who knows how to think. But like millions of others—including many who call themselves Christian—he must have sensed something missing in his life, something that money and career success couldn't provide. So he chose to become a babalawo. Others seek to fill their spiritual hunger by forming their own mixtures of Eastern religions, combined with bits and pieces of Christian theology, "varying degrees of occult, considerable measures of New Ageism, self-help, and pop psychology, along with a dash of Western optimism, [all] justified by whatever current scientific theories can be assumed."[6]

COMMON STRANDS

In the midst of this diversity and unorthodoxy there are similar strands in new spirituality devotees. Their spiritual journeys are so unique that they cannot be pigeonholed into neat categories, but almost all are looking toward a new age for humanity in the twenty-first century. Many have moved away from traditional religion and are searching, often passionately, for something fresh, relevant, and hopeful. Many have looked for new spiritual awareness by turning to the ancient religions and philosophies of the East. These philosophies form the common themes in spirituality books that rise to and remain at the top of best-seller lists. The familiar strands of the new spirituality make their appearance in seminars and therapy rooms. It is likely that some of the new spirituality basics have entered your thinking, and you haven't even noticed.

Turning Off the Mind, Looking for Experience

The first of these basic themes has been mentioned already: *the new spirituality is nontraditional, nonrational, and often focused on experience.* It is not like the Judeo-Christian religion that has characterized our culture for centuries. When I was a professor, my work involved teaching students to think logically, to look for solid facts, to fine-tune their minds. We debated issues, reasoned together, and tried to avoid inconsistencies and contradictions. Everybody assumed that clear thinking would open the doors to everything we needed to know. We agreed that solid arguments, logically presented, would move spiritually hungry people toward answers to their questions and commitments to spiritual views like the ones we held in those classrooms.

This intellectual approach doesn't fly anymore. Many people, even scholars and college students, believe that rational thinking limits one's ability to soar spiritually, to be more aware of the sacred, and to reach higher stages of enlightenment. Rational thinking can't help us cope with life's biggest issues, such as the meaning of suffering, the choice of values, the reasons for living, or the significance of death. If you want spiritual enlightenment, we are told, then move from reason to intuition, let your mind drift into emptiness, and turn within yourself to be guided by the soul-companion (sometimes called the daimon, spirit guide, or angel) who can expand your consciousness and increase your spiritual awareness. The rational arguments of theologians or the carefully crafted sermons of preachers often fail to reach people involved in the new spirituality. They don't want to be chained by logic and rational thinking. They want to empty the mind of facts or memories so they can experience whatever inner knowledge their intuition will reveal. They resist converting to somebody else's ways of thinking. They are willing to end up wherever we end up. If we all reach different conclusions or have different religious experiences, that is okay.

Unlike the active classroom debates, study of books, and scramble to complete assignments that characterized my graduate students, the new spirituality urges people to quiet the mind, meditate, and try blocking out sensations. One morning near a busy departure gate at O'Hare International Airport, I noticed a sharply dressed young woman in a business suit sitting ramrod straight in one of the chairs, her feet planted firmly on the floor, her eyes closed, her body motionless. At first I wondered if something was wrong, but soon I concluded that she was meditating, able to shut out the world for a while and concentrate on something within, at least until she heard the call for people to board the aircraft.

Getting in Touch with Something Bigger than Ourselves

For the first half of their lives, a generation of baby boomers embraced political activism, pushed to build careers, and was fueled by materialism, hedonism, and fitness. But all of this has left a feeling of emptiness. Many of us sense it, even if we are people outside the baby boom generation or entrenched in busy churches. We wonder if we are missing something, if there is more to life than what we experience. We can understand the hunger for something more, something better than what we've got. In response to this emptiness, *the new spirituality involves a seeking for enlightenment and intimate contact with the supernatural.*

Betty Jean Eadie has pointed millions to something that she considers enlightening, supernatural, and bigger than themselves. In November 1973, Eadie was lying in a Seattle hospital, recovering from a routine hysterectomy. Suddenly she began to hemorrhage, and shortly thereafter, the thirty-one-year-old woman "died."

But there is more to the story. For the next five hours, Eadie claims to have been in the world beyond, and then she "returned to life" with "an almost photographic view" of what she had experienced. Soon she began telling her friends and family about this "near death experience," and before long she was speaking to small groups in libraries and churches. In 1992, almost twenty years after her experience, Eadie told her story in a book published by a small Mormon press. When it was introduced to the wider public, however, *Embraced By the Light* hit the best-seller list and the author became a celebrity.[7] Eadie appeared on the major talk shows, was interviewed by newspaper and magazine writers, and began speaking to sellout crowds of eager admirers. People of all religious persuasions rushed to buy the book that one reviewer called "an odd mixture of Christian theism, and New Age/metaphysical pantheism," mixed with Mormon doctrine, Eastern philosophy, and the occult.[8]

Eadie's reported experience with "the light" has brought encouragement to thousands. After we die, each of us will have a "life review," she concluded, but there will be no future judgment, except the judgment that we make of ourselves. Even then, the Savior will prevent us from being too hard on ourselves. Hell, according to Eadie, is no more than momentary suffering felt when the life review reminds us of the grief we have caused others. Sin is not something bad when viewed in the light. Instead, it's an opportunity to learn. "I knew that he [Jesus] was aware of all my sins and faults," Eadie wrote in describing her experiences, "but all that didn't matter right now. He just wanted to hold me and share his love with me."[9] For people seeking enlightenment and greater awareness of the supernatural, this is a book of reassurance and hope, without religious dogma, guilt, or demands for changed behavior.

Dealing with Life Force Energies

Betty Eadie's popular book points to a third common theme of the new spirituality—the existence of a powerful life force or basic energy. Known by different names, including *Ki, Chi, prana, universe, the Force, universal life energy,* and sometimes even *god force,* this energy is assumed to run through all of creation and the universe, and flow into and out of our bodies and minds. *The new spirituality seeks to tap into and control the basic energy that is assumed to support and permeate all of existence.*[10] This life force concept originated centuries ago with Hinduism in India, but modern writers often give it a newer, more contemporary-sounding name: *bioenergy.*

Eadie is among those who believe that the life force consists of two kinds of energies, positive and negative. Positive energy is good and just; negative energy is harmful. The two energies are assumed to work in opposition to each other, but all operate according to metaphysical "laws" that we can learn to obey and control for our own good. "When we recognize these laws and learn how to use their positive and negative forces, we will have access to power beyond comprehension," according to Eadie.[11]

Learning to manipulate the energies also brings healing. Much of popular holistic healing assumes that pain is an accumulation of energy in some part of the body. If the energy can be correctly redistributed and brought back into harmonious balance, health is restored. In his best-selling novel *The Tenth Insight,* James Redfield writes about the main character spraining his ankle. A woman passing by wraps a wet towel around the swollen limb and then gives her philosophy of healing: "I believe the first step in the process is to identify the fear with which the medical problem seems to be connected; this opens up the energy block in your body to conscious healing. The next step is to pull in as much energy as possible and focus it on the exact location of the block."[12] Illness and even accidents come when the energy is out of balance, sometimes as a result of wrong thinking.

Crystals are assumed to help. Hold a crystal in your hand and look at it for a few minutes and you will begin to balance your energies, advises Brett Bravo, a psychic counselor, teacher, and healer. He says, "Lie on your back, put the crystal on your solar plexis, and place one hand over it." Then "cosmic rays will penetrate, and physical rays will stimulate your emotional body," and presumably bring greater health.[13] Something called crystal healing, which involves lying on stones, has been called "one of the most advanced and effective methods of cleansing the aura, releasing suppressed traumas, and connecting the person with his/her own source of truth and power."[14] The crystals can also help people meditate, gain energy, eliminate repressed memories, resolve mental conflicts, change attitudes, sharpen psychic powers, and replace sadness and depression with joy and enthusiasm.[15] As long as the positive and negative energies are balanced, with or without crystals, everything is fine.

If you are a Bible-totin' fundamentalist, a devout Catholic, an atheist with minimal interest in spirituality, or almost anyone else, you might find this talk about life forces, energy balance, and crystals to be nothing more than creative fantasy. But millions of people take it seriously. Dressed in more contemporary language, these views appear in medicine, movies, motivational seminars, and myriads of novels, articles, and counseling offices. Books on spirituality have dominated the best-seller lists for several years, and many advocate variations of the life force approach to life. Many people, perhaps including some of your neighbors or relatives, find these explanations to be enlightening, insightful, encouraging, and helpful.

Getting Through Life with a New View of God

Most of the people I know are busy—too busy. We run from place to place and commitment to commitment, squeezing more and more into our hectic days, trying to balance demands and keep on top of the E-mail, voice mail messages, and faxes that were supposed to make our lives simpler. We dream of quiet times that never appear and suspect, within our hearts, that life was never intended to be this chaotic. For many among us, the current fascination with spirituality represents a grasping to find stability, meaning, and tranquillity in a culture dominated by breathless rushing.

Marty Kaplan—screenwriter, producer, author, former political speechwriter, Hollywood studio executive—needed tranquillity in his busy life. He grew up as "a nice Jewish boy from

Newark," but abandoned his religious tradition and became an agnostic as he got older. "Of course I didn't like it," he wrote in describing his spiritual journey. "Who wants to face death without God? Who wants to tell kids that the universe is indifferent to them?"[16]

Then he stumbled onto meditation. If it could help people facing serious physical illness like cancer, he reasoned, why couldn't it help him deal with the troublesome tooth grinding that was evidence of his stress? Soon he found himself engaging in a practice that has been at the heart of religious mysticism for millennia. "What attracted me to meditation was its apparent religious neutrality," he wrote in *Time* magazine. "You don't have to believe in anything; all you have to do is do it. . . . To separate 20 minutes from the day with silence and intention is to worship, whether you call it that or not."

Kaplan concluded, "I used to think of psychic phenomena as New Age flimflam. I used to think of reincarnation as a myth. I used to think the soul was a metaphor. Now I know there is a God—my God, in here, demanding not faith but experience, an inexhaustible wonder at the richness of this very moment."[17] He even gave his god a name, Tetragrammaton, something equivalent to Nothingness, Spirit, or Being.

This personal, religiously neutral, self-created god of Marty Kaplan is the kind of deity that many spiritual seekers want. *The new spirituality has diverse views of God, often concluding that God is a power or force within ourselves.* This may be a god like Kaplan's, a god that makes no demands and can be accessed or turned off at will like the light switch on a wall. It is a god that gives human beings a sense of unlimited power. For increasing numbers of people, especially women, the new deity may be a goddess. Worldwide, a women's spirituality movement is growing, attracting many who mix the I-can-be-like-God message with a new brand of feminism. Some seek to discover a goddess within who gives special power. Others, coming from more traditional religious traditions, delete references to God the Father from their vocabulary and talk about Mother God or God as female.

Other people view god as a higher power or a spirit guide who can be reached through *channeling*, often with the assistance of spiritual helpers known as channelers. Russell Chandler, former religion writer for the *Los Angeles Times*, describes channeling as "yesterday's séance medium, palm reader, crystal ball-gazer, and fortune-teller dressed up in high-tech drag and often packaged by Madison Avenue."[18] Sometimes in exchange for payment, channelers go into trances to establish contact with a spirit, higher consciousness, or different otherworldly entity that is called to give guidance, messages, and enlightenment. Today, testimonies to the impact of a higher power are proclaimed not so much in churches as in twelve-step programs, wellness centers, cancer support groups, sports arenas, and hospital rooms.

Making Connections and Commitments

The new spirituality often believes that human beings are not alone and that we must make commitments to causes greater than ourselves. Some assume that all parts of nature—people, animals, and things; bodies and minds; things tangible and things material— are interconnected. Philosophers call this *monism,* the idea that all is one, one is all. "Today's spiritual awakening not only reveals the hidden interconnectedness of things, it prompts people to pledge themselves to a host of new causes, from saving the planet to helping the disenfranchised," writes one observer of the new spirituality.[19] Although many spiritual seekers are self-centered and not interested in looking beyond themselves, others find that their spiritual awakenings lead to a new kind of selflessness. They have new determination to clean up the planet, save endangered species, help the homeless, feed the hungry, build the body with natural foods, heal with herbal medicines, relax with meditation, and visualize a peaceful, better world. Along with a new quest for inner peace and personal spiritual experiences, there is a new sense of caring for the earth, for animals, and for other human beings. And pulling all of this diversity together, there is an ongoing search.

SEARCHING

Twenty or thirty years ago, if you had picked up a book on spirituality, you might have expected to read about something Christian. At least in our culture, most people assumed that spiritual issues involved prayer, Bible study, worship, and the sacraments of the church. Today, many people are fed up with the church. They dislike the rules, the politics, the scandals, the apparent irrelevance, the system. Disenchanted worshipers feel that traditional churches and long-established Christian religious practices are not meeting the needs of those they exist to serve, so people are looking elsewhere for the answers to life.

In some parts of the world, most notably in Latin America, people are leaving the Catholic church in droves and flocking to pentecostal and other experience-oriented forms of Protestantism. These new converts like the enthusiasm, the informality, the evidence of God's presence, and the camaraderie that come apart from Christian traditions. "I don't want to hear about who Jesus is," one man told his pastor. "I want to know what Jesus can do for people like me." Others, especially younger people and North Americans, Europeans, and Australians, have given up on the churches and stopped attending altogether. But they haven't stopped their interest in spiritual things. As one twenty-seven-year-old said to me recently, "My generation is into spirituality; we just aren't into church."

Decades ago, when Freud wrote about religion, he predicted that interest in spiritual things would fade as people embraced science. How could he have known that the opposite would occur, that we would reach the end of a century with millions of people disillusioned with science, but searching for something more? These people are dominated by technology, distrustful of their governments, disenchanted with their educations, disappointed by their careers, and often damaged by their families. They are coming to realize that the hedonistic and materialistic philosophies of previous decades have failed to deliver on their promises.

Consider Rich and Karen as two examples.[20] Radically different in their philosophies and spiritual pathways, both desire greater peace of mind, an experience of something bigger than themselves, a way to make sense of a world that seems to be spinning into chaos. Both hunger for clear and convincing moral values. Both are concerned about suffering and poverty in the world where we live; both harbor deep-seated insecurities about the future.

Rich grew up in a home with deeply religious, morally upright parents who called themselves evangelical Christians and who took their children faithfully to their "Bible-believing" church. Rich attended Sunday school for years, was part of the church youth group, and went to religious schools for an education that his parents struggled to afford. Once he even considered becoming a preacher, but that changed when he reached young adulthood and discovered a broader world, a world with less-rigid morality and greater tolerance for religious diversity. It was a world filled with people who claimed to be spiritual but who ignored the God of the Bible. They were people interested more in caring for the earth than in making money. They were open-minded, tolerant, willing to try new religious experiences, and not caught in the narrowness that Rich had seen in his home church. Rich isn't a rebel, intent on throwing over the religion of his parents. Sometimes he even goes to church with them. But he senses an emptiness in his life, and he hungers for something more than the catchy choruses, old-fashioned hymns, and cliché-filled sermons that he has heard all his life.

Karen knows nothing about the religion that permeated Rich's growing-up years. Her parents were successful professionals whose lives revolved around their careers and whose only gods were the trappings of success. As Rita McClain described earlier, Karen has tried a variety of spiritual experiences and traveled on a number of sacred pathways. Recently she has joined with a group of seekers on the Internet. "Welcome to sacred journey," says the group's home page on the World Wide Web. "Many of us are discovering that humankind is undergoing an exciting spiritual transformation. We are learning to take segmented religions and merge them together into a unified truth. The East and the West, the scientific and the spiritual, coming together to form a new spiritual culture on the face of the earth. This means each of us should do our best to cultivate an open mind, a loving heart, and an enlightened spirit." The Web site is for people interested in the "spiritual, ecumenical transformation taking place on our planet." Will Karen turn away from this computer religion, disillusioned as she has been so often in the past? In contrast, will this new search for enlightenment lead to the soul satisfaction that she craves? For Karen, it is too early to know.

We will return to Rich and Karen in the following pages, but their search for the sacred might cause you to think about yourself. Do you ever rush about your work or other daily activities and wonder if something in your life is missing? Do you see people who seem to be genuinely enthusiastic about worship, excited about their churches, consistently cheerful even in the midst of pain or disappointment, seemingly in touch with God, then wonder why this never seems to be your experience? Do you long for intimate friendships with other people who could understand your problems and deepest concerns, give you encouragement, and travel alongside you on your spiritual journey? Do you struggle with questions about the meaning of your life, the reasons for suffering and injustice, the future of your career, the source of real inner peace or consistent joy? Do you ever wish that you could experience a genuine oneness with a God who knows you, forgives you, loves you, and cares about you?

If you are like me and can answer yes to some of these questions, you can begin to understand why so many people turn to the new spiritualities. We are a rich nation, with technology that our grandparents could never have imagined, with access to unlimited information and sources of entertainment. But millions are empty, lonely, isolated, stressed, and looking for something different, something better than what they have. A *Newsweek* writer states that we are a nation of people searching for "some sense of harmony with the cosmic order and communication with its source."[21] Most of us would throw out such fancy language and say we are searching for purpose in life, for inner peace, for a sense of security, for intimacy with other human beings, for something sacred, something more than what we have now. We don't want stuffy theological language, outdated tradition, ecclesiastical rigidity, and irrelevant long-winded sermons. We want something worthwhile to believe in, something that will give us hope and purpose as we live in this confusing, increasingly complex, and ever-changing world.

Disillusioned with organized religion and frustrated with cold rationality, people are looking for experiences and opportunities to express themselves. They like the freedom to find their own forms of worship and ways to experience the sacred. Living in an era of supertolerance, many go their own ways, let others go their ways, and assume that what works for you is good for you—regardless of whether it is logical, scientifically tested, or believed by other people. So here we are, living in the midst of a genuine spiritual awakening, surrounded by people searching for different things, and all of us, it seems, are searching in different directions and in different ways.

I am writing the last words of this chapter on Christmas Eve. In other parts of the world it already is Christmas Day, and many are celebrating the birth of Christ. He came, said the angels, to bring peace on earth. He came to enable his followers to have abundant life at present and eternal life in the future. He came to die, to take the punishment for our sins, and to offer forgiveness. It's an old message that has sustained generations of believers. But it is a story that largely is buried in the bustle of Christmas and the plethora of voices looking to a new spirituality that will move us into a new century. Two thousand years after the coming of Christ, it is worth considering why so many people will look beyond Christ this Christmas and seek renewal in a new spirituality. Does this describe you? How did we get to this place in our history? What are the roots of the diverse spirituality puzzle that we keep encountering? Read on.

— 3 —

Roots of the Spirituality Puzzle:
Why Is There a New Spiritual Awakening?

When Russell Chandler's family retreated to their mountain cabin one holiday season, they took a giant jigsaw puzzle to occupy their spare time and provide mindless amusement during their vacation. It wasn't a simple puzzle. It had a jillion tiny pieces that all looked alike except for the few that formed the border. The family started enthusiastically, but soon their attention drifted to other things. The puzzle sat unfinished for months, a rough outline of two edges, some interlocking pieces in the center, a jumble of unmatching squiggly shapes heaped to the side. Sometimes, if they were bored or walking past the puzzle, a family member might fit in a piece or two, but more than once somebody remarked that parts of the puzzle probably were missing.

When he began his award-winning survey of the New Age movement, Chandler likened his quest to putting together that giant puzzle. Eventually the pieces began to fall in place, but the task was horrendous and the diversity overwhelming. While he was researching his book, Chandler went to visit a "gray-bearded, owlish-eyed, cap-wearing, researcher-author" named Brooks Alexander who headed an organization that examines and critiques new religious groups and their leaders. "You can do one of two things," Alexander cautioned when he learned about Chandler's book. "You can either keep up with the New Age movement, or you can write about it—but not both."[1]

Today, we talk less about the New Age movement and more about the new spirituality, but the underlying philosophies are the same. I am easily overwhelmed by the piles of books, articles, and resources that surround me as I write. If you plug into the World Wide Web as I did and search with words like *spirituality, New Age,* and *mysticism,* you will be inundated with the complexity, prevalence, and variety of new spirituality resources. The pieces in the big spirituality jigsaw puzzle are increasing, and so are the numbers of new spirituality searchers. Disenchanted both with their materialistic lifestyles and with traditional, patriarchal religion, the people of the new spirituality—people like Rich and Karen—are looking for something better.

Some of the counselors and religious leaders I know are able to retreat to their offices or churches and pretend that the new spirituality is limited to college campuses where professors and students wander around with their heads in the clouds and their feet rarely touching reality. But you don't have to look far to see that religions rooted in pantheism, syncretism, pluralism, monism, and experience-centered therapies are springing up everywhere. We cannot ignore the explosion of interest in nontraditional spirituality and the ever-growing collection of techniques that promise to bring instant spiritual transformation. The new spirituality puzzle may have thousands of pieces that don't appear to fit together. Some pieces may seem to be missing. But the new spirituality has captured the attention and devotion of the masses, and it cannot be dismissed or overlooked.

If you are like me, you might wonder how this new interest in nontraditional spirituality became so popular. The answer is not found in theology. Instead, the roots of the new spirituality are grounded in psychology and history.[2] Together these form the foundations on which the new spirituality house is built.

PSYCHOLOGY AND THE NEW SPIRITUALITY PUZZLE

A few years ago, my wife and I had the opportunity to spend a half day walking with some friends through the Nazi prison camp at Auschwitz in southern Poland. Our Polish friends had tried to prepare us for what we would see, but no words could have softened the stark reality of what we encountered. We stood in the room where thousands entered, naked, prepared to take a shower, only to die as deadly gases came from the spigots instead of water. We saw the place where the bodies were loaded into incinerators. We gazed at the wall where prisoners were shot and killed every day. We saw the cramped living facilities, the piles of eyeglasses and suitcases that the prisoners had left behind, the indescribably inadequate toilet facilities, and the places where some unfortunate souls were isolated in cells so small and confining that there was no room to sit on the floor. The old prison now has thousands of visitors every day, but it is a tourist attraction unlike any that we had seen before. On the morning of our visit, we saw no vendors selling cheap and gaudy souvenirs. There was no tourist laughter at Auschwitz. Instead, all the visitors who walked through that death-saturated prison camp wore sober expressions on their faces.

When I returned home, I went to my bookshelves and retrieved a faded, dust-covered paperback book that I first read many years ago. Titled *Man's Search for Meaning*, it was written by a survivor of Auschwitz, an Austrian psychiatrist named Viktor Frankl.[3] During my years as a student, that little book was on everybody's reading list. For three grim years the author had remained a prisoner of the Nazis, observing himself and his fellow prisoners, hoarding little pieces of paper on which he formed an outline for the book that would impact me and many others years after his release. Thousands died because of the whims of their guards, but among those who escaped the gas chambers, some handled prison life better than others. The difference, Frankl concluded, depended on each person's inner life.

In the midst of incredible suffering, a few rare individuals walked through the huts comforting others, giving away their last pieces of bread. Frankl saw these people as "sufficient proof that everything can be taken from a man but one thing: the last of the human freedoms—to choose one's attitude in any given set of circumstances, to choose one's own way."[4] The prisoners who survived maintained an inner strength by looking toward a future goal, something to sustain them until they could be released. Like Frankl, who was determined to write a postprison book, the survivors tried to find hope for the future and meaning in their suffering. They were realistic about the depths of their tragedy, but at times they were able to retreat mentally from the terrible surroundings to a life of inner richness and freedom. For them, and for us, mental health does not depend on freedom from tension, according to Frankl. We can live and even flourish in the midst of great suffering if we have a reason to keep going. He wrote, "The prisoner who had lost his faith in the future—his future—was doomed."[5]

Frankl, Freud, Jung, and Two Americans

Frankl was trained in Vienna. He knew of Freud's teachings and probably knew Freud. But the psychiatrist from Auschwitz disagreed with the founder of psychoanalysis. Frankl thought that Freud was too introspective, concerned about the past, and focused on technique. In contrast, Frankl wanted to help people escape the emptiness of their lives by finding meaning, even in times of suffering.

Emptiness, meaninglessness, and suffering didn't concern Freud. He was more interested in understanding the unconscious. He wrote about religion, but Freud had greater faith in his brand of science. He dismissed religion as a narcotic, a crutch, "infantile helplessness," and an illusion that would no longer be needed when science advanced.

Carl Jung, Freud's onetime friend and later critic, disagreed. The son of a Swiss pastor, Jung grew up in a home where his mother was warm and accepting, but his somewhat distant father was plagued with doubts about the faith. The older man often turned to his son for reassurance and the courage to keep on preaching to others what he questioned in himself. All of that led the younger Jung to conclude that Christianity was lacking and ultimately wrong. Ever curious, the pastor's son looked for alternative approaches to spirituality in psychotherapy, Eastern and ancient religions, and occult practices. Jung's god was not the transcendent, sovereign Lord of the universe who is righteous, omnipotent, omniscient, omnipresent, and worthy of our praise and obedience. Jung concluded that god was a part of the "collective unconscious" that all human beings possess. To find "him," we look within ourselves and use active imagination to visualize the image of the deity. There is no need to worry about churches, absolute truth, doctrine, objective moral standards, or obedience. From Jung's perspective, the Bible and other religious books could be interpreted subjectively and used as one of many ways to map the unconscious.

Within recent years, Freud's influence has faded and few people today talk about Frankl. Jung, in contrast, has emerged as a hero of the new spirituality. His emphasis on a subjective, demand-free, psychologically astute spirituality is popular among people who distrust authority and prefer to search for answers within themselves. Most of the classic approaches to psychotherapy have no answers to the ultimate questions of why we exist, where we go after death, what the source of evil is, or how we make sense of emotional and physical pain. Jung was different, willing to face these issues. He didn't claim to have answers to the most pressing questions of life, but he encouraged self-exploration, involvement with seers and mystics, and serious consideration of the ancient religions and other forces that formed the collective unconscious where god is assumed to dwell. He took part in séances and once wrote a book on flying saucers, claiming that UFO's had religious and psychological significance.

Unlike Freud, Jung didn't consider religion and spirituality to be negative forces that would be abandoned when our civilization reached greater maturity. Jung proudly proclaimed that spirituality and mystical experience could be vital parts of the personality. He believed that the meaning of human history could be found not by scouring historical documents, but by looking within. Influenced by his knowledge of Eastern thought, he didn't think about God and sacred things as something apart from human beings or up in the heavens. Instead, he pulled god deep inside us and concluded that the sacred would be found not by looking without, but by searching within. And he popularized the concept of *synchronicity,* the idea that when two seemingly unrelated events occur in close proximity, they may be related after all. Maybe you think of somebody you haven't heard from in years and at that point the person phones you. "It must be mental telepathy," both of you conclude, but Jung and many in the new spirituality would call this synchronicity.

Before Jung died in 1961, two American psychologists—Abraham Maslow and Carl Rogers—had risen to prominence with messages that furthered the New Age–new spirituality message. Abraham Maslow wrote about human potential and the ability of people to develop the possibilities that are within. An atheistic humanist who had little interest in God or the supernatural, Maslow nevertheless published a whole book about religions, values, and "peak-experiences."[6] These experiences were called ecstatic, "God-like," pleasurable, desirable, and available to anybody. They give meaning to life, bring inner peace, make people less selfish, and help us see the universe as an integrated and unified whole. When I first discovered the book as a young psychologist, I was excited because a respected leader in my profession was saying what few had said before: spirituality, spiritual values, and religion were legitimate topics for study, and not "the exclusive possession of organized churches."[7]

The other American psychologist, Carl Rogers, developed an approach to therapy still used by many practitioners today. Convinced that each person has the potential to solve his or her problems, Rogers emphasized human experience and taught that "self-realization" and fulfillment could come apart from other people, traditions, or an objective God who makes moral demands. As a young man, Rogers abandoned the study of theology to become a psychologist, but he never seemed to leave his religious roots. Near the end of his life, especially as he faced the death of his wife, Rogers looked beyond psychology for answers to his questions and guidance for his future. He turned to séances, Ouija boards, and a medium in Brazil who claimed to put the famous psychologist in contact with his departed wife. As much as any other person, this pillar of American psychology took his profession and many of his admirers in the direction of the new spirituality that would emerge later.

The Psychological Society

All of these therapists and academics helped to create what one journalist called the *psychological society*. Writing twenty years ago, Martin Gross argued that the church had grown weaker in the West, so confused citizens turned to the only alternative they knew: psychological experts who claimed to have a new scientific standard of behavior to replace fading traditions. "Armed with what it claims are the hidden truths about . . . behavior," modern psychology was described as a movement that "has impressed its philosophical stamp on virtually all of contemporary life."[8] Americans are in a desperate search for psychic understanding and repair, Gross continued, but with the weakening of Judeo-Christian values, we have created a new society, a psychological society:

For many, this Society has all the earmarks of a potent new religion. When educated man lost faith in formal religion, he required a substitute belief that would be as reputable in the last half of the twentieth century as Christianity was in the first. Psychology and psychiatry have now assumed that role. They offer mass belief, a promise of a better future, opportunity for confession, unseen mystical workings and a trained priesthood of helping professionals devoted to servicing the paying-by-the-hour communicants.[9]

Throughout the 1970s and 1980s, the psychological society grew like an aggressive cancer, extending into the worlds of media, business, education, entertainment, medicine, therapy, and religion. Voices that were often isolated and sometimes reactionary cried out that psychology was becoming too influential, too powerful. But it was not the alarmists who tamed the spread of psychology. The cost-cutting machine known as managed care sliced into the fees of therapists, cut out the long-term approaches to therapy, and carved away at the bloated claims of therapeutic success. Researchers increasingly demonstrated the value and effectiveness of therapy, but aggressive reporters, zealous lawyers, hypercritical pastors, and cost-conscious insurance companies all questioned whether psychology was as powerful as its promoters claimed.

From within its own ranks, increasing numbers of mental health practitioners—psychiatrists, psychologists, social workers, counselors—began concluding that psychological science, despite its proven effectiveness, could do little to meet deep inner spiritual needs. Recently conscientious therapists have begun talking about "soul therapy," trying to understand the spirituality puzzles in their clients. Some are embarking on new therapies that look for ways to heal our culture as well as the inner crises that people bring to their doors. These new therapies are going beyond the treatment of symptoms, suggests one writer. They are helping clients "connect with forces of spirit, body, and creativity . . . shifting the boundaries between the self and the world, the soul and the society."[10] The psychology that did so much to introduce the new spiritualities only a few years ago in turn is being shaped by the sacred searching that has captivated many members of modern society.

Pop Psychology

Along with the psychological society and the new therapies came a host of popularizers, each bringing a unique self-help formula that promised to change people forever and that slid in various degrees of Eastern thought. One of the most influential and bizarre was Erhard Seminars Training, abbreviated as *est*, and developed by a used-car salesman who influenced hundreds of thousands of business executives, educators, clergy, therapists, and entertainment personalities including the late John Denver, Yoko Ono, John Travolta, and Diana Ross.

Born during the depression to an Episcopalian mother and a Jewish father who converted to evangelical Christianity, the founder of *est* was Jack Rosenberg. After deserting his first wife and four children, he flew with his girlfriend to St. Louis searching for a new identity. On the plane he read an article about West Germany and decided to name himself Werner Hans Erhard after some of the people mentioned in the article. Erhard read the writings of Maslow and Rogers, familiarized himself with the possibility thinking books, dabbled in Zen Buddhism and Scientology, took the Dale Carnegie personality development course, and was trained in the martial arts. In the midst of all this, Erhard claimed to have a peak-experience that gave him the principles for *est* and launched him on a seminar circuit aimed at the business market.

A few years after its start, *est* was repackaged and given a new name, The Forum. Billed as "a powerful, practical inquiry into the issues that determine our personal effectiveness," The Forum promised to "produce an extraordinary advantage in your personal effectiveness and a decisive edge in your ability to achieve." In exchange for $525, participants were crowded into two consecutive weekend seminars (9 A.M. to 11:30 P.M.) where they had limited food and toilet breaks but lots of verbal abuse that challenged trainees to question and even dislodge their basic assumptions. Visualization and self-hypnosis exercises were part of the program intended to "change your life totally" and teach participants that "you will get in touch with yourself" and be able to "experience yourself as the creator of your own circumstances." The seminars elevated experience and taught, "You are god in your universe. There is no God unless it is self." In 1984, Erhard developed Transformational Technologies, Inc., aimed at the training management market, but the foundation was still the Zen Buddhism and Scientology basic to the whole movement.

Several years ago Werner Erhard disappeared. Some speculated that he was trying to avoid the Internal Revenue Service seeking back taxes; others assumed that he was wanting to avoid the Scientologists or running from a number of personal problems including charges of family abuse—which he denied. Prior to his departure, Erhard's seminars probably helped many people find new direction and purpose. In the process he developed a popular psychology that pulled many people in the direction of Eastern thought.

Consumer-Driven Spirituality?

Despite their excesses, the Erhard seminars illustrated the partnership that has emerged between Western consumerism and some segments of contemporary spirituality. In consumer-driven cultures, like those of the United States and Australia, upwardly mobile people flock to personalities and programs that promise power, prominence, and peak performance. Erhard is gone, but a handful of master motivators have appeared in his place, each offering high-energy, expensive programs for "finding that inner force that sustains you throughout the course of your life." A few of the sold-out seminars that pop up around the country bring religion and spirituality into their presentations; others are like the seminars and tapes of a youthful dynamo named Anthony Robbins. He preaches a message of unlimited personal power without much thought of God.

Still in his thirties, Robbins has been described as a man "definitely wired up differently than the average person. He is passionate, compassionate, real, mega, rigid, and flexible—all rolled into one imposing and impactful package," according to one of his close associates.[11] Energetic, tall (six feet seven inches), articulate, and dynamic, Robbins has proclaimed his personal power message to almost two million people who have attended his seminars. His book *Personal Power* sold more than twenty-four million copies in the first five years. His popular videos and tapes can be ordered on the Internet by typing in a credit card number and clicking once or twice on the computer keyboard.

Robbins taps into the dissatisfaction that many people feel today by bringing a message of self-mastery, positive action, inner personal power, self-motivation, and hope. The promise of a better future is extended to all who unleash the giant of unlimited power that each of us is assumed to have within.[12] Sometimes Robbins quotes the teachings of Christ, cites Scripture, and draws on the insights of Gandhi and Buddha, among others. But he probably wouldn't consider his unlimited power concept to be a spiritual message, and few would call him a spiritual leader. By mastering the arts of salesmanship and mass marketing, however, he has preached to millions that meaning, fulfillment, peak-experiences, and lasting happiness don't depend on any god or supernatural influence. All we need is to uncap the flowing source of inner power and master the resources within. It all starts when we pull out a credit card.

The Steps to Recovery and the Roads Less Traveled

Two additional influences are worth mentioning as we dig for the roots of the new spirituality. We need to consider the now-fading recovery movement and the ongoing popularity of psychiatrist-author M. Scott Peck.

The recovery movement reached the height of its impact and popularity in the 1980s, but its beginnings go back to the founding of Alcoholics Anonymous (AA) fifty years earlier. The twelve steps of AA were not intended to cultivate spirituality or to teach Christian principles, but group members were taught to recognize their need for a "higher power" to help them overcome alcoholism. With the initial (and ongoing) success of AA, similar groups appeared to help people overcome and recover from substance abuse, compulsive gambling, and a host of other addictions. Each assumed that people with problems were victims, usually not responsible for their difficulties, best able to recover by joining a group of others with similar problems all going through twelve-step programs of recovery. And almost all of the recovery programs assumed that we need some power other than ourselves to bring recovery.[13] For Christians, who embraced the recovery movement with gusto, this higher power was assumed to be God. Recovery enthusiasts often concluded and boldly proclaimed that everybody needed to be in recovery from something. Those who disagreed were dismissed as being in denial.

But many counselors have challenged the idea that we are all victims and either in denial or in need of recovery. Theologically minded critics have noted that participants in recovery have been able to ignore the issues of sin and forgiveness. Psychological rituals in recovery groups have replaced the more orthodox church rituals, and people in recovery have been able to build their identities on a pilgrimage of recovery rather than on anything more religious. Even the critics agree, however, that twelve-step programs have been helpful to innumerable people—and will continue to help. Recovery groups have offered more authentic community than many people find in churches. The groups have provided safe havens where struggling people have felt free to unburden their shameful secrets, find genuine accountability, and still be accepted.

Even so, the faddish popularity of recovery in the 1980s, the production of endless recovery books, and the explosive proliferation of recovery groups have all combined to overexpose and weaken the recovery movement. Many people got tired of hearing about twelve-step programs. Books promised to help individuals get free of their addictions to recovery groups. One author proposed a thirteenth step for people who never wanted to go through the first twelve steps again. While that was going on, however, there was continuing emphasis on the need for some supernatural power to help us meet needs and solve problems. With this emphasis, the recovery movement has joined with the other psychological influences to point people to a new spirituality.

But no individual or whole recovery movement can match psychiatrist M. Scott Peck as a molder of the new spirituality. His 1978 book, *The Road Less Traveled*, remained on the *New York Times* best-seller list for six hundred weeks and "initiated the entire psychology-spirituality movement," according to Richard Abancs, who has written a critique of Peck's work.[14] An article in the *SCP Journal* notes that Peck single-handedly "helped to spark a spiritual revolution that is still going on today."[15]

Peck claims to be a Christian whose books are "divinely inspired." He is a captivating writer who deals with common distressing emotions, gives easy-to-understand ways to deal with problems, sprinkles his books with fascinating case histories taken from his private practice, and isn't afraid to tackle taboo subjects like evil and exorcisms. His writings are insightful, interesting, rich, and often genuinely helpful. Admirers of Peck include both Christian and non-Christian readers, but critics have noted that his Christianity sometimes is far from orthodox. In one of his books, for example, he divides spirituality into four levels. Lower levels view God as an external, transcendent Being—the kind of God that most Christians worship. The most mature top level of spirituality is much more pantheistic. It is a stage "of unity, of an underlying connectedness between things: between men and women, between us and the other creatures and even inanimate matter as well, fitting together according to an ordinarily invisible fabric underlying the cosmos."[16]

Conclusions like this are not far removed from the thinking of many modern people who embrace the new spirituality. This thinking has been described as a modern resurgence of the ancient religion of Mother Earth, where all of nature is seen to be alive, filled with divine energy, and interconnected. From this perspective, true spirituality seeks to find energy and unrealized potential within ourselves and within nature. It is a spirituality that is slipping into many parts of the society, including the churches and mainstream psychotherapy.

Some people argue that psychology is like a Trojan horse smuggling a whole army of new spirituality ideas into an unsuspecting society. This is an unfair, inaccurate, and sweeping condemnation that fails to recognize both the complexity and the diversity of psychology. Writing as a psychologist, I have tried to show that some trends and people in my field have been influential in stimulating the new spirituality. But this new awakening has come as well through people in art, literature, business, education, media, theology, and most other segments of the society. And all of this is possible because of recent and radical historical changes in the way we think about life and about the universe where we live.

SOCIETY, HISTORY, AND THE NEW SPIRITUALITY PUZZLE

The Malden Mills fire was spectacular. I remember seeing the pictures and reading about the thirty-one hundred employees who silently watched their jobs go up in smoke. Aaron Feuerstein, the mill's seventy-one-year-old chief executive, must have watched as well. His family had built and operated the textile mill, but over the years they had built something even more valuable: loyalty from their employees and a reputation for being fair and doing what was right. Feuerstein's Orthodox Jewish faith had convinced him that God wants his people to do the right thing, even in situations where there are no clear ethical guidelines. In the hours after the fire, the family must have debated how they could do what was right when their business was in ruins and their faithful employees were faced with forced unemployment.

Those employees didn't have to wait long for word about their future. In an announcement that stunned the business world and attracted immediate international attention, the silver-haired Feuerstein indicated that most of the employees would be kept on the payroll even though there would not be enough work to keep them busy while the mill was being rebuilt. In part, the decision was inspired by the words of Rabbi Hillel, a Jewish sage who lived about the time of Christ. The rabbi had said that not everyone who acquired great wealth is wise in God's eyes. Feuerstein and his family had been financially successful, and they did want to be wise in God's eyes. That meant doing the right thing for the employees, despite the cost.

To his surprise, Feuerstein's generosity made him a hero. In the year following the fire he was profiled in the media, given five honorary degrees, flooded with speaking invitations, and presented with numerous awards. His favorite came from the students at a Hebrew day school who made a patchwork quilt with eleven panels depicting biblical injunctions to do good. Above them all were these words: *Who is honored? One who honors others.*

Aaron Feuerstein's Jewish spirituality is far different from the new spirituality that is sweeping the world today. The textile manufacturer built his life and his business on universally accepted, traditional principles derived from the Scriptures and from the authoritative wisdom of giants like Rabbi Hillel. Despite his dependence on traditional orthodoxy, Feuerstein's systematic approach to building the business suggests that he, like most of us, thinks and lives in accordance with a worldview that goes under the name *modernity*.

The Modern Mind

Beginning about two hundred years ago, near the time of the French Revolution, modernity assumed that the world we live in is orderly and able to be understood. Our task is to use our minds to "unlock the secrets of the universe . . . and create a better world."[17] Modern thinkers, probably including you, assume that knowledge is desirable, objective, and available to the human mind. We value education because it trains us to think rationally and logically, teaches us independence, and helps us build our careers. Most of us agree that the ability to reason has allowed human beings to make great advances through science and technology. This absolute faith in human rational capabilities even influences our religions. Earlier I mentioned my years as a professor in a theological school. We all agreed that there were solid reasons for what we believed, and students were taught to defend their faith factually and logically through a rational way of thinking that theologians call *apologetics*.

This rational kind of thinking has its downside. With the emphasis on facts, logic, and objective conclusions, modern thinking has elevated science but given less prominence to beliefs, feelings, religion, art, ethical values, and the humanities. I found that as an undergraduate at a university in Canada. My literature teachers defended their course content as being valuable even though it was not scientific or precise like mathematics. My psychology professors talked about the science of human behavior and underscored the importance of measurement, statistical analyses, and precision in our conclusions about people.

Since science and logic are supreme in modern thinking, there can be little room for supernatural beings, an external authority like God, or debates about ethics and moral absolutes. Instead, modernity has assumed that each person can make his or her individual moral decisions based on the facts at hand (this is called moral relativism), and there tends to be buoyant optimism about the future. We see this in churches, universities, businesses, and politics. During the 1996 presidential campaign, Bob Dole called himself the most optimistic man alive, and Bill Clinton wrote a book that inspired optimism about the future. This thinking "leads to the belief that progress is inevitable, that science, coupled with the power of education, will eventually free us from our vulnerability to nature, as well as from all social bondage."[18] At the core of modern thinking, reason is assumed to be supreme, humans have limitless possibilities for progress, and God really isn't necessary. It is unlikely that the new spirituality movement would have grown if this modern type of thinking had continued to dominate the universities and the society.

But a change is under way. You might not notice, but it is seeping into almost every part of our lives. "Our culture is in the throes of a cultural shift of immense proportions," according to Regent College professor Stanley Grenz. The modern era is crumbling. "As modernity dies around us, we appear to be entering a new epoch."[19] It is called *postmodernism*.

Enter Postmodernism

Postmodernism (sometimes called *postmodernity*) is not a passing fad that can be fun to discuss but has no relevance outside college classrooms. It is at the core of contemporary art, architecture, literature, fashion, and even rock music. It is revolutionizing education, media, psychotherapy, and Hollywood films. Historian Arnold Toynbee, writing long before the idea became popular, concluded that postmodernism would end Western dominance in the world and lead to the decline of individualism, capitalism, and Christianity.[20] Already it has begun to impact our morals, reshape our views of marriage and the family, influence interpersonal relationships, and seep into churches and synagogues. It is certain to make people like Aaron Feuerstein appear to be relics from the past. And postmodernism is the foundation undergirding the new spirituality.

As you might expect, people who embrace postmodernism aren't all the same, and writers describe postmodernism in different ways. Even so, a few features appear in almost all the descriptions.

A New View of Reason

For decades we have relied on reason and science to help us uncover truth, make discoveries, and build a better world. Now, postmodernists tell us to forget about being rational and get used to the idea that emotions and intuition are valid sources of knowledge. The world is not something objective and "out there," waiting to be discovered by science and understood intellectually with our brains. According to postmodernism, there is no such thing as objective truth or facts that we can all accept. What is true for you might not be true for me. It all depends on the individual, on the way we perceive the world, and on the communities where we live.

Think about what it means to reject rational thinking. Scientific thinking based on order, rationality, and progress is no longer relevant or useful. One person's view of reality is as valid as another's. There can be no such thing as objective truth, and there is nothing wrong with contradictions. If you want to mix classic Christian doctrines with non-Christian views such as occultism or belief in the healing power of crystals, that's valid if it makes sense to you. Nobody can ever be wrong about what he or she believes. Both Rich and Karen can be right, if that is what they want to believe, and so are Rich's parents who go to that traditional church and know nothing about sacred journeys or enlightened spirits. And if anybody—a religious person, for example—claims to have a message that is true, that person is thought to be intolerant and arrogant.

Recently I attended a conference where the speaker, an abuse counselor, was talking about people who believe they have been abused by their parents. "I'm not interested in whether or not the abuse really happened," the speaker said. "If somebody thinks it happened, then that is reality to the person." This is postmodern thinking and an insight into the postmodern view of history: we don't need to worry about the facts; each of us constructs our own reality. If an individual thinks something is true, viewed from his or her perspective, then for that person it is true. Taken a step farther, it follows that if a person in a mental hospital has what we used to call bizarre and irrational thoughts, they are true, at least to the patient. There is no separation between reality and delusion.

Postmodern thinking tends to be pessimistic. There is widespread dissatisfaction with a culture that has embraced rationalism and lauded technology, only to see increased evidence of war, violence, poverty, and environmental pollution. Things aren't getting better with all our technology, postmodernism claims. Things are getting worse. Grenz summarizes this concisely: "For the first time in recent history, the emerging generation does not share the conviction of their parents that the world is becoming a better place in which to live. From widening holes in the ozone layer to teen-on-teen violence, they see our problems mounting. And they are no longer convinced that human ingenuity will solve these enormous problems or that their living standard will be higher than that of their parents."[21] The postmodern generation even believes that the survival of the human race is at stake.

Some sociologists have looked at our culture and argued that this is an in-between time. Our future direction is unclear, but old dreams about endless progress and the superiority of reason have faded. Now that the cold war is over, the clear struggle between the East and the West has gone. Instead, we are faced with unpredictable, seemingly uncontrollable local skirmishes in places like Latin America, the Balkans, the Middle East, and the African continent where whole countries teeter on the edge of anarchy.[22] Uncertainty about the future captivates people of all ages: violence and poverty are on the increase, the church is declining in prestige and influence, politicians seem more concerned about their egos and chances for reelection than about the good of the people whom they are supposed to represent. With all of this discord, many are looking for a spiritual reality that goes beyond the despair that surrounds us.

A New Look at Morals

Probably you can guess the postmodern view of morals. It assumes that there can be no such thing as right or wrong. Everything depends on the perspective of the individual and the community where one lives. Personal pragmatism is the basis for deciding what is right or true. If my perspective works for me, then it is valid. Essentially the view is stated, "What is right for us might not be right for you," and "What is wrong in our context might in your context be acceptable and even preferable."[23] If Aaron Feuerstein thinks it is right and honorable to keep his idle employees on the payroll, that is right for him. If another employer had let them all go and moved his business to another location, that would have been right too. This thinking can lead to the dangerous conclusion that people can never be wrong about their values or moral standards. And they can never be wrong about religion. It isn't surprising that postmodern thinking clashes with religious viewpoints that claim to know the truth or that hold absolute standards of right and wrong.

All of this has many implications for the new spirituality. In an age of tolerance and antidogmatism, we are free to believe whatever we want. Nobody has an edge on the truth; no one religious belief or practice is better than another. And there is nothing to stop us from changing religions if we so desire: "Since faith is rooted in practical matters of personal taste and experience, people tend to adopt and abandon beliefs according to the demands of the moment. After all, when truth is a human creation rather than something independent of ourselves, we may casually move on to some new 'truth' whenever it suits us."[24] It is no more appropriate to question the validity of a person's religious beliefs than it is to evaluate his or her choice from a dinner menu. And it makes no sense to debate issues together, seeking to discover truth or arrive at a consensus based on logical thinking.[25]

It is easy for a former professor like me to be critical of postmodernism without acknowledging its strengths. Postmodern despair and pessimism about the planet have validity. Even some of my more conservative Christian friends agree with postmodernist hopelessness and despondency about the harmful effects of technology, the stubborn persistence of poverty and violence, the disappearance of the sacred from everyday life, and the seeming futility of human efforts to bring world peace and higher standards of living. The Old Testament writer of Ecclesiastes spoke to the postmodernist with a similar voice of cynicism and despair although he reached a different conclusion—that with God everything is meaningful. Even Jesus seemed to be a little postmodernesque at times. He was nontraditional, nonscientific, a nonconformist, and inclined to speak in parables, even though he was never illogical and never deviated from his anchor in the Scriptures.

A New View of Community

Community plays a major role in postmodernism. Unlike the preference for individualism that characterized modernism, the postmodernists sense a need to belong. It is in a community that we discover ourselves and find well-being.

Suppose two people are evaluating a controversial issue such as abortion. How we see the abortion issue depends a lot on where we are and the persons we are with. If they are consistent with their opinions that dogmatism is out and tolerance is in, postmodernists would have to agree that the pro-life stance taken by a community of people who oppose abortion is as valid and as truthful as the pro-choice stance taken by members of the National Organization of Women (NOW) or other groups that support a woman's right to choose what will happen to her unborn baby.

HOW DOES THIS TIE IN WITH
THE NEW SPIRITUALITY?

I'm old enough to remember the Second World War and the optimism that swept the Western world following the defeat of Hitler and his allies. Everybody hoped that war would be gone for a long time, maybe forever, and millions of people had hope for a brighter tomorrow. Soon, however, the iron curtain of communism cast its shadow over the entire globe. Within a few years, a generation of postwar babies reached young adulthood and turned the world upside down with an experientially oriented counterculture revolution in the 1960s. Instead of getting better, the world seemed to get worse—more violent, more expensive, more uncertain. The age of anxiety gave way to the "me generation," and by the late eighties there were widespread despair and recognition that the halcyon days of the fifties were gone forever.

As we moved into the 1990s, many corporate climbers, especially baby boomers, were hitting glass ceilings. Growing numbers were seeing the futility and the cost of their relentless pursuit of success. There was talk of downshifting to simpler lifestyles. More and more of us now realize the value of slowing down and building character instead of driving to build careers and accumulate more stuff. The middle-aged boomers are realizing that their parents and their children are getting older. Their parents are experiencing retirement or impending retirement, no longer concerned about careers but wondering what the future holds. Near the other end of the age spectrum are members of Generation X, who want connectedness more than career success but who wonder if they will be left with the debt and massive social problems that older generations have created. In all of these age-groups, including the cadre of teenagers and younger people who are growing up today, there appears to be what Mother Teresa called the greatest problem of this generation: loneliness. There are also anxiety, uncertainty about the future, and a search for answers.

At one time families, churches, and governments gave clear answers, accepted morality, and proven stability, but not any longer. Families are falling apart, thousands of churches seem to have lost their relevance, and almost nobody trusts or respects the government. We are a mobile people, often without roots, trying to find meaning and stability in a world that is changing, confusing, and dumping on us with tons of new information every day. For years we have looked to psychology for help—many still do. But as we have seen, even the mental health practitioners admit that they don't have answers to the search for meaning, and the need to understand evil, suffering, and death. So we hurry to read books about near death experiences, angels, inner tranquillity, or channelers and spirit guides who claim to show us the way to go.

When these guides and the gurus of the new spirituality tell us that enlightenment comes from within, we are tempted to respond with relief. When postmodernists tell us there is no need to worry about truth, order, consistency, rules, rituals, belief in the right things, or adherence to somebody else's religious dogmas, many people respond enthusiastically. It can be encouraging to hear that people can control their lives and their overwhelming circumstances if they can look within themselves and find enlightenment, unlimited power, and inner knowledge. Some new spirituality teachers tell us that humans can control angels, repeat lives, never have to say they're sorry for past behavior, and even view life as a story that evolves. It all sounds very attractive, even plausible, to people living in a whirlwind of crammed schedules, incessant demands, and cascading change.

GETTING BACK TO THE NEW SPIRITUALITY

In one way or another, all of us are interested in spirituality, and most of us want more in-depth spiritual experiences for ourselves. We have been exposed to the new spirituality smorgasbord and may be confused by the diversity. But in our searching for the sacred do we need to consider all of this psychology, philosophy, and history? Is it really necessary to take long digressions into topics such as the recovery movement and postmodern thinking, to ponder the teachings of Anthony Robbins and Scott Peck, or to consider the concerns of baby boomers? Maybe not. But familiarity with issues like the ones in this chapter can give us a much surer foundation on which to grow in our communion with God. Now we begin to understand why the new spirituality is so popular and widely accepted. Now we see why so many people are searching for the sacred and where they are looking.

One of my Generation X friends interacts daily with people—maybe like you—who are attracted to the new spiritualities. "A lot of people seem to be longing to find meaning in everyday life," my friend told me. They want to gain peace of mind and learn how to cope in a society that breeds anxiety. They want to find a worldview that makes sense of suffering, one that is honest about the difficult chapters in their lives—the tragedies they have encountered, the ways they have been hurt, their struggles to find hope. My friend talked about a psychologist he knows who is "into various forms of Buddhism and has no interest in 'Western religions,'" but who longs for a relationship with a God who is personal and relational rather than simply gaining a peaceful consciousness.

Both Rich and Karen would resonate with these goals. The Christianity that Rich has rejected focused on a personal relationship with Jesus Christ, but the people in his church seem uncomfortable with questioning and unwilling to understand and come alongside younger members of the congregation who struggle to find meaning in their lives. Suffering is sometimes mentioned in Rich's former church, most often in sermons about Job, but the tragedies and injustices of life tend to be explained away with syrupy language and covered with placid smiles. Rich wants something real. He is attracted to the passion and inspirational energy of Anthony Robbins, notices when the dynamic motivator mentions the Bible, and is encouraged with the idea that all one needs for life is to release the personal power within. But Rich is not into making money or making sales, and he wonders if Robbins is too slick, too optimistic, and too motivational to speak to people who struggle to find meaning in the humdrum of everyday life.

Karen knows the emptiness of the success that Robbins exemplifies; she has seen it in her career-driven parents. She resonates more with the self-exploration, inner probings, and spiritual journeys of her friends who embrace Jung. She likes the subjectivism, moral freedom, and sense of community that she finds in postmodernist ways of thinking. But she still feels alone, searching for the sacred in a lonely pilgrimage, surrounded by others who are equally lonely and grappling for spiritual fulfillment. As she searches, Karen is committed to simplistic living, healthy eating, and the alternative approaches to healing that we will discuss in the next chapter.

When Russell Chandler's family began to work on their giant jigsaw puzzle, we can almost guarantee that they started by looking at the picture on the box. They could see the bigger picture and get some idea of what they were trying to accomplish. In a similar way, we now have glanced at the bigger picture. It is time to return to the pieces and start making progress in putting the spirituality puzzle together for our lives.

— 4 —

Healing and the Spirituality Puzzle:

Does the New Spirituality Improve Our Health?

Before I tell you how a new breed of doctors is changing the face of medicine, I'd like to make a confession: I believe. I believe in the brilliance of Western medicine, in the technological wonders of organ transplants, brain scans, and laparoscopic surgery—and I also believe that shamanic healers from indigenous cultures have discovered treatments for illnesses that traditional medicine can't touch, that the mind alone can trigger and then reverse illness, that dietary changes, along with vitamin and herbal supplements, can powerfully impact the course of disease. I believe in merging the best of both worlds—the orthodox and the alternative. I'm not alone in my belief.[1]

With those words, the author of a popular magazine article began her summary of one of the most distinctive features of the new spirituality: the growing acceptance of meditation, shamanism, prayer, acupuncture, and a host of other alternative approaches to treating illnesses and maintaining health. The movement began at the popular level, far removed from medical schools and doctors' offices. Today, the rush to embrace alternative medicines is breaking into mainstream medicine where respected physicians are risking their reputations and security by blending prayer, spirituality, and nontraditional methods with their high-tech treatment procedures.

Dr. Howard Fuerst is one of these physicians. He didn't expect to become a believer. Trained at University of Pennsylvania Medical School, the doctor became an internist and built a successful practice in Florida. When his stepdaughter give him a book by an Indian spiritual healer named Deepak Chopra, the busy doctor looked at it briefly, then put it aside. Chopra's thesis that the human body and the human spirit are intimately connected was of little interest to Dr. Fuerst. That idea didn't appear in his medical journals, and it hadn't been part of the curriculum of his med school training.

Everything changed when the doctor learned that he had prostate cancer so advanced that surgery was not possible. He was put on standard hormone therapy and given two years to live. Faced with that crisis, he picked up the Chopra book and began reading that meditation, the right diet, and a Westernized version of Hindu mysticism could prevent and even reverse disease. Dr. Fuerst started meditating thirty minutes a day. He prayed, recited Chopra's 10 Keys to Happiness, and showed up at every Chopra speaking engagement within two hundred miles. And the doctor's tumor disappeared. This happens sometimes; the medical profession calls it *spontaneous healing*. But Dr. Fuerst has no doubt that his recovery came because he had applied the teachings of Deepak Chopra.

SPIRITUALLY NEUTRAL TREATMENT?

Chopra is among the latest in a long line of healers combining their views of spirituality with the nonmedical treatment of disease and illness. But we shouldn't assume that all nontraditional approaches to healing are tied to the new spirituality. Many illnesses—such as high blood pressure, acute anxiety, depression, backaches, cardiovascular and gastrointestinal disease, and chronic headaches—are related to stress and the way we live. Surgery or medications can help, but people with these conditions may be more likely to get better when they slow the pace of their lives, take time for relaxation, eat in healthier ways, or hook up with others who can give support and encouragement. These approaches to healing have little to do with the sterile and high-tech world of medicine. And more often than not, these approaches make no reference to anything religious or spiritual.

Isadore Rosenfeld is an expert in these new methods. Distinguished Professor of Clinical Medicine at New York Hospital/Cornell Medical Center and attending physician at both the New York Hospital and the Memorial Sloan-Kettering Cancer Center, Dr. Rosenfeld has impressive medical credentials. He is also a clear and captivating writer whose *Guide to Alternative Medicine* is not intended to be a book about spirituality.[2] The physician-author looks at a variety of nontraditional approaches to healing, evaluates the scientific evidence to support the claims of each, and tries to guide readers in distinguishing between competent and quack practitioners. But if you read his discussions about acupuncture, chiropractic, enzyme therapy, applied kinesiology, reflexology, neurolinguistic programming, and two dozen others, you begin to see how so many of these popular approaches are less neutral than they might appear at first. Often these treatments are built on new spirituality theories and views of life. For many of the alternative medicines, spirituality and physical health are intertwined, sometimes subtly. This point brings us back to the impact and popularity of Deepak Chopra.

CHOPRA'S SPIRITUALITY

Bright and articulate, Chopra was only seventeen when he was accepted at the prestigious All India School of Medical Sciences. Following graduation, he moved to the United States, interned at a small hospital in New Jersey, was recruited during the Vietnam-era doctor shortage, and eventually became an endocrinologist and chief of staff at a Massachusetts hospital.[3]

The doctor was ambitious and successful but dismayed at the lifestyle that came with his job: rushing through his days, drinking endless pots of coffee, smoking packs of cigarettes, and using Scotch each night to calm down. He began to feel like a legalized drug pusher, prescribing medication to a never-ending line of patients, ignoring long-term prevention, and dispensing short-term cures in the form of pills. One day he picked up a book on transcendental meditation (TM). Using its principles, he quit smoking and drinking, and soon found himself on a spiritual journey back to his roots in India. He visited the founder of the Hindu-based TM, Maharishi Mahesh Yogi, and eventually became a salesman for the Maharishi's Indian herbal cures known as Ayur-Veda. The *Journal of the American Medical Association* was critical of Ayur-Veda, but Chopra became a millionaire salesman and found the freedom to turn his attention to writing.

His *Ageless Body, Timeless Mind* became a six-million-copy bestseller.[4] On the day following Chopra's appearance on Oprah Winfrey's television show, his book sold 137,000 copies. I bought one copy several months after that, plowed through its contents, and later read *Time* magazine's description of Chopra's book:

> A remarkable work, it is a hodge-podge of personal anecdotes, unfootnoted references to scientific studies, literary allusion, commonsense wisdom and spiritual speculation; it features Dostoyevsky, the Rig Veda, bar graphs, German physicist Werner Heisenberg and exercises you can perform at home. At its core, and repeatedly in seemingly endless permutations, is a religio-philosophical thesis that runs something like this:

> Our bodies, which seem so solid and finite, are not. For one thing, we replace most of our component cells regularly; thus, rather than collections of aging organs, we are works in constant progress. On the subatomic level, moreover, we are no denser than the air around us and indistinguishable from our

surroundings. Finally, since quantum physics asserts that matter and energy are interchangeable, we are not individual beings at all but merely local expressions of an infinite, universal field of energy. A smart field of energy; "All of us are connected to patterns of intelligence that govern the whole cosmos. Our bodies are part of a universal body, our minds an aspect of a universal mind."[5]

Chopra's approach to health and healing involves meditating, reducing stress, and following Ayurvedic practices. Since nothing holds more power over the body than beliefs in the mind, Chopra reasons that we can change the conditions of our bodies and the course of disease by changing our perceptions and refocusing our minds. If your vigor and energy decline as you get older, that is because you are expecting them to decline. According to Chopra, loss of vigor means that you have "unwittingly implanted a self-defeating intention in the form of a strong belief, and the mind-body connection automatically carries out this intention." You can prevent the losses of age by "consciously programing your mind to remain youthful, using the power of your intention."[6]

In the article about Deepak Chopra, the *Time* journalist identified four categories of new healers. First, the Physicians, like Andrew Weil and Larry Dossey, try to relate spirituality to Western medical science. Second, the Synthesizers seek to adapt mysticism, Zen Buddhism, visualization, and other Eastern worldviews to fit the approaches to healing and stress reduction that are used in the West. Third, the Expressionists, like Marianne Williamson and Louise Hay, touch the heartstrings and passionately describe how thought patterns can cure illness. Hay, for example, writes that hernias may be caused by ruptured relationships and may be cured by thinking, *I love myself and am free to be me*. Fourth, the Visionaries see visions, promote the messages of their spirit guides, and "use mind energy, connected with universal God energy," to bring healing. According to the *Time* article, Chopra is strong because he is a combination of all four of these approaches: an endocrinologist, a synthesizer of Indian

75

medicine and quantum physics, a writer of great passion, and a visionary propagator of magic and mysticism.[7]

This is not as far removed from your life and spirituality as it might seem. Alternative approaches to healing, many based on Chopra-type new spirituality, are sweeping into medical schools and being accepted as legitimate forms of treatment by dollar-conscious health-care providers and insurance companies. Even governments are considering the financial and healing benefits of alternative medicines, but doctors who practice mainstream medicine have been slow to accept the new approaches. Still, "it's not fulfilling to practice medicine as if human beings are machines," suggests Dr. Larry Dossey. "Doctors are spiritually hungry, they are becoming seekers, and this is more than an intellectual adventure. It has become a personal search" that is changing the doctors and affecting their approaches to treatment.[8]

The spiritual hunger and the personal search that Dossey attributes to physicians extend to the rest of us as well. Every week I talk with friends who are facing serious illness—failing kidneys, multiple sclerosis, advancing cancer, cardiovascular problems, persisting depression. I know two couples whose infant children are fighting losing battles against terminal illnesses that seem certain to snuff out young lives while their grief-burdened parents watch helplessly. I have a colleague with a brain tumor, a lifelong friend who has had a stroke, and another acquaintance who lives with the lingering effects of a near fatal automobile accident. As I watch all of them, I stand amazed and grateful for the health that has been with me all of my life. I have never been seriously ill or in the hospital, so I don't know how I would react to a life-threatening disease. But I can guess.

Like most of my friends who have illnesses, I surely would seek the best medical treatment possible and rationalize a way to pay even for what I could not afford. If the doctors offered little hope, I might look for alternative treatments or clinics that were outside the sphere of modern, technologically based medicine. In all of this I would pray about my condition and ask others to pray as well. Probably I would ask the leaders of my church to pray for me and maybe anoint me with oil, as the New Testament directs. I would never visit a shaman and I don't think I would go to a faith-healing meeting—they are not part of my theology—but if I were desperate, maybe I would look for hope and healing in places and with people whom I dismiss today when I have good health and buoyant energy. Alternative healings, many with a spiritual basis, are not remote and far-fetched to people who are in pain and in dire need of healing.

We may be in the midst of a health-care revolution that could stitch mainstream and alternative medicines into one integrated medicine. If so, then you and I will be impacted by the new spirituality when we visit the doctor in the future. It is already happening.[9] And it is influenced by a new interest in the healing powers of faith and prayer.

CAN FAITH HEAL?

Ten years ago, two unusual articles appeared in the *Southern Medical Journal,* a technical magazine for doctors. One article described a study of 393 patients from the coronary care unit at San Francisco General Hospital. Without their knowledge, those people were divided into two groups as part of a research project. To reduce bias, the patients, their families, and the doctors and nurses who treated them were not told that they were part of an experiment until it was over. One group was prayed for consistently by a number of committed Christians; the other group was not prayed for. When medical records were compared later, patients in the prayed-for group had fewer incidents of congestive heart failure or other complications during recovery. In addition, when compared to the other group, patients who had been prayed for were less likely to get pneumonia, less often in need of diuretics, less frequently connected to tubes or ventilators to help breathing, and five times less likely to need antibiotics. Stated differently, the prayed-for people were more likely to get better, and their improvement was smoother and faster.[10]

The other article concerned patients who were severely burned. Even though recovery for these people is painful, prolonged, often depressing, and always stressful, doctors and nurses know that some patients cope very well in contrast to those who do not. Part of the difference concerns religion. There is growing evidence that people who are religious cope better with severe burns and other physical problems and are more likely to show improvements in physical and mental health.[11]

During the past few years, numerous other studies have shown that religion is good for your health:[12]

- A Dartmouth Medical School research team studied patients preparing for elective heart surgery. Nonreligious people were three times more likely to die within six months than patients who found strength and comfort in their religious beliefs. Of the thirty-seven patients who called themselves "deeply religious," none died.
- Family medicine researchers in North Carolina discovered fewer medical complications for maternity patients and their newborns if the mothers had a religious affiliation.
- One study of thirty female patients recovering from hip fractures found that those who regarded God as a source of strength and comfort and who normally attended religious services were able to walk farther upon discharge and had less depression than patients who had few religious beliefs.
- A thirty-year study on blood pressure showed that churchgoers had lower blood pressure even when the statistics were adjusted to account for smoking and other risk factors.
- A National Institute of Aging survey of four thousand randomly selected elderly people living at home found that the people who attended religious services were less depressed and physically healthier than those who worshiped at home or watched religious services on television. It is possible, of course, that the people who went to church were less depressed because they were healthier and better able to get out. Nevertheless, the researcher (a Duke University psychiatrist) concluded that participating in religious services,

praying together in a community of believers, and using Scripture reading as a comforting and coping device all had a positive impact on physical health—more positive than "do it yourself at home" or television religion.

Dr. Larry Dossey, the physician-author of a best-seller titled *Prayer Is Good Medicine,* has been described as "the doctor who almost single-handedly legitimized the study of prayer in medicine."[13] Born in the Bible Belt and steeped in fundamentalism, Dossey became an agnostic as he got older, but he never lost his fascination with prayer. He became a physician and found himself as a battalion surgeon in Vietnam, amazed to be offering prayers of thanks to a God he no longer believed in every time he missed being hit by a mortar shell. Back home after the war, Dossey stumbled onto the Randolph Byrd article on the healing power of prayer. Soon he discovered the writings of Dr. David Larson, whose work at the National Institute for Healthcare Research is demonstrating conclusively that religious practices, including prayer, can have health benefits. Dossey gradually immersed himself in the tenets of Buddhism, particularly Zen, discovered the mystical traditions of Christianity, read the works of Jung, and became convinced that we can use our minds to influence other people's behavior and even promote or inhibit the growth of bacteria and fungi at a distance of several miles.[14] More recently the prayer doctor has turned his attention to what he calls negative prayer. If we can pray for the good of others, including their healing, he argues, then why can't we pray that others will be harmed, or that people will be defeated who don't share our views? Dossey doesn't seem ready to admit the existence of a literal Satan, but he acknowledges that there may be what Jung called the devil in the form of "an archetypal force in the human mind."[15]

Many researchers are vague in what they mean by *prayer, belief,* or *religion.* Some have a Christian view that defines *prayer* as bringing petitions before a sovereign, divine Being. Others, like Dossey and Harvard professor Herbert Benson, see prayer and belief in a much broader sense. Having faith—whether in God, in Allah, in an invincible force, or even in medicine—is assumed to be what's important. Praying to Jesus, praying the rosary, using a mantra, and meditating with crystals are thought to be equally valid, as long as the person believes. In a major article on the healing power of prayer, Christian physician Dale Matthews noted that "being devout provides more health benefits than not being devout." Science has demonstrated this convincingly. But, Matthews conceded, "we haven't shown that being a devout Christian will make you healthier than being a devout Buddhist" or being a devout believer in anything else.[16]

Despite this uncertainty about the meaning of prayer, it would seem that doctors should be enthusiastic about all of these results showing the positive impact of faith on health. If prayer were a drug, like Prozac, the medical world would be excited about its potential for bringing wellness and healing. That excitement doesn't exist, however, at least not yet. For decades, physicians, especially psychiatrists, have viewed religion as irrelevant for treatment and sometimes even harmful. Some doctors have looked at the research results and concluded that religious belief is not nearly as important as the social support that religious patients get from other believers. Several polls have supported the idea that doctors, as a group, are more skeptical than their patients about the healing power of prayer, faith, religion, and spirituality.

In the United States—other countries would be different—one survey found that 79 percent of nonmedical people agreed that spiritual faith can help us recover from disease, injury, or illness. The same poll found that 56 percent believe that their faith already has helped them recover from illness. Almost 76 percent of those questioned thought it was good for doctors to talk to their patients about faith, but only 10 percent said that a doctor had ever mentioned anything spiritual or religious.[17] In a *Time*/CNN survey, 82 percent of the respondents said they believe in the healing power of prayer, 77 percent agreed that God sometimes intervenes to cure serious illness, and 64 percent believed that doctors would pray with patients who request it.[18] But few doctors are comfortable in that role. Many don't even believe in God, and prayer is never part of their treatment.

The insurance companies and the managed care groups who pay the bills are less hesitant. Increasingly they see prayer and spirituality as low-cost, effective treatments that clients want and that doctors will have to accept, sooner or later. Prayer doesn't always bring healing, of course, but group studies continue to show that, taken as a whole, patients who are prayed for tend to do better than people who don't get prayer. In a society that rarely mentioned religion a few years ago, prayer has come out of the closet. It has stopped being a private or embarrassing topic and is emerging as a significant part of the new interest in spirituality.

A DIFFERENT KIND OF HEALING

Ann Cannady prayed, but ultimately she found healing in a different way. When test results confirmed that she had advanced uterine cancer, Ann and her husband, Gary, "spent the next eight weeks scared and praying, praying and scared." Gary's first wife had died of the same illness, and he wondered if he had the strength to go through it all a second time. "Please, if I'm going to die, let me die quickly," Ann prayed. "I don't want Gary to have to face this again."

One morning, three days before his wife was scheduled for surgery, Gary answered the doorbell and was greeted by a very large man, taller than Gary's six-foot, five-inch height. The visitor was black, with deep azure blue eyes. He introduced himself as Thomas and told Ann that her cancer was gone.

Thomas announced to the astonished couple that he had been sent by God, and when he raised his right hand, Ann felt incredible heat coming from his palm. "Suddenly I felt my legs go out from under me and I fell to the floor," she said later. "As I lay there, a strong white light, like one of those searchlights, traveled through my body. It started at my feet and worked its way up. I knew, then, with every part of me—my body, my mind, and my heart—that something supernatural had happened." Then Ann passed out.

When she awoke, Gary was leaning over his wife's limp body, pleading for her to speak. Thomas was gone and Ann felt weak. But she was able to crawl to the phone, call her doctor, and tell him that she had been cured and didn't need the surgery. The doctor replied that she was showing signs of stress and fear, but she insisted that the surgery wouldn't be needed. In the end they reached a compromise. Ann would show up at the hospital as scheduled, but before operating the surgeons would do a biopsy.

When she woke up after the biopsy, Ann was in a regular hospital room with the doctor at her bedside. "I don't understand what has happened," he said. "Your test came back clean." In the following weeks, as she returned for further tests, the doctor confirmed that the cancer was gone and acknowledged that he had witnessed a medical miracle. To this day, Gary and Ann are convinced that the miracle came when they were visited by a black angel named Thomas.[19]

ANGELS AMONG US

It's no secret that angels have been known for centuries. In addition to Christianity and Judaism, angels are a part of Islam. Angelic figures are painted in the tombs of Egypt, and similar beings are found in Buddhism, Hinduism, and Zoroastrianism. Despite their longevity, these supernatural beings have rarely attracted much popular attention. The Bible mentions them often, picturing angels sometimes as individual messengers (the word *angel* means "messenger") and other times as heavenly hosts who worship God and carry out his divine purposes. Sometimes they are powerful creatures who strike fear in people who meet them. In Genesis, angels with flashing swords guarded the gates of Eden. In Ezekiel, they overpowered the prophet with awesome visions. In the Gospels, a host of angels appeared to shepherds who fell to the ground in great fear. In Revelation, they came together in luminous beauty, raising their magnificent voices in a powerful crescendo of praise to God. They also did battle with a dragon—and won. Biblical people who encountered angels were changed dramatically. Similar experiences have come to people like Ann Cannady and others who claim to have met angels in more recent times.

How different are the angels who are part of the angel mania craze that recently swept the nation and still attracts millions of devotees. "In the past few years angels have lodged in the popular imagination," concludes a writer in *Time* magazine. There are angels-only boutiques, angel newsletters, angel seminars, plays and movies about angels, and a host of best-selling angel books. What are these modern angels like?

> Glancing around the gift shops, one might imagine that their role is purely decorative. Holiday angels are luscious creatures, plump and dimpled, all ruffled and improvised. In their tame placidity they bear no resemblance to the fearsome creatures in the Bible. . . . In their modern incarnation, these mighty messengers and fearless soldiers have been reduced to bite-sized beings, easily digested. The terrifying cherubim have become Kewpie-doll cherubs. For those who choke too easily on God and his rules, theologians observe, angels are the handy compromise, all fluff and meringue, kind, nonjudgmental. And they are available to anyone like aspirin. . . .They're nonthreatening, wise and loving beings. They offer help whether we ask for it or not.[20]

And they're taken seriously by people searching for the sacred. One survey found that 69 percent of respondents believed in the existence of angels; 46 percent believed they had a personal guardian angel.[21] To the distress of Christian theologians, the angels that grab the popular imagination and appear in lapel pins or dainty statues are light-years away from the celestial beings that have characterized more traditional religion. Hollywood sometimes pictures angels as "regular people" who pull pranks, drink with the guys, and even have sex with willing partners on earth.[22] Some popular authors have turned angels into personal genies, available at our beck and call to solve problems and work magic. Other writers invite each of us to get in touch with the personal inner angel, to summon our "angel psychotherapist," or to view ourselves as angels.

Angels help us conquer illness. "Angels are healers as well as messengers," writes one popular author. She adds that angels "can also rearrange your cells on a microscopic level, with the help of your own imagination." Healing is promised to those who "visualize angels programing your immune system with healing messages and charging it up with energy."[23]

Angel Popularity

Why have angels become so popular? What has led to their eager acceptance by so many spiritual seekers? One answer suggests that angels are attractive because they offer a spirituality that does not involve rules or commitment to God.[24] By re-creating angels to make them look friendly, lovable, and accepting, we can deal with the supernatural on our own terms, without having to bother about God.

With angels we can also find a way to get help with our problems. At the First Church of the Angels in Carmel, California, minister Andre D'Angelo (I wonder if that is his real name?) calls on "angel power" to help his clients work through "unresolved traumas." Often, angels are assumed to give us guidance and protection in the midst of a changing and dangerous society. "Angels are popular now because the ordinary ways of coping are not working," suggests a professor at Chapman University. "People are lost in the machinery of society and are getting chewed up. So you need someone you can trust, maybe your own guardian angel, someone you can call down on yourself."[25] Sometimes these angelic creatures help us escape the realities of the present and build fantasy images of a celestial world where everything is okay.

Life becomes more meaningful and worth living when we ask the angels into our lives, according to angel author Terry Lynn Taylor. "They provide us with unconditional happiness, fun, and mirth. They also help us with romance and wealth. And they help us extinguish worries that plague our lives."[26] When our lives end, they assure us that life will go on after we die.

But does it seem strange that the popular conceptions view all angels as benevolent, as promoting our health and self-esteem? Is this largely a spiritual fad bred by wishful thinking? Theological researcher Ron Rhodes suggests that much of what we read about angels in many best-selling books would seem to have more to do with fallen angels (demons) than with God's holy angels. Christians believe that fallen angels act as benevolent helpers and bearers of insights. In this way they hide the fact that they really are impostors, luring innocent people into a destructive spirituality without God.[27]

FOUR UNIQUE SPIRITUALITY SEEKERS

Stories of healing and spirituality, angels and changed lives, seem to be endless. The cover of *Common Boundary*, a magazine dedicated to "Exploring Psychology, Spirituality, and Creativity," recently showed a smiling picture of Caroline Myss, who comes across as a warm and charming woman described in the magazine as a medical intuitive. That, readers learn, is a person "who can perceive the state of health or illness in another's body, using a skill similar to telepathy." Myss is given a person's name and birth date, then "without drama or fanfare, she begins to receive a series of intuitive impressions. She translates these impressions into specific medical diagnoses such as pancreatic cancer, diabetes, or even an illness that is in such an early stage that medical tests pick it up only months later." Myss's medical colleague, who probably is not the most objective observer, reports that the diagnoses exceed the accuracy of conventional medicine by at least 10 percent. All of this works, according to the magazine article, because Myss is able to read the flow of energy in the human body and pick up the currents in a body's electromagnetic field.[28]

Carol Wilken has taken another approach to spirituality. Her spiritual quest began in earnest when she was diagnosed as having a brain tumor. It was small, benign, and operable, but as she lay on the operating table, Wilken sensed a "feminine presence," assuring her that everything would be all right. This encounter with "goddess energy" launched Wilken on a search for what she calls the "Sacred Feminine." One major difference between this female spirituality and more traditional religion is that mainstream religions view God as being "out there, somewhere in the heavens." The Sacred Feminine "is the imaging of the divine as it exists within each of us and the belief that the earth is alive, that everything comes from and is relative to the earth."[29] Other forms of feminine spirituality have focused on worship of the goddess Sophia and rejected Christianity as a male religion of violence and masculine oppression. Jung fueled some of this thinking with his theory that deep within all of us there is a "Divine Woman archetype." This feminine spiritual part of our personalities has been pushed down for centuries. Women have been forced to live their lives through the aspirations of men. Men, in turn, have squelched this feminine part of their lives and been less complete as a result. Wilken's feminine spirituality seeks to correct this imbalance.

Judith Fein encountered a different type of spirituality. Born into a Jewish family, she left the synagogue behind and became a successful screenwriter in the secular world of Hollywood. In preparation for a documentary film series, Fein went to New Mexico. She entered a Native American world where twentieth-century Americans live in developing-country poverty and where people appear to cling to a culture stubbornly set in its outdated ways. To her surprise, Fein found something else—a way of life "from children's stories to celebrations, that is imbued with spirituality and mortared with subtle lessons in kindness to others, reverence for the earth, patience and generosity." In touch with this Indian spirituality, Fein discovered a new focus and meaning to life. She was healed, she believes, from a neurotic lifestyle once marked by a fear of heights, fear of nature, fear of the future, and fear of what other people think. Among the Native Americans she was with people who feel safe on the planet, secure in Mother Earth, and not bound by a constant state of anxiety and insecurity.[30]

Three decades earlier, a psychologist at Columbia University heard an inaudible voice that claimed to be Jesus. Declaring herself to be an atheist and a reluctant scribe, the psychologist, whose name was Helen Schucman, took notes on what she was hearing. "This is a course in miracles," the voice began, and Schucman started writing. For seven years the note taking continued until the writer had a 1,200-page work that promises to bring people to increasingly deeper experiences of God. The Course resembles the ascent up a spiral staircase, according to its page on the Internet. "The reader is led in a circular pattern, each revolution leading higher until the top of the spiral is reached, which opens to God" and leads ultimately to the perceptual and experiential transformation that is the aim of the Course. Schucman died in 1981, but her *Course in Miracles* remains popular; at last count more than a million copies of the three-volume set had been sold.

How do you respond to what you have been reading? Over and over again, we hear about diverse approaches to healing, about endless theories and fantasies concerning angels, about medical intuition, the goddess movement, Indian spirituality, and even about miracles. A magazine in my mailbox tells me that I can "discover the pulse of life and find renewal" in the shamanism based in the Huichol Indian tradition. While I was writing this section, a friend faxed me an article about sacred sexuality—the idea that sexual ecstasy is the best route to deeper spirituality. The articles, books, and seminars on spirituality continue to inundate almost all of us.

For seekers like Rich and Karen, or for people like you and me, it can be lonely and confusing trying to make our way through this spirituality maze. Each movement, each spiritual leader, each promise of enlightenment or route to spiritual awakening, comes with enthusiastic endorsements and guaranteed offers of success. Karen tries to pick and choose, cafeteria style, hoping to piece together a belief system that will work for her. Rich struggles with guilt and discomfort about forsaking his Christian roots, but he wonders if a personally crafted spirituality really would be better. Others may read about all of the spiritual diversities and feel increasing frustration and bewilderment.

This brings us to an important question that, until now, we have not faced directly: What is spirituality? For centuries, Christians defined *spirituality* in terms of one's relationship with God, but within recent years the term has become much broader, increasingly vague, and maybe so diverse that it is meaningless. Modern discussions of spirituality often abandon the concept of God, redefine the meaning of God, urge us to look within ourselves if we want to find God, or even suggest that each of us is a god.

WHAT, THEN, IS SPIRITUALITY?

For many years I was on the faculty of a large Protestant theological seminary. I taught classes and spent a lot of time with students who were interested both in their own spirituality and in ways to encourage spirituality in others. We talked about the secular psychology in which I had been trained, we discussed theology and its relevance (or its lack of relevance) to modern society, and we learned together about personal and spiritual growth. Looking back on my days as a professor, I wish I had prayed more with my students, worshiped more often with them in community, and been more sensitive to where those young lives were going on their spiritual journeys. Too often, I think, we studied prayer but took little time to pray, talked about helping but overlooked opportunities to help, read books about spirituality but were too busy with our studies and term papers to apply what we were reading to our lives.

One of my students left with his diploma and went to work in a church-sponsored counseling center. Moving from there into a private practice, he later worked at a cancer treatment center and then at a psychiatric hospital. Through all of those experiences, my former student—his name is Andy—found that he had no distinctive approach to doing his counseling. As his professional career developed, so did his spiritual search. He explored charismatic approaches to healing and became "a reluctant charismatic." He tried to understand something of the "signs and wonders" movement, but it left him feeling dissatisfied. Eventually, to his surprise, he landed in the ceremonial and ritualistic arms of the Episcopal Church. Andy's counseling began to combine the importance of God's inspired Word drawn from the evangelical church, the emphasis on healing and spiritual gifts from the charismatic church, and the liturgical reverence of the Episcopal-Catholic tradition. Working, planning, and praying together with fellow believers, my friend developed a new mental health program modeled on the writings of a sixth-century monk named Saint Benedict. The new spiritual approach to helping and healing involves worship, lectures, spiritual direction, group therapy, prayer, journaling, and personal study.[31]

This Christian approach to healing and spirituality is far removed from the new spirituality that we have discussed in this book thus far. Andy's Benedictine perspective points to the sometimes forgotten fact that many spiritual seekers don't look to the mystical religions of the East or to the teachings of modern psychology. Instead, they go back to the Christian roots that many followers of the new spirituality seem anxious to jettison. My friend looked at his Christian foundations, decided to explore alternatives within the broad area of Christendom, settled in a church that was far removed from the congregation of his youth, but still concluded that true spirituality could be found only in Christ.

Neither Rich nor Karen would make that kind of commitment. Christian spiritualities, in all their diversities, are what Rich has sought for so long to grow beyond. He has had little interest in alternative medicine, maybe because his youthful body rarely gets sick and he hasn't considered the healing power of prayer or the nontraditional ways of healing. Karen, in contrast, frequently visits health food stores, carefully monitors what she eats, and is steeped in the health-giving powers of herbs, alfalfa, and various types of grains. She is attracted to the feminine spirituality that has captivated people like Carol Wilken, and she takes angels more seriously than the more free-spirited Rich. For both of these seekers, Andy's Benedictine spirituality would seem far removed from more modern approaches to the sacred. But while Andy has found inner peace and tranquillity, Rich and Karen still search for true spirituality.

In later pages I will argue that true spirituality is more than getting in touch with a higher self, developing one's inner potential, finding a divinity within, exploring a world of angels, getting in touch with cosmic energy, completing a course in miracles, or finding security in a goddess or in Mother Earth. I will argue, too, that spirituality is not something added on to our lives like the P.S. on a letter. True spirituality penetrates every part of life—our careers, relationships, lifestyles, sexuality, emotions, thinking, hopes, and plans for the future. The spiritual is not an isolated segment of life that can be pushed to one day or one hour of the week and otherwise ignored or accessed whenever we need a spiritual fix. Spirituality is not something we possess, like a book of techniques or a set of rules that we can apply to ourselves to make us spiritual. Neither is spirituality something that looks the same in every person. We are unique individuals with unique personalities, interests, abilities, and emotional makeups. We can't assume that all of us will be spiritual in the same one-brand-fits-all way. But neither can we assume that spiritual people will be loners, developing their inner spiritual lives, oblivious to others. True spirituality comes in community as spiritual seekers grow, serve, care, and mature together, even while each of us retains individuality within the body of the group.

The spiritual life is a journey, a pilgrimage of becoming more and more like the individuals and the community of believers that God wants us to be. *Spirituality*, according to one definition, is "the human response to a mysterious, transcendent Other who for unknown reasons cares enough about us to initiate a relationship with us."[32] Another definition describes *spirituality* as the "ways in which people seek, make, celebrate, and apply meaning to their lives."[33] But spirituality is more personal than these vague words suggest. It involves personal intimacy with God, a process of being conformed to the image of God for the sake of others. The spiritual journey is an ongoing experience of being shaped by God toward wholeness, according to Robert Mulholland. It is "a move against the grain of our do-it-yourself culture and our powerful need to be in control of our existence" or circumstances.[34]

In this book, I am trying to present a broad picture of contemporary spirituality in a way that respects those with whom I disagree and invites readers to explore and search for the sacred along with me. But I would be deceptive and disrespectful if I didn't reveal my perspective on spirituality, a perspective that is alert to contemporary trends and concerned about the radical uncertainty of our age, but still unashamedly Christian. I am impressed with the words of Rowland Croucher, an insightful Australian writer whom I met in Melbourne several years ago. "Christian spirituality is about the movements of God's Spirit in one's life, in the community of faith, and in the cosmos," Croucher wrote. "It is concerned with how all realities relate, enlivened, enlightened, and empowered by the Spirit of Jesus." Spirituality—and spiritual formation—is *"the dynamic process whereby the Word of God is applied by the Spirit of God to the heart and mind of the child of God so that she or he becomes more like the Son of God."*[35]

I cannot say it any better. For me, it is more than a definition; it is an expression of the spirituality that I want to guide my life. I realize, of course, that many of my fellow spiritual journeyers will not agree, but this disagreement leads to another piece of the spirituality puzzle: the issue of individual differences. Why do we differ in what we believe? What causes some of us to embrace alternative medicine enthusiastically while others are skeptical or resistant? Why do some of us build our lives around one kind of spirituality while others move toward something very different? How can we make sense of these differences? To answer, we need to look at what motivates each of us to believe and what leads us to different conclusions about our spirituality.

— 5 —

Making Sense of the Spirituality Puzzle:

Why Do People Believe the Way They Do?

My first teaching job was at a small college in Minnesota where I taught every psychology course in the catalog. When I arrived on campus, one of the older professors was leaving for a sabbatical year, and he offered to let me teach his favorite course while he was gone. I didn't have the courage to tell him that the course didn't interest me at all. It was titled "Individual Differences" and had something to do with distinctions between people in their personalities, intelligence, and interests. I had never taken a course like that and I had no idea how to teach it, but I was new on campus and wanted to make a good impression, so I agreed. Then I did what beginning college teachers often do. I got two books, assigned one to the students as a text, and used the other to prepare my lectures. After that first semester I gave the course back to the older professor and never taught it again.

Despite my disinterest, one part of that course fascinated me, and it still grabs my attention. What accounts for our religious differences? Why might you get involved with one form of spirituality while I commit to something different? Why do any of us embrace one view of God or the universe and reject all the others? When I was a boy growing up in Canada, we lived next door to a family of devoted Catholics. Our families were good friends for years, but I can still remember my mother's perspective on their religion. "Why do they eat fish on Fridays and listen to all that Latin gibberish?" she wondered. We never discussed it, but I suspect our neighbors had questions about us. They might have wondered why we didn't observe Lent or go to dances and why we went to church on Sunday morning and again that night.

Today, we could put this into more modern terms. Why are there different denominations? Why are so many people not interested in religion at all? What accounts for the growing popularity of do-it-yourself spirituality? What motivates some intelligent people to shake off their roots and forsake their families to join new religious movements? Why do others stay put, stick with the churches or synagogues where they grew up, and never even think about moving? Why has Rich, the man whose name we have used before, moved away from his spiritual roots but without completely rejecting the religion of his parents? Why has Karen never settled into much of anything spiritual but has continued to move from place to place, still searching for soul satisfaction?

These questions about individual differences aren't like the dull stuff I taught in my first year of teaching. Years after that course, I still want to know why and how people choose their spiritual beliefs from a cafeteria of spirituality alternatives.

To help answer these questions and to get a better grasp on our spirituality, we will focus on two issues. The first concerns the misunderstood, dangerous, and fascinating world of cults. The other is one of the hottest and most divisive topics in modern psychology and psychiatry, the issue of buried memories of abuse.

Both can shed light on why we might choose differing spiritual pathways.

NEW RELIGIOUS MOVEMENTS

The newspaper heading gave the basics: "THE DEADLY RIDDLE OF HEAVEN'S GATE: The 39 people found dead near San Diego apparently believed they were going with God into space. To get there, they ate drugged pudding and applesauce, drank some vodka and waited for death to lift them up."[1] The victims packed for the journey, dressed in black from head to toe, and died in waves; only the last to die were without the purple shrouds that neatly covered the faces of the others. Led by an elderly, unlikely guru named Marshall Applewhite, the Heaven's Gate participants were promised fulfillment and joy if they would follow their leader by taking their lives and joining the "spacecraft from the Level Above Human" to find their home in the heavens. They ranged in age from twenty-six to seventy-two. Apparently all believed that they were chosen, angelic presences who would escape the gritty bonds of earth and rise to be with God by joining a spaceship just behind the brilliant tail of the Hale-Bopp comet that was making dramatic nighttime appearances at the time of the suicides.

They were sophisticated seekers who used the Internet to spread their message rather than pass out brochures at airports. Their deaths shocked their families and led commentators, cult experts, and ordinary people around the world to ponder *why*. Hundreds of media reports reminded us that cults are common around the globe, that an estimated six million people are past or present members of these groups, and that they have streamlined themselves to appeal to a broader population from every background and age-group. Some—like the Heaven's Gate members or the people who died in Jonestown, Guyana, or Waco—have beliefs and behaviors that make no sense to onlookers. Others are more like the groups of spirituality seekers that cover the land and often attract young people who have no strong previous ties to religion, but are fascinated with UFO's, space aliens, angels, or promises of better lives ahead.

Twenty-one-year-old Donald-Justin Pressley watched the media reports about Heaven's Gate with special interest. Months before the suicides, Pressley and his university roommate spotted a flyer advertising a lecture titled "Evolutionary Steps Beyond Humankind." The roommate went to the lecture and became a member of the group, but Pressley turned to other things and gave the issue little thought until he received a phone call from a man who probably was Marshall Applewhite, the group's leader. "I've never been a cultist or anything like that, but at that time in my life I decided I needed something to grasp on to," Pressley said later. He agreed to watch a videotape and later talked to his friend who had joined the group. "He said he really liked the group and they were the nicest people he ever met in his life," Pressley told a newspaper reporter. "It's not like they were all weirdos." They were "more like intelligent people who went for it—seekers."[2]

Within recent years, these groups of spirituality seekers have been called *new religious movements,* and the term *cults* has been used less often. I've learned a lot about them from reading books, but I've learned even more from several of my friends who have been involved. None of these people ever met a stranger on the street who said, "Hi, I'm a Moonie, and I'd like to invite you to join our cult." I'm sure there are exceptions, but none of my ex-cultist friends were ever argued into a religious group. Usually the process was more subtle, characterized by encounters with attractive, persuasive people who used charm, flattery, and promises to pull their unsuspecting victims into the group's activities.

Tricia was an example. Recently divorced, lonely, and facing a future that wasn't expected, she worked in a small cosmetics boutique, hoping to get a better job that would meet her needs.[3] Her divorce settlement had been sparse, and her savings were almost nonexistent, so she was interested in a notice tacked on the wall of a coffee shop. It announced a seminar on ways of thinking that could enable anybody to prosper, regardless of circumstances. Each participant would learn how to "gather money, power and love," the notice said. It was an opportunity to "learn to think from a place of *having,* not from a basis of needing."

When she called for information, Tricia was told that the seminar would begin on the day of her call. The meeting was in a well-furnished home with about twenty-five people present, plus two seminar leaders named Glenda and Jonathan. Jonathan was handsome, suave, seductive, and attentive to Tricia and her fellow participants. Glenda was expensively dressed, articulate, and outgoing. She explained that people who struggle financially have made decisions "coming from poverty rather than from abundance." She preached that poverty was a matter of the mind and that people could learn to "materialize money" if they came to subsequent seminars, each offered at a cost of fifteen dollars.

In the following weeks, Tricia was welcomed warmly, accepted unconditionally, and affirmed continually. She attended numerous group events, each at a cost, and soon was taking private lessons from Glenda to learn relaxation and breathing exercises to "produce mental prosperity." Before long, Tricia was spending two hundred dollars a week for lessons and other programs. The pay-as-you-go instruction about prosperity was sliding her deeper and deeper into debt. She borrowed from relatives, used up her credit card balances, and eventually moved into the group's house, giving all of her furniture, her valuables, and her car to Glenda and the group.

After two years, Tricia once again began to pressure her mother for more money. Instead of cash, the mother gave Tricia the opportunity to meet ex–group members who helped her see that she was in a prosperity cult that actually was increasing her poverty. Tricia quit.

In many cultlike groups, leaving is not that easy. The methods differ from group to group, but most of these new movements try to find people who are lonely, needy, in transition, and looking for companionship. Tricia fit all of those categories. With excessive friendliness and lots of affirmation, the potential recruit is invited to a place where he or she is surrounded by congenial, attentive people—most of whom are long-term members in the group. Slowly the newcomers are charmed, manipulated, or tricked into making increasing commitments. Almost always, the groups have a teacher or leader who is held in high esteem and assumed to possess unusual insights or wisdom. As they listen to the teacher and assimilate into the group, the new members withdraw from their families, talk and dress like the other group members, and accept the leader's teachings without question (most cult leaders discourage doubt or questioning). Often these group members become trapped, so they cannot leave without guilt, harassment, fear, and sometimes physical harm. If they do break away, they may miss the camaraderie and certainty of the group. Some ex-cultists would never have left and might have gone back into the security of the group if they did not have supportive friends on the outside.

I remember giving a lecture about new religious movements in a small city in New Zealand. Somebody in the audience indicated that the existence of cults was an American thing, that no groups had formed in New Zealand. Several people immediately challenged the statement, describing cultlike activities throughout their country. Groups like these exist to entrap unsuspecting people throughout the world.[4] Sometimes they abuse people sexually or physically. Others abuse people financially, like Glenda's group that took money from Tricia. Almost all abuse people psychologically, promising to bring enlightenment and freedom, but instead delivering enslavement and mindless submission to a self-centered, hedonistic leader. In their extreme forms, the groups lead people into death, all with the promise of better things to come. Outsiders look on with dismay and wonder why anybody could willingly accept beliefs and go on sacred journeys that the rest of us consider to be weird and bizarre.

Does a similar change in thinking occur in people who go to therapists looking for help with their problems and end up accepting beliefs about horrible abuses presumably done to them by their family members?

SUGGESTIONS AND MEMORIES OF ABUSE

Several years ago I was the guest on a talk show that began with the host asking some provocative questions: "Is it possible for a person to have an emotionally disruptive experience and be so distressed by this that the event is completely forgotten and pushed out of memory? Has this ever happened to you? If so, how did you learn about your hidden memories?"

Almost immediately the phones began to ring. One after another the callers poured out stories of abuse and other traumatic experiences that had been forgotten at first, but remembered later. One woman described her depression and lifelong difficulties in relating to other people, especially men. She had gone to a therapist and discovered that her problems as an adult stemmed from long-buried incidents of being abused as a child. Another caller told how she and her husband had been cut off from their children and grandchildren because one of their daughters had concluded that she had been abused by her father. She had "discovered" it in therapy and convinced her brothers and sisters to have no contact with the parents until they were honest enough to confess the acts that, according to the caller, never happened.

One of the most widely publicized cases of apparent repressed memories concerned the former Catholic archbishop of Chicago. A man in another state concluded during counseling that his problems as an adult arose from hidden memories of being sexually abused by Cardinal Joseph Bernardin years earlier. The presumed victim took his charges to the media. Months passed before he admitted that none of the abuse had ever happened. In the meantime, the cardinal struggled to answer the incessant questions from reporters, to retain his otherwise impeccable reputation, and to deal compassionately and honestly with the young man's charges, knowing that they were false.

Within recent years, all across the country and in other parts of the world, people have been "discovering" hidden memories of terrible things that presumably occurred, most often during childhood. According to some psychologists, these memories are so painful that they get pushed out of awareness but they don't fade away. Hidden someplace in the brain, they continue to fester and interfere with day-to-day activities. A child who has been abused may grow up to become like the caller on that talk-show radio program, constantly depressed and unable to trust men. She couldn't understand the reasons for her problems, so she went to a counselor. During therapy, she was able to uncover a distressing but plausible reason for her current difficulties.

People who discover repressed memories at first tend to doubt that the alleged abuse or other trauma actually happened, but with the help of their counselors they become more convinced. Once they assume that the newly discovered memories are true, they react with understandable anger. They are encouraged to confront their abusers—often their parents—and to no longer interact with them. As a result, families (and sometimes careers and reputations) are destroyed almost overnight and opportunities for reconciliation are thrown away.

The issue of repressed memories has become highly controversial, and as we will see later, it is not as far removed from spirituality as you might think. Convinced that many problems stem from repressed memories that must be uncovered and dealt with, large numbers of counselors use memory recovery techniques. They are intended to uncover the traumatic memories so that healing can result and the abusers can be forced to face the consequences of their actions. But there is almost no way to prove that the assumed abuse really happened. And there is increasing research evidence that most of us, including people in counseling, can be persuaded to believe events that never occurred. Is it possible, then, that untrue memories can be created and false beliefs implanted by well-meaning, but misinformed therapists who influence the thinking of their clients, even without meaning to do any harm? In many cases, it seems, the so-called repressed memories of abuse really are suggestions of abuse coming from therapists.

Nobody remembers everything that happens in life, but if you have a traumatic experience, isn't that more likely to stick in your memory and stand out without being forgotten? And knowing as much as we do about the unreliability of memories, surely it is unrealistic to claim that events from years ago can be hidden in the brain, then remembered with 100 percent accuracy. Unlike the computer that files and keeps an accurate record of these words as I type, our memories are prone to distortions and errors.

We have seen the terrible effects of abuse and have become more aware of the needs of abuse victims. As a result of their compassion and sense of justice, therapists and emergency room physicians look so hard for evidence of abuse that they are likely to see abuse when none actually occurred. If an abuse-conscious counselor suggests even the possibility of past abuse to somebody who is emotionally distressed, that person can easily believe that the counselor's suggestion is correct. This has been called a "magic bullet argument."[5] It assumes that if only we can find one single cause of a problem, then everything falls into place, all of life's difficulties can be explained, and mental health is on the way. This magic bullet idea overlooks the complexity of life and pins all our adult problems on one or two past events.

In my work as a psychologist, I have come to accept the idea that memories of abuse sometimes do get buried in the mind. Sometimes genuine—but probably faded and distorted—memories are uncovered in counseling sessions. I am equally convinced that, deliberately or without intending to do this, many counselors make suggestions of abuse that never occurred.[6] They implant false memories that become the basis of false accusations against innocent family members or people like the religious leader in Chicago. The physical, sexual, and psychological abuse of individuals, especially children, is a terrible sin that ruins many lives. But equally wrong and often equally destructive is the abuse heaped on innocent family members and others accused falsely of being abusive.

Do you ever wonder if you have been abused? One popular—and harmful—book states that "if you think you were abused and your life shows the symptoms, then you were."[7] But the list of symptoms is so vague and general that it can fit almost everybody: headaches, arthritis, poor self-esteem, a preference for baggy clothes, difficulty in relationships with the opposite sex, drug or alcohol abuse, being overweight, anxiety, depression, avoidance of mirrors, and even a desire to change one's mate. Abuse survivors have many of these traits, but in themselves they do not indicate abuse. I have some of these "symptoms" and probably you have some as well, but that doesn't mean that we have been abused. Yet, some counselors use this or similar vague lists to diagnose abuse and lead people to believe new and often inaccurate ways of looking at their lives and families.

MEMORIES OF ABUSE, CULTS, AND SPIRITUALITY

An expert on suggestibility, Dr. Michael Yapko sees a similarity between leaders of new religious movements who lead people to believe in false teachings about life or enlightenment, and counselors who encourage clients to believe in false memories. Consider the young man who grows up in a rural area of the Midwest and goes off to college where he becomes a Hare Krishna.[8] Nothing in the man's background, growing up on a farm, suggests that he would join a cult. At the university, however, he is lonely, impressionable, and searching for answers to life's toughest questions. *What is the meaning of my life?* he wonders. *Why am I on this earth at this time, and where am I going?* One day he meets a new friend on campus who introduces him to a group that appears to have answers. The members welcome the visitor warmly and say things that are helpful as he considers his purpose in life. The student doesn't join the group at first, but he keeps going to the meetings. He learns how to think, dress, conduct relationships, pray, contribute, and do everything else in the "right" way, the Krishna way. If he needs or wants to believe that there is more to life than what he experiences, he might be attracted to the idea of reincarnation, finding it enlightening, reassuring, and true. He abandons his Midwest values, family, old friends, way of life, and career aspirations as he draws closer to the group that gives answers and truth that he thinks others are too blind to see.

There are similarities among this young man who joined a cult, people like Tricia, who was lured to Glenda's group, others who accept the reality of false memories, people who convert to new religions, seekers who embrace one of the new spiritualities, and—I have to be honest—people who come to Christian churches seeking answers and acceptance from Christian believers. In general, these people aren't mentally unstable, unable to think clearly, or psychologically weak. Most are not deprived, socially inept, or misfits. Many come from stable homes with caring parents, good educations, and sometimes solid church backgrounds.

But there are times in life when all of us are more open to change and less resistant to persuasion. When I joined the navy and went to a training base, I was away from home, out of contact with my family and friends, filled with uncertainties about whether or not I was cut out for military life, and very much wanting to be accepted by my peers. As I mentioned earlier, I didn't follow their example, but I watched as several of my young navy friends reveled in their newfound freedom, slid into behavior and language that would not have been tolerated in their homes, and experimented with out-of-uniform lifestyles that reflected their search for a new identity. If we had been together on a college campus, the young recruits might have dabbled in new religions, partially out of curiosity and partially out of a desire to find something to replace the older beliefs of their parents.

All spiritual seekers have not rejected these older beliefs. Many find lively, relevant, caring Christian churches that meet people at their places of need, show them acceptance, answer their questions, recommend small groups for them to join, and encourage them to become followers of Jesus Christ. The methods of recruitment and persuasion may be similar in the new and old spiritualities, but as we will see in later chapters, the Christian groups have a number of uniquenesses. And the best ones do not force people to join, manipulate them to stay, or seek to arouse guilt in those who leave.

There is evidence that a lot of people get into a religious movement, conclude that it isn't what they are seeking, back out quickly, and go on with other things.[9] The people who stay and are most susceptible to new ideas are those who are in transition—like Tricia who was recently divorced, individuals who struggle with problems, young adults like those military recruits, college students seeking direction in life, or older people uncertain about their futures. Often these people are without close friends, lonely, and longing for acceptance. Sometimes they are in crisis, looking for direction, maybe a little depressed, and open to guidance and suggestions from people who appear stronger and able to give answers. At such times, it is easy to be more vulnerable, less cautious, and more inclined to believe therapists, religious leaders, seminar speakers, or others who give affirmation, acceptance, guidance, and hope for the future.

Maybe you see yourself in this picture. We all do at times because we all face periods of transition, crisis, and uncertainty. It could be argued that our whole society is in transition, leaving most of us with the challenge of coping with uncertain futures, ongoing change, radically shifting moral values, and an increasing avalanche of information that we can't handle. Until recently people dealt with change and instability by retreating to the security of the home, putting their confidence in the government, and finding direction and hope in established religions. Now our homes are unstable, our trust in the government is at an all-time low, and too many of our churches seem irrelevant and old-fashioned. So there is a grasping for something new. Some counselees find answers and comfort by believing that past abuse accounts for their present distress. Others look for enlightenment and stability by aligning with groups that later appear to be cults. Some give up on religious answers and try to find direction in their work or families. Others drift into new spiritualities that offer hope and new ways of viewing the universe. Many move into church groups that offer ecstatic experiences and promises of healing, deliverance, health, wealth, and prophetic revelations about the future.

A SHORT LOOK AT A LITTLE HISTORY

New religions and approaches to spirituality seem to appear at regular intervals throughout history, especially when there is widespread uncertainty about the future. The new movements give guidance about lifestyles—sometimes by suggesting rigid rules, at other times by proposing very lax standards. Often there is enthusiasm in the religious groups, a searching for ecstasy, a quest for enlightenment, and an elitism that assumes "we have something that others don't possess." Like Christianity in its early days, these new belief systems are criticized and rejected by established religions. But the arrival of new spiritualities forces the traditional religions to look at themselves and make changes if they are to survive during periods of social transition and beyond. Eventually most of the new movements fade as quickly as they came on the scene.[10]

More than two centuries ago, America experienced what has been known as the first Great Awakening, arising from the preaching of Jonathan Edwards. Most of it was centered in New England where the Republic was getting established in the New World. As a result of the spiritual revival—most Christians would agree that the Holy Spirit was the power behind all that happened—a new wave of churches appeared up and down the northeastern coast. In the 1800s, when the country was focused on the new frontier, a second Great Awakening occurred in what now is the Midwest. People spoke in tongues, were "slain in the Spirit," claimed miraculous cures, and participated in various types of trance behavior. That was the time when denominations gained their largest number of converts. In the 1960s another spiritual awakening occurred. It came as the baby boomers were reaching young adulthood, throwing off the values of their parents, and disrupting the whole country. Countercultural thinking and behaving were a worldwide movement, but much of the focus was in California. That time, however, the awakening moved beyond organized religion. New teaching based on Eastern religion came via gurus born or trained in India. The drug culture brought new chemical ecstasies, and hedonistic lifestyles brought rejection of traditional morals and old religious traditions.

Mollie Stone was engulfed by this 1960s awakening.[11] Today, she is a single mother living in Massachusetts, but she has fond memories of the sixties. "That era changed my entire life," she exclaims enthusiastically. "It was the culture that I liked . . . the sixties' culture and everything that it represented."

Mollie liked the political activism, the demonstrations and protests that created a sense of oneness, and the feeling of being involved in something exciting and potentially earth-changing. She wasn't heavily into drugs, but she liked the way hallucinogenics expanded her consciousness, provided a means of escape, and gave her a high experience of psychic adventure. Most of all, Mollie liked the freedom, breaking away from her traditional religious background, her hollow middle-class roots, and her family's acceptance of materialism, capitalistic values, and the American way of life.

When she was interviewed thirty years after her countercultural experiences, Mollie frequently used the word *spiritual*. She was critical of her religious upbringing because it seemed impersonal and empty, rigid and limiting, removed from everyday life, insensitive to racism or poverty, and inclined to squelch anything spiritual. Mollie described herself as a free spirit, a deeply spiritual person, concerned about her children's spirituality, and shaped by the experience-based spirituality of the sixties.

Mollie doesn't view spirituality as anything religious or otherworldly. She defines *the spiritual* as "something very worldly, having to do with relating to the earth and sky and animals and people; something very bodily, having to do with health, happiness, and feeling good about herself. Mollie's spirituality arises out of her own experience." According to a man who knew her well, "It has to do with feelings, with the power that comes from within, with knowing our deepest selves and what is sacred to us."[12] Spirituality, for many in Mollie's generation and those who have come later, involves self-knowledge and the inner self being connected to others, to the world, and to nature. In this era of chaos and change, Mollie's ideals are unity, peace, and harmony, both within herself and in the universe.

I am not a philosopher, but I see the old philosophy of Gnosticism in Mollie's spirituality and in most of the "new" spiritualities mentioned earlier. Gnosticism has been around for centuries. It infiltrated the early church and was criticized by several of the New Testament writers. Stated briefly, Gnosticism maintains that salvation is not achieved by the grace of God; it comes from the individual's self-understanding, knowledge (*gnosis*), and effort. Redemption is not found in being delivered from sin. According to Gnostic thinking, we are freed from our confining and nonspiritual bodies by means of special knowledge or enlightenment that comes from within and is best comprehended by an intellectual elite who have insights into the profound mysteries of the universe. Catholic professor John Saliba believes that the new spiritualities and the old Gnosticism have both been criticized for their elitist attitudes, their nontraditional social and moral behaviors, their attempts to reconcile good and evil, their belief that human beings can achieve salvation and enlightenment through their own efforts, and their unusual rituals.[13] Some observers are convinced that the old Gnosticism is enjoying a revival in contemporary society. It influenced many new spirituality leaders, especially Jung. And it also may be infiltrating the modern church, undermining its doctrinal purity, and keeping it from reaching people like Mollie, who apparently feel no need to be interested in a spirituality related to Jesus Christ.[14]

WHY BELIEVE?

We come back now to the questions raised earlier. Why do intelligent people get involved in new spiritualities or other ways of thinking that seem unusual and even weird to onlookers? Why do others abandon spirituality altogether or stay with more traditional groups of believers and styles of worship? Complex questions like these rarely have simple explanations, but the answers may have something to do with our deepest human needs and desires.[15] We have a need to believe in something greater than ourselves. Our minds need to understand where we are in this universe and where we fit. We are social creatures who need to be accepted. And in times of uncertainty and transition, we have a need to be in control of our changing circumstances. Depending on our backgrounds and other factors, we try to satisfy these needs in different ways, which lead us into different forms of spirituality.

The Need to Believe

It is easy to prove that human beings need food, water, and air to breathe. But we can't prove beyond a shadow of a doubt that people have a need to believe. Again and again, however, we read about generations of people searching for something bigger than themselves. Remember the God-shaped vacuum deep within that Pascal wrote about? It is an emptiness that can't be filled by success or things or pleasures. We can try to ignore it, deny it, or look for creative ways to fill it, but sooner or later we are left with the reality that life without God ultimately is hollow. Nobody knows this better than the people of Mollie's generation, who had everything—money, freedom, sex, drug-induced highs—but still are searching for something more, something fulfilling beyond themselves.

Like Mollie, Linda Kramer lived through the sixties, but her spiritual journey has been very different.[16] Linda grew up in a small Ohio town, far from the countercultural activities of the big cities. Like the majority of her generation, Linda didn't embrace the "sex, drugs, and rock-and-roll" mentality of Mollie's peers. The product of a Christian home and a family who "loved the Lord and worshiped regularly," Linda went to a small college before she moved to the city. Confronted with the permissiveness and liberal values of her workplace, Linda recognized her need for a closer walk with God to give her life direction and stability in the midst of her stormy environment. She found an active church and reinforced her commitment to God. Her world was rocked by political assassinations, riots, hippies, cults, Vietnam, Watergate, feminism, and the gay rights movement, but Linda found acceptance, stability, and support in the arms of her church and her beliefs. Today, she is married, seeking to raise her children to walk with the Lord and to maintain a commitment to Christ in the midst of temptations to pull away.

Linda believes in Christ as the only guide for living, the only One who can forgive sin and provide a way to heaven, the only way to truth and life in its abundance. In contrast, Mollie thinks that "there are so many great teachings in all the religions, how could you ever choose one or the other?"[17] So she keeps searching. Psychologists enter the search by providing nontheological objects of belief such as archetypes, erroneous zones, Peter Pan syndromes, Cinderella complexes, and the inner child.

"'Healing the inner child within' has become the goal of therapists across the country, and a handy, highly publicized framework from which to launch their clinical practices and workshops," writes Michael Yapko.[18] Inner child talk has become so common among some counselors and so enticing that some people actually believe that the inner child exists when, in fact, there is no such thing. It is only a suggested way of thinking about yourself. Say this in some circles, however, and you will get angry and defensive protests because you have attacked a precious belief that gives an explanation for actions that might be incomprehensible otherwise.

We all believe in something, even if we prefer the inner child in place of belief in God. Our conclusions about the supernatural differ, depending on what each of us has experienced or heard, but there appears to be a need to believe in something greater than ourselves, something or someone able to give answers, guidance, and purpose for living and dying.

The Need to Understand and Make Sense of the Universe

Many people make little distinction between psychology and spirituality. Both claim to give answers to people who are searching for meaning and trying to make sense of their lives. Popular authors—psychiatrist Scott Peck is the best example—write about evil, sacrifice, and sin, but recast these religious ideas into psychological language that is more convincing to readers who are skeptical of religion. Spurred by writers such as Peck, many of these readers are willing to explore unfamiliar approaches to spirituality and self-help.[19] The result is a willingness to believe in astrology, reincarnation, witchcraft, herbal medicines, crystals, channeling, repressed memories, cultic teachings, or anything else that promises to give fulfillment and answers to life's complex questions. People who are confused and searching are starved for clarity, so many accept the suggestions of an author, a speaker, or a therapist without pausing to consider whether these conclusions might have any validity.

Suppose you decide to go to a therapist for help with a personal problem. The counselor reflects stability and appears to have his or her life in order. As you pour out your problems, inadequacies, hurts, fears, and symptoms, you feel very vulnerable and willing to accept and apply whatever your trusted counselor recommends. If the counselor talks about your repressed memories, past abuse, inner child, feminine archetype, karma, underlying sin, or dysfunctional family, you may be skeptical at first, but slowly you begin to talk and think like the therapist. Perhaps you are introduced to group counseling sessions where you meet others with problems similar to yours, who are talking the therapist's language and seeming to get better. You don't take the time to critically evaluate the counselor's theory—especially if you are influenced by postmodern thinking. The theory is working for others; why shouldn't it work for you? If it is plausible and able to explain your problems, then maybe you don't much care if it is accurate.

Replace the words *therapist* and *counselor* in the preceding paragraph with *religious leader, seminar speaker, cult leader,* or *guest on* Oprah, and you can see how any of us, in a state of need, might accept teachings that appear to answer questions and give help. When people are confused, uncertain, in transition, or looking for direction, they are more responsive to the influence of others. They especially are attracted to spiritual leaders, therapists, or authors who seem to have it all together, who radiate confidence or authority, and who appear to understand life. If we assume that millions today are needy and searching in the midst of turbulent change, we can understand why so many are captivated by new, esoteric spiritualities that make few demands but offer hope and enlightenment.

The Need to Be Accepted

Most of us want to be accepted by other people. Combined with our common feelings of insecurity and inadequacy, our need for acceptance can push us into extreme and irrational behavior. We all know about teenagers who dress, talk, and act in ways that get approval from their peers, but that doesn't stop with the passing of adolescence. No doubt you've heard about people who spend money they don't have, for things they don't need, to impress people they don't like. Everybody who has been involved in a wedding has seen some of this urge to impress others and bolster one's self-image. If it isn't in the bride or groom, it usually appears in at least some of the relatives. By looking good, we hope to gain approval from others.

When I was teaching that course on individual differences (and working hard to be accepted as a good teacher), many of my students were reading a book that asked in the title, "If you really knew me, would you still like me?" That question lurks in the minds of people who debate about revealing themselves to their counselors, accountability partners, or friends. No one wants to appear weak, vulnerable, or inadequate. People have a great need for acceptance and approval.

All of this has a bearing on spirituality. People in churches, cults, or new spirituality movements may resist the pressure to conform, but many go along with the group's teachings because they value approval. That midwestern college student who joined with the Krishnas was looking for friendship to offset his loneliness and answers to counter his confusion. To keep the acceptance of the group members, he had to chant and dress and think like the group members, even if that meant casting off his old values and closing down the ability of his brain to think critically. If you had tried to discuss his irrational beliefs in a logical manner, you might have had little success. Searching people will believe almost anything and rigidly cling to their beliefs if they are looking as well for acceptance and approval from people who appear to be credible.

The Need to Be in Control

Even though my health has been good over the years, like everybody else sometimes I get sick. When that happens, I try to ignore the symptoms, swallow a couple of aspirin tablets, and determine to keep going. I don't like to admit that I'm not in control of my body. I try to be cooperative when I must go to the doctor, but I get frustrated and sometimes annoyed when I have to submit to the questions and probings of medical people, especially when they have no inclination to hurry and no awareness or concern about my time. I like to control my schedule, my finances, my career, and my lifestyle. If I am not careful, I can try to control other people, and sometimes I even want to control God.

People like me have a strong desire to be in control. It is frustrating when I cannot control the interruptions that come into my life, the sales of my books, or the ways in which God handles my prayers. All through the Bible I see evidence that God isn't in a hurry, doesn't fit into human agendas, doesn't see the same urgency that we see, and can't be manipulated or talked into going along with our creative plans. Several biblical personalities became impatient waiting for God, took things into their own hands, and courted personal disaster as a result.[20]

It is easy to see how all of this applies to spirituality—including Christian spirituality. Impatient, out-of-control people eagerly grasp on to spiritualities and spiritual leaders who promise instant relief, ready answers, health and wealth, inner stability, enlightenment, power over demons, and a host of other quick-fix remedies. Tell people that they can control their destinies, get what they want, find new insights, or avoid taking responsibility for their actions, and there will be takers.

A PLACE FOR CAUTION

All of this points to one conclusion: every one of us is spiritually vulnerable. We are motivated to believe something, to make sense of our circumstances, to be accepted, and to have control of our lives. As a result, we are easily swayed by persuasive speakers and writers, psychological and spiritual gurus who speak to our needs, and overtly caring people who proffer acceptance and philosophies that seem to make sense. If I have learned anything from reading and talking to people who have been in new spirituality movements, it is this human vulnerability. Every one of us can be swayed by new spirituality arguments, some of which appear to be sweeping into the church and slipping into sermons, sometimes without being noticed even by the preacher.

Not long ago I read about an anthropologist named Michael Brown who decided to study channeling, "a subculture within the New Age Movement that even most New Agers consider fringe." Brown spent many hours with people who believe they can use themselves as conduits for messages from other planets, spirits, or epochs. One group claimed to channel Kana, a force or being who "lives on a future dimensional plane, parallel to ours but ahead of us by many thousands of years." Brown watched all of this with as much of an open mind as he could muster and then wrote a book describing channeling as a modern form of spirituality for an anxious age.[21] It began centuries ago, the anthropologist discovered, but it has filtered into "self-help groups full of mall-going, middle-class Americans."[22]

Despite the beliefs of channelers who assume their messages are valid, channeling is like free association, according to Brown. "It's like friends sitting around a room late at night and saying, 'Let's talk about the first thing that pops into our heads.' You are moving away from rational thought, experimenting with a different way of being in the world. It's actually kind of fun, if you aren't worried about where it's headed." Sometimes, however, it's headed toward "self-important babble," fantasies about the world where we live, reports of strange personal experiences, and predictions about the future that nobody dares challenge. It taps into the contemporary belief that every person has the limitless potential to experience the sacred without any middlemen— especially middlemen or middlewomen in the church.

In the preceding chapters we have explored the terrain of modern spirituality and ended with one of the most controversial— the activities, beliefs, and predictions of channelers. We come now to a more personal look at the search for spiritual intimacy. And we begin with the church.

PART 2

True Spirituality: Intimacy with God

The New York Academy of Sciences hosted a three-day meeting for two hundred scientists, doctors, philosophers, and educators who had become concerned about the "flight from reason" in American society. These scholarly people met to discuss the postmodern attacks on logic. There was discussion about the current stampede to alternative medicines that have no scientific basis, the widespread fascination with angels and out-of-body experiences, the interest in demons and aliens, and the popularity of astrology, reincarnation, channeling, and other parts of what we have been calling the new spirituality. The New York meeting was intended to battle back against the critics of science, logic, technology, and medicine.

On the other side of the Atlantic, many years before those scholars met in New York, G. K. Chesterton predicted that when people stopped believing in the God of the Bible, they would free themselves to believe in "anything and everything." Earlier, Nietzsche had predicted that when God is assumed to be dead, there would be a "rain of gods," each vying for attention and pulling people in a variety of directions. We would move to a new

Buddhism, Nietzsche suggested, often combined with a belief in nothing. That would lead us to cynical despair.

This is where many people find themselves in their searches for the sacred. They go in different directions and seem to believe in anything and everything—or in nothing. This book has not used the word *superstition* or *charlatanism*, but as I have read about the plethora of new spiritualities on the market today, I have often thought that many searchers have become superstitious, caught in magical thinking, and manipulated by shrewd charlatans. I don't put much stock in the proclaimers of panic who frantically shout about culture wars, worldwide conspiracies, or power encounters. Maybe I am wrong and insensitive, like the proverbial frog that sits contentedly in the kettle while the water gets hotter, oblivious to the warming trends until it is too late to jump. But I do agree with some of those New York scientists that we have become a superstitious, experience-centered culture of people who don't think very deeply or critically.

I believe, too, that many of those who are looking for the sacred and searching for spirituality are looking in some wrong places. In the midst of all the spiritual scurry, a surprising number of seekers are finding new life in the church and in their Christian roots. Most of these seekers aren't looking to return to the dead religion that they knew in the past. They want a new and fresh type of spirituality that is relevant, up-to-date, and Christian. They want a new Christian spirituality for the new century.

As we explore this Christian spirituality in the second part of the book, I hope you will stay with me—whether you are grounded in the church or more like those people mentioned earlier who are into spirituality but not into church. After looking at the modern church and considering some of the magical thinking that has captivated many religious people today, we will discuss the Christian approach to spirituality. The book will close with a new look at the spiritual life that is intended to pull everything together in a way that will be refreshing and practical for anybody who wants to walk closely with God. I hope our trek through the following chapters will be helpful, even for people who long ago bypassed Christianity or rejected it altogether.

— 6 —

Religion and the Spirituality Puzzle:
What Does the Church Have to Do with Spirituality?

I was at a conference in Florida when I remembered one morning that NASA was planning to launch another group of astronauts into space around 7:30. I had planned to go for breakfast about that time, but decided to turn on the television set to watch the launch before leaving my room. I sat on the edge of the bed and saw the live news coverage before making my way to the restaurant on the top floor of the hotel a few minutes later.

The hostess was the first to tell me what I soon heard again from my waitress and from several excited voices in the restaurant. The hotel had a clear view of the launch site. At the time of liftoff all of the diners and staff had gathered at the windows and watched together as the rocket soared into the air. I hadn't realized that the hotel restaurant was a perfect viewing place. I could have been there had I not chosen at the last minute to stay in my room, watching the events on television. I didn't know any better at the time, but I had settled for the images on the screen when I could have seen the real thing.

In viewing the spirituality landscape, I think too many people are settling for something of lesser value and missing the real thing. They aren't doing this deliberately.[1] Like me in that hotel room, they are experiencing what they think is the best there is because they haven't gone to a different level and seen something better. Many are looking in all the wrong places, searching for soul satisfaction, true spirituality, enlightenment, or intimacy with God, and finding only fading images. Sooner or later they will be disappointed as I was in that restaurant. They will have looked intensively, only to realize later that they missed the real thing.

FINDING THE REAL THING

Every year, college students descend in droves to Florida not to see a shuttle launch, but to find fun and sunshine during the annual spring break from classes. When he was a senior in college, a friend of mine decided to do something different. He was a Christian, interested in spirituality. His roommate was studying medieval history and had a special interest in the traditions of the Catholic church. So while most of their classmates headed to the Florida beaches, my friend and his roommate drove north to a Benedictine monastery.

They had made prior arrangements to spend a week living like the monks and learning whatever they could. Before the trip they decided to stay in separate rooms to prevent late-night discussions that would distract from their monastic experience, and they decided to exist on only bread and water. Their decision distressed the monks, who thought that the diet was too strict and unhealthy and who were afraid that the students would return to their evangelical Protestant world carrying a wrong impression of how the Catholic brothers really lived and ate.

Several years have passed, but the former roommates still talk in glowing terms about their week in the monastery. For them, it was a significant spiritual experience that both would like to repeat sometime. Today, they continue on their spiritual journeys, but unlike most searchers involved with the new spiritualities, these young men are looking within the church. They are familiar with the new spiritualities of the New Age, but they believe that the real thing is more likely to be found in the spirituality that is emerging from the diverse folds of Protestantism. The methods, approaches, and expressions are different and constantly changing, but the new Christian spirituality might be reduced to one question: *How can I walk in closeness to God today?*

SPIRITUALITY AMONG CHRISTIANS

I would need an encyclopedia to summarize the new interest in spirituality sweeping through Christendom today. In some parts of the world, especially in Latin America and Africa, an experiential, pentecostal-type spirituality is rolling across the land, even penetrating the Catholic church, sometimes to the distress of the hierarchy in Rome. In India, the work started by Mother Teresa has attracted international attention and given rise to a worldwide Missionaries of Charity movement. It is a spiritual path that balances the prayerful, contemplative life with the practical outreach of love in action. Monasteries, like the one my friend visited on his spring break, may be fewer and smaller, but they continue to exist and thrive not because the nuns and monks are unwilling to face the daily grind that the rest of us encounter, but because they believe that their lives of prayer can change society.

Go into any Christian bookstore and you will see shelves full of books on spirituality. The authors write from various theological perspectives, but in their different ways they all focus on how people can walk with God. Some of these books are more mystical and contemplative, often drawing on the works of Catholic writers like Augustine and Thomas Merton. Other books take a more intellectual approach to spirituality, like the writings of C. S. Lewis, J. I. Packer, and R. C. Sproul.[2] A few are like the books of Richard Foster, who comes from Quaker roots and emphasizes simplicity and spiritual disciplines of prayer, solitude, and fasting. Many of the most popular books are written by people from the pentecostal-charismatic camp who often fill their books with words of encouragement, inspiring stories, and formulas for Spirit-filled lives marked by miracles, healings, signs, and wonders. Some books, including many of the more popular novels, picture the spiritual life as a raging battle against the forces of Satan where believers "bind" or "take authority" over demons. Much different are the writers who bring a psychological perspective and focus on inner peace, freedom from anxiety, or steps to conquer dysfunctional pasts that hinder spiritual growth in the present. Others, like Henri Nouwen, have written reflectively, sharing their journals or writing about their struggles and spiritual journeys.

The list could go on. There are novels, spirituality workbooks, guidelines for finding your spiritual gifts, books about prayer, biographies of spiritual giants, collections of sermons, and endless devotional and Bible study guides. Even agnostics are getting into the shelves of Christian bookshops. "I am neither a Christian nor a theist," states one professor of economics who has written a book about religion. But he argues that we are in a moral crisis that will lead to our destruction unless there is a revival of religion, especially the Christian religion, as a bulwark against our social ills.[3]

Considering all of this diversity, we may conclude that we are creating a modern Christian Tower of Babel, constructed not of bricks, but of books, interspersed with compact discs of the latest contemporary Christian music. Some of these books and discs are very good. They have solid content, are based on careful study of the Scriptures, and are intended to meet the needs of people who want to know God and grow spiritually in the midst of their breathless lifestyles. But the gems are buried within towers of self-oriented, do-it-yourself spirituality books that concentrate less on God and draw more attention to the authors and their readers. Too often there are spiritual confusion and confused language, similar to what the builders of that Old Testament tower experienced. By their own efforts, they tried to reach heaven and build a name for themselves, but they ended up confused and scattered.[4]

With the growth of spirituality babble in the marketplace, it is not surprising that non-Christian new spiritualities have begun to seep into the church. Sometimes they have been paraded into the Christian community and proclaimed from the pulpits. Some churches put such an emphasis on self-centered experiences that there is no place for doctrine. God is seen as a buddy rather than the sovereign Lord of the universe, religion is largely subjective and private, and faith focuses on what God can do for you, especially if you know the techniques for getting God to give you what you want. Writing with passion and deep conviction about these issues, theologian Michael Horton argues that a new Gnosticism is taking over mainstream Christianity.[5] Like the old Gnosticism mentioned earlier, this new form of spirituality pulls bits and pieces from various sources, underscores the subjective, distrusts institutions such as the church, emphasizes personal revelations from God, is suspicious of history and anything from the Old Testament, and concludes that "heart knowledge," or personal experience with God, is more reliable than "head knowledge," or correct beliefs about God.

I find this trend disturbing and maybe you do too. I am a son of the church. I grew up surrounded by church activities. My closest friends, then and now, are firmly planted in their churches. I spent most of my teaching career helping to prepare men and women to serve in the church, and I'm still involved actively. But if the church is becoming more and more like the cafeteria-style new spirituality of the secular world, then why do we need to bother about the church? Many healthy churches have a positive impact on the spirituality of millions of people, but interspersed with the good is the destructive influence of pathological churches. They promote a toxic faith that undermines spirituality instead of building it. Even worse, these unhealthy congregations turn away genuine spiritual seekers who then bypass the church and continue searching for the sacred in places where they'll never find the real thing.

PASSING THE CHURCH ON THE ROAD TO SPIRITUALITY

In what must have been an unusual gathering, Jesus found himself standing on the edge of a lake, probably in danger of being jostled into the water by the large crowd that had come to hear him speak. In the midst of the shoving, he got into a boat, pushed out a short distance from the shore, and gave one of his most famous sermons while the people listened on the bank.

Jesus told a story that day about a farmer who went into his fields to sow his seed. Some was swallowed up immediately by the hungry birds that followed the sower. Some fell on rocky ground and sprang up quickly, only to die in the hot sun because the little plants had no roots. Other seeds took root and grew until they were choked out by thorns and weeds. The seed that produced the harvest fell on good soil and produced crops, a hundred, sixty, or thirty times more than what was planted.[6]

Beginning when I was very young, my parents took me every Sunday to the Philpott Memorial Church where they were members. Later, as a teenager, I would take the bus every weekend, making my way to the church-sponsored youth activities that taught me about the faith and helped me get through a difficult time in my life. Today, many years later, I have lost contact with most of the people who were in my Sunday school classes and youth group activities, but I know that Jesus' story from that lakeside pulpit was an accurate predictor of where many of us went. As they reached adulthood, some of my peers were enticed and swallowed up by the lifestyles and attractions of the worlds where they were building their careers and raising their families. Others sprung up with great enthusiasm about their beliefs and spiritual vitality, only to cast it all aside because they had no roots to sustain them when trouble or temptations came their way. I can think of several others who reached adulthood intending to go on in their faith but whose spiritual interests were choked out by life's worries and disappointments or by the pursuit of success, wealth, and personal pleasure. Only a minority of my church friends appear to have taken in and understood the spiritual teachings so that their lives became fruitful, impacting others, sometimes in major ways.

Why did I stick with the minority and stay with the church? I don't have any concise answers apart from the grace of God. When I was in college, I attended a living room–size church led by an overbearing and dogmatic pastor whose sermons rambled and who didn't pay much attention to quality. I stayed because I admired the man's dedication, knew that I needed spiritual roots to support me during my secular studies, and found some of my closest friends among the little congregation. Many of them were as dissatisfied as I was, but there weren't other churches in the neighborhood, so we stuck it out.

A few years later, as young parents, Julie and I went to a church that wasn't much better. We both believed that Christians need to be involved with other believers and we wanted our kids to experience Sunday school, but I felt like a misfit. Many times I sat in a back pew and hid a magazine between the pages of a hymnbook so I could do something with my mind while the preacher spoke. At times I felt there was no depth or practical relevance in the churches we attended. More than once I concluded that the church was out of contact with the high-energy world where we all lived during the week.

In recent years I have had much better experiences, involvements with churches where the music is upbeat, the messages are relevant, the people are real, the old clichés are gone, the leaders are less domineering or self-focused, and the worship experiences direct more genuine praise to God. Today, most of my friends are anchored in some way in the church. I've built friendships with a number of church leaders and have come to understand and admire their dedication, commitment to serve, and willingness to persist in a job that rarely is easy. It hasn't always been this way for me, but I can't imagine that I would grow spiritually without being part of a body of fellow believers where everyone can serve, learn, be nurtured, encourage, worship, and find both fulfillment and accountability in the company of others.

In times like ours, when spirituality is such a popular topic, why do so many people ignore or bypass the church and rush with the crowds to embrace one of the new spiritualities? There are thousands of good churches, like the one where I grew up and some that I have attended recently. They are filled with committed people who are concerned about spiritual issues and guided by dedicated leaders. Even so, the church is considered irrelevant and outdated by a whole generation of spiritual searchers who settle instead for "new" spiritualities that are based in Eastern religions and philosophies that are far older than Christianity.

The lakeside sermon of Jesus gives some reasons why people turn away from the church or pass by when they are searching for the sacred. Some get distracted by their troubles, life difficulties, worries, pursuits of wealth, or the influence of what Jesus called "the wicked one [who] comes and snatches away" (Matt. 13:19 NKJV) the spiritual messages that they learned, often when they were very young. No doubt, some seekers bypass the church completely without considering what it has to offer. They proudly proclaim their tolerance and openness to every idea, but they draw the line when it comes to being open to a spirituality that might be church related. Others take a closer look but walk away because they see the church as an archaic institution, out of step with the times, irrelevant to modern needs, and too often characterized by psychological hang-ups in the members and hypocrisy in the leaders.

TOXIC FAITH AND ABUSIVE CHURCHES

These criticisms have validity. In a book that attracted attention and aroused criticism, Stephen Arterburn and Jack Felton took a careful look at the church from the inside and concluded that many believers have what they termed a *toxic faith*.[7] Some people show this in their compulsive church activity, rushing from one meeting to another, serving on committees, feverishly working around the church, determined to please God by doing his work while their families suffer and their bodies wear out. Others build fantasies about God, creating in their minds a deity who is at our beck and call, eager to bring quick fixes and easy solutions. Very different are the people burdened with guilt, self-condemning and convinced of their inadequacies because they cannot meet the expectations of their demanding pastors or tyrant God. In too many churches, people are taught to squelch their feelings and believe that anger, sadness, loneliness, and depression show a lack of faith and need to be hidden behind a mask of happiness and never-ending joy. Others are confused and angry, wondering why a loving God would allow sickness, sorrow, or injustice to come into their lives when they expected ongoing spiritual ecstasy and freedom from pain and pressure.

"Faith becomes toxic when individuals use God or religion for profit, power, pleasure, and/or prestige," write Arterburn and Felton.[8] Any one of us could drift into poisonous thinking that distorts our view of God, undermines our faith, and leads to inconsistencies and destructive behaviors in our lives. While this happens, onlooking critics see the harm that comes to some in the church, naively conclude that this is the norm, and decide to look elsewhere for spiritual direction.

Sociologist Ronald Enroth became an expert in cults before he started writing about unhealthy churches.[9] He traveled around the country, conducting interviews, listening to sermons, and surveying churches that abuse people through a combination of intimidation, guilt, fear, insensitivity, manipulation, and sometimes humiliation. Most often these unhealthy churches are led by self-centered, adversarial, rigid, domineering pastors who claim to have a corner on the truth, refuse to tolerate dissension, and expect blind loyalty from their flocks. Addicted to their own power and need to control others, these pastoral leaders are accountable to no one and resistant to any outside scrutiny. When there is dissension, these churches squelch it. When there is criticism from the outside, they call themselves victims of persecution.

When disgruntled members want to leave, there may be condemnation, intimidation, and dire predictions about life apart from the church.

All of the churches and church leaders that Enroth studied appear to be extreme in their unhealthy influences on people. More common are the churches that slowly instill unhealthy attitudes and ways of thinking into their members, often with nobody, not even the church leader, realizing the harm that is being done. Compulsive religious activity may be seen by everyone involved as a sign of devotion and a way to please God. Some believe that by giving more and more to God, we will be more inclined to receive wealth and other blessings in return. In this age of psychology, many churches encourage believers toward an excessive focus on their own needs, hurts, desires, struggles, and pressures. A self-centered religion often follows, concentrated on how God solves our problems but with little emphasis on worshiping God, engaging in spiritual disciplines, or caring for others. Even in established churches—maybe the one that you attend—there can be an unhealthy elitism that assumes "we are better than any others" and shows intolerance for individuals or churches that are "not like us." More recently there seems to have been a growing desire for religious ecstasy. Arterburn and Felton warn of an overemphasis on highly arousing emotional experiences that become so attractive that people forget God in the midst of the frenzy and euphoria:

> The adrenaline rush actually energizes and stimulates them, alters the mood, and provides relief from real pain. The hysteria is repeated any time they need to escape or feel differently. These "instant religious experience" practitioners might as well take a drink, swallow a pill, or inject a drug. The intent of their actions is not to worship God [even though they might argue otherwise] but to alter their perception of reality. They are religious junkies, obsessed with mood alteration and a quick fix to face life.[10]

I read about a survey that asked people to identify the "sleaziest" occupations in America. Drug dealers and crime bosses topped the list, but television evangelists came third, just ahead of prostitutes, street peddlers, and politicians.[11] Too many people base their views of Christianity on what they see in a few television speakers or a handful of disgraced pastors. Often the more flamboyant evangelists preach and demonstrate all of the unhealthy characteristics that I have been describing. On the television screen and in their coworkers or neighbors, skeptics see the compulsions, rigidity, legalism, manipulation, and hyperemotionalism that characterize the worst of the church. Sometimes there is little awareness that Christian spirituality more often is healthy, pointing people away from the pathology and toward life-enriching stability, in-depth spiritual experiences, and authentic community.

HEALTHY RELIGION AND HEALTHY CHURCHES

When my wife took an evangelism course, she sat for several weeks not far from a woman who had been a skeptic all her life but had recently become a Christian. Prior to that, at a time of desperation she had decided to slip into the back row of a big church where she determined to hide in the crowd and check out whether religion might help her with her problems. For several months she kept returning, week after week. The people were friendly, but there were no embarrassing efforts to draw attention to visitors. The congregation was large, so she was able to have the space that she needed.

"This church made me so mad," she told the evangelism class. "Everybody seemed to be genuinely enthusiastic about their faith, but there was no crazy behavior, and no pressure for me to be like them." The woman was surprised that the pastor could talk simple language without a lot of religious jargon. He spoke about real-life issues, lived as if the Bible was a book that mattered to his life, explained how people could become Christians, but showed no inclination to manipulate people. He admitted that the Christian life often carried problems and disappointments, even for him. It took a while, but the visitor became a believer— attracted, in part, by the healthy religion she saw in church people who were concerned about others, honest about their spiritual journeys, and not bogged down by the symptoms of toxic faith.

There are at least eleven characteristics of healthy religion. They are summarized in the table "Marks of Healthy Religion." First, *people who have healthy religion know what they believe* and often know why they believe as they do. They hold these beliefs firmly, as convictions, but they are not so rigid that they would never change or be modified. Sometimes the beliefs come from parents or religious teachers, but they are not latched on to half-heartedly as the secondhand faith of somebody else. When they get to adulthood, people with healthy religion adopt the beliefs as their own. Healthy believers have confidence that their beliefs are valid, and as a result, they strongly hold the convictions.

Second, *people with healthy religion behave in ways and show attitudes that are consistent with their beliefs*. Hypocrisy occurs when people claim to believe one thing but build their lives on values that are different. Jesus strongly condemned the pious religious leaders of his time who looked lily-white on the outside but were egotistical, self-righteous schemers inside. No one is perfect in keeping beliefs and actions always aligned, but healthy religious people strive for this consistency. They know that hypocrisy is not healthy.

Third, *healthy religion is marked by religious practices that are consistent with what one believes*. Prayer, worship, Bible study, and periods of solitude or meditation are all part of the Christian's life. If these are missing, then something is wrong. By his words and actions, Jesus demonstrated that religious practices are important. To call oneself a follower of Christ and then not to follow his teachings is inconsistent and spiritually unhealthy. Also wrong, in the Christian view, are involvements with mediums, fortune-tellers, horoscopes, psychics, and other occult activities that claim to predict the future and give enlightenment at the same time as

130

they forget God or ignore biblical injunctions against such practices.[12]

MARKS OF HEALTHY RELIGION

People with healthy religion

1. know what they believe (and often why they believe as they do).
2. act in ways and show attitudes that are consistent with their beliefs.
3. have religious practices that are consistent with their beliefs.
4. have a balance between reason and emotion.
5. have a realistic and essentially positive self-concept.
6. respect others and are not judgmental or defensive.
7. take responsibility for their actions.
8. are willing and able to forgive.
9. are willing and able to postpone immediate pleasure so that greater satisfaction can come in the future.
10. are characterized by love that influences relationships and reaches out to others in acts of service, compassion, social justice, and evangelism.
11. are involved in community.

This acceptance of some spiritual practices and rejection of others is known as *spiritual exclusivity*. People like Rich and Karen wonder why Christians aren't open to embracing all of the offerings of the spiritual cafeteria. The answer concerns the Christian's commitment to God. When we commit to a romantic partner, we agree to exclude some relationships and activities that would interfere with the commitment. The husband, for example, agrees to remain faithful to his wife and to exclude other sexual partnerships, legal entanglements, and competing financial commitments. In a similar way, the committed Christian agrees to avoid practices that bypass God and ignore his teachings and instructions.

Fourth, *in healthy religion there is a balance between reason and emotion*. It has been said that some seminaries turn out intellectual giants and relational dwarfs. When they graduate and enter the ministry, these pastors know how to be intellectual. They can discuss theology, but they don't know how to relate to people and they aren't very comfortable with emotion. The result is unbalanced religion that squelches feelings and becomes coldly intellectual. In contrast to this dead orthodoxy, there are churches where emotion reigns supreme, and the mind is held in check. Healthy religion seeks a balance between the knowledge of what we believe and the expression of emotions in praise, worship, and singing.

Fifth, *healthy religion stimulates a realistic and essentially positive self-concept*. People with a healthy faith feel good about themselves. This is not because they are egotistical, self-focused, and proud. In the Christian faith, we assume that all are sinners, but we are valuable in God's sight. He created us in his image. He didn't make us robots, but respected us enough so that we were given the freedom to ignore him, go our own ways, and engage in other sinful behavior. When that happened, he showed his love for us by sending his Son, Jesus Christ, to die in payment for our sins. He extended forgiveness, and for those who accepted his offer, he promised restoration into God's family. Even now, he never forces anyone to accept his gift of forgiveness, and he leaves us free to believe or to forget about him and take whatever consequences follow. Those who do believe are adopted as God's children and given special "spiritual gifts" and opportunities to serve—not because we are so great but because God is great. He is so good that he makes believers over, molding us into the people that we eventually will become.

Please reread the preceding paragraph. It is the basis for Christian spirituality, and it gives us reason for a positive self-concept.

My value and yours are not based on our wonderful abilities and personalities or on the things we have done. We are valuable and we can accept ourselves as people of value because of what God has done and is doing in our lives. As Christians, we believe that we are children of God. That's reason for accepting and valuing ourselves positively.

Sixth, *people with healthy religion respect others and are not judgmental or defensive.* I hold strong religious convictions. I am convinced that my beliefs are right. I have tried to build my beliefs on the Bible, a book that I consider to be the Word of God. But I am not omniscient—somebody who knows the truth without error and can pronounce with authority that I am right and that everybody else is wrong. As a Christian, I am compelled to tell others what I believe is the Word of God, but I am not to judge people, to show them disrespect, or to get defensive and threatened when others don't agree with my convictions.[13] If you have read the previous pages, I hope you have seen a writer who is respectful, even of people and ideas that I don't accept. Healthy religion is not wishy-washy—having no firm convictions—but neither is it condemning, combative, and judgmental.

Seventh, *people with healthy religion take responsibility for their actions.* We all make mistakes, and more often than most of us might like to admit, we say and do things that are blatantly wrong. Healthy believers don't try to pass the buck, pin blame on somebody else, or refuse to acknowledge our actions. There are times, of course, when the actions of others do cause our problems. We don't deny this. But people with healthy religion also admit errors and sinfulness, seek forgiveness from God and from others who might have been harmed, make restitution when possible, and go on—determined not to let a similar situation happen again.

Eighth, *healthy religion involves a willingness and ability to forgive.* Many people know the story of Corrie ten Boom, the Dutch woman who was imprisoned in a Nazi prison camp where she was badly mistreated and watched as her sister died. Following her release, she traveled around the world, describing her experiences to many audiences. One night she was approached by a man whom she recognized as one of the guards who had treated her so badly. "I am a Christian now," he said as he extended his hand. "I want to ask for your forgiveness." The former prisoner froze in hesitation, but then she extended her hand and forgave the guard. Immediately she sensed an overwhelming peace. Strengthened by her God, she was able to forgive.[14] That is a true test of healthy religion.

I wonder if that guard who approached Corrie ten Boom was able to forgive himself? As a counselor, I have seen people who have engaged in blatantly sinful and destructive behavior, confessed it to God, and accepted his forgiveness. Often these people can freely forgive others, but many struggle with the inability to accept this forgiveness and to view themselves as forgiven. Sometimes they need somebody to come alongside, to give them encouragement, to guide them as they let go of the past, and to help them see that the God who forgives freely can help them to apply that forgiveness to themselves. As a Christian, I don't believe that any individual has the moral authority to forgive oneself—only God can forgive. But when we accept that forgiveness and no longer condemn ourselves, this is a sign of healthy religion.

Ninth, *healthy religion involves a willingness and ability to postpone immediate gratification so that greater satisfaction can come in the future.* I am not very athletic, but I know that nobody gets into shape overnight. The athlete in good physical condition has avoided harmful eating and subjected the body to workouts and other exercise over a period of time. Some of the workouts aren't very pleasant as we do them, but the sacrifice at one time brings better physical shape later. Teenage abstinence programs work on the same principle, and so does a lot of education. We postpone some things now so that we can have something better in the future.

Healthy religion calls us to forsake self-indulgent, self-centered living and to commit instead to purity, love, giving, unselfishness, discipline, and sometimes uncomfortable lifestyles. This is not intended to steal away our joy and make life miserable. In contrast, a life of devotion brings inner peace, fulfillment, and the promise of better things to come in the future.

My friend Lee Strobel once researched the very different lives of Mother Teresa and rock star Madonna. Mother Teresa gave her entire life to serving others but reached the end feeling incredibly fulfilled and satisfied. The star focused all her energies on trying to please herself and said that she didn't know anybody who was happy.

Tenth, *healthy religion is characterized by love that influences all relationships and reaches out in acts of service, compassion, social justice, and evangelism.* Some of the most angry, hate-filled people in this world claim to be spiritual but spew venom in the name of their religions. Cult leaders aren't known to be very loving, and almost every day we hear about the terrorist tactics of extreme Islamic fundamentalists. But there is hatred in the Christian community as well, in direct contrast to the love that Jesus proclaimed and demonstrated. Healthy religious people aren't perfect in their ability to love—nobody is. But the person with a healthy religion seeks to be a compassionate, caring, serving, loving individual who helps and builds up others rather than tearing people down. Even if you have only a passing acquaintance with the revivals of people like John Wesley and Charles Finney, you know how they led to significant social action that changed their societies. That is healthy Christianity in action.

Finally, *healthy religion is community based.* There is a side of Christian spirituality that is very personal and involves pulling away from others. Jesus took time to withdraw from the crowds so that he could pray in lonely places. Times of solitude, reflection, and private communion with God can be spiritually and personally refreshing. But Jesus always returned to the crowds and to his disciples. He worshiped regularly and expected his followers to do the same. Later, the early church met together, shared together, and worshiped in community. We are expected to do the same, reaching out from our religious communities with acts of encouragement, love, and good deeds.[15]

My wife and I live next to a pond that recently overflowed its banks following heavy rains. The whole lower level of our house was under a foot or more of dirty water that ruined the carpet, seeped into the walls, corroded the electrical and telephone wires, destroyed a lot of my books, and soaked into the furniture. Julie and I spent a day trying to clean up, but we hardly made a dent in the mess. Then, one morning, a group of seventeen people appeared from our church. They ripped up the carpet, carted out the damaged books and furniture, tore off the wallboard, and mopped up the water. Then they put fans and dehumidifiers in the basement and ended their work by spreading out a great lunch in our kitchen. About the time they were there, my phone rang and a friend from another church offered to "get a group of guys together" to come over to help clean up. I was overwhelmed to the point of tears. With no thought of payment or anything else from us, these believers (including my friend who called) demonstrated love in action pouring forth from a community of believers. That day, in my soggy basement, I stood in amazement and gratitude, watching healthy religion in action.

MATURE FAITH

The Search Institute in Minneapolis is a research organization interested in teenagers and how they can be helped to mature through the efforts of churches and community leaders. In a study of mature Christian faith, the institute identified eight core characteristics that differ a little from what we have been discussing. According to the researchers, a spirituality that is healthy and mature

1. trusts in God's saving grace and believes firmly in the humanity and divinity of Jesus.
2. experiences a sense of personal well-being, security, and peace.
3. integrates faith and life, seeing work, family, social relationships, and political choices as part of one's religious life.

4. seeks spiritual growth through study, reflection, prayer, and discussion with others.
5. seeks to be part of a community of believers in which people give witness to their faith and support and nourish one another.
6. holds life-affirming values, including commitment to racial and gender equality, affirmation of cultural and religious diversity, and a personal sense of responsibility for the welfare of others.
7. advocates social and global change to bring about greater social justice.
8. serves humanity, consistently and passionately, through acts of love and justice.[16]

A list like this can be intimidating, especially for anybody who wants a healthy religion and a mature spirituality but who comes up short when these guidelines are applied personally. Don't despair. Most of us fall short of the ideal, but for the Christian, the spiritual walk is a slow, often uneven, but steady progression to greater maturity and Christlikeness.

THE SPIRITUAL DIVIDE

It must have been at least twenty-five years ago when I accepted an invitation to lead a weekend seminar at the Fourth Presbyterian Church in Bethesda, Maryland, just outside Washington, D.C. I was told that many members of congress and government officials attended that church, but I don't remember meeting anybody famous except one person—the church's pastor. I can still remember visiting in the office of Richard Halverson. I had read one or two of his books and knew of his outstanding reputation, but I wasn't prepared for the visit with him. He was warm and cordial. Our brief time together was like the meeting of two old friends, even though that was the only time we ever met.

In 1981, Halverson was appointed chaplain of the United States Senate where he served for fourteen years. In a city where image is very important, the chaplain drove to work in his old car and roamed Capitol Hill greeting everyone—elevator operators, janitors, secretaries, Capitol police, and prominent senators. He learned their names, inquired about their families, treated them as friends, and often stopped to pray with them. "He was a spiritual giant," former Congressman John Dellenback said when Halverson died. "I always thought, 'He is a man who walks the walk, who lives what he talks.'"[17]

Once known as a conceited and arrogant young man with an enormous ego, Halverson began to change when he became a Christian. The people who knew him best were impressed with his deep humility, compassion, and concern for others. He was a man whose faith was genuine, whose spirituality was healthy, and whose adult life was spent close to the church.

Like Richard Halverson, many people who search for the sacred also stay within the confines of the church. A survey of more than 2,500 baby boomers concluded that 42 percent drop out of the church and stay out, but 33 percent are loyalists who never leave their religious moorings and the remaining 25 percent are returnees who have come back to organized religion. Most often they come to churches perceived as being more healthy, sensitive to people, up-to-date, and better able to meet their needs than the churches that they previously abandoned.[18]

In his landmark book about the spiritual journeys of baby boomers, Wade Clark Roof concludes that there is a "great spiritual divide" between the seekers of spirituality.[19] A small number of people are in the middle, never thinking about religion or spirituality, giving little thought to making sense of life, dealing with life's hard times by blaming fate or finding scientific or psychological explanations. More often, the baby boomers, and perhaps the generations that surround them, cluster toward one of two religious-spiritual extremes with a deep gulf between.

At one extreme are the new spiritualities that we discussed in the first half of this book. People who seek spirituality on this side of the great divide never darken the door of a church. For them, the spiritual quest is personal, self-focused, based more on feelings and experiences rather than on intellectual understanding. God, if he or she exists, is assumed to be a force, found by looking within, most likely experienced when one is open and receptive to the spiritual powers that will bring harmony. People on this side of the divide talk about centeredness, connectedness, harmony, and the oneness of human beings, nature, and the universe. Karen is in this camp and so, at least for a while, is Rich, who crossed the divide to explore new spiritual alternatives.

Very different is the spirituality perhaps best represented by the evangelical Protestantism of people like Richard Halverson. This spirituality is very sensitive to individual needs and how people walk with God. But truth and authority are not sought by looking within; they are assumed to come from an external source—a transcendent God who has revealed himself through the Bible and through his Son, Jesus Christ, who alone provides salvation. This theistic spirituality is rooted in the church, based on an understanding of scriptural truth, but open to expressions of emotion and contemplation. It is a spirituality that involves corporate worship, clear moral guidelines, awareness of sin, and compassionate service. Personal discipline, faithfulness, regular Bible reading and prayer, witnessing for Christ, worshiping and growing in the company of other believers, seeking the guidance of the Holy Spirit, and walking the Christian walk all define what spirituality is like for people on this side of the great gulf.

People on this side of the divide are on a pilgrimage with God; a walk with God that integrates expressions of worship, personal discipline, inner joy, communal love, and social justice. It is unlike the pilgrimage of people on the other side whose ongoing introspection leads them to explore the spirituality within.

Despite these vast differences, Roof suggests some unifying themes and points of agreement between the two extremes. Both want "a *genuine* spiritual experience that transcends the dry, external set of behaviors, dogmas, and forms associated with organized religion."[20] Both seek to endow life with religious and spiritual meaning. Both are concerned about personal needs, compulsions, problems, dysfunctional families, recovery, spiritual healing, and growth. Roof continues,

> Both ends of the religious spectrum appeal to a popular, do-it-yourself mentality, reflecting a voluntaristic religious climate where people of almost all persuasions increasingly choose their own private forms of religion rather than rely on the authority of a tradition or a religious community. Both give expression to turning inward, an introspection that empowers individuals to take responsibility for their own spiritual lives. Both see physical health and material prosperity as signs of blessings. Both express . . . faith in an abundance of spiritual power available to human beings, if only they make right use of it. . . .
>
> At both ends of the spectrum we find apocalyptic visions of the future. Both mystics and evangelicals, along with charismatics and pentecostals, often see the world as in the last stages of disintegration before the dawning of a new era. The scenarios differ in detail, but they agree on the imminence of a worldwide breakdown and the establishment of a new, spiritually transformed community. Lifted up is a vision of a new people and a new world.[21]

How do we make sense of this in our lives? Do we stay secure on one side of the great divide (or try huddling in the middle), nod in friendly fashion to people on the other side, and go about our daily activities and spiritual quests, each one searching alone or with a few like-minded spiritual travelers? As a Christian who follows one who described himself as the way, the truth, and the life, I am convinced that people find genuine spiritual satisfaction only by coming to God through Christ.[22] I stand on one side of the divide and so, probably, do you.

CHRISTIAN SPIRITUALITY

In a book that seeks to give a "road map for spiritual formation," Robert Mulholland sees Christian spirituality as a *process of becoming conformed to the image of Christ for the sake of others.*[23] This implies that spirituality is an ongoing, ever-developing, lifelong growth process; it is not a static possession that we achieve as a result of a dramatic experience, religious encounter, or participation in a twelve-step program for spiritual growth. Spirituality is a pilgrimage of becoming more like Christ, a journey of deepening responsiveness to God's control of our lives.

Seen this way, spirituality is not something added to a person's personality to supplement his or her physical, psychological, and social nature. Christian spirituality is at the very essence of the being. When we live seeking to be conformed to God's will for our lives, every part of the personality is affected.

Furthermore, Christian spirituality cannot be packaged into a form that fits everybody. We are unique individuals, and the Holy Spirit, who guides our spiritual growth, often molds us in distinct ways and into unique followers of Christ. From this it does not follow that true spirituality is so private and individualized that we withdraw into ourselves, pull away from other believers in the church, and have no concern for the needs of others. Christians who are growing spiritually are Christians who are becoming more like Christ and more holy. But as John Wesley emphasized, when there is personal holiness, there also will be social concern and responsibility. If we assume that God wants all of us to be spiritual, we must begin with ourselves, seeking ways by which we can be "conformed to the image of Christ for the sake of others." That becomes an important piece in putting together the spirituality puzzle.

— 7 —

Magic and the Spirituality Puzzle:
How Do We Play Games with the Spiritual?

Wh-hen I started my car one morning not long ago, I discovered that the radio was tuned to a religious program with an impassioned preacher. I reached out to turn to a different station but changed my mind and listened as I drove away from the house. The speaker was a woman, highly articulate, seemingly very sincere, and clearly zealous about her topic. Lacing the talk with Bible quotations, she urged her listeners to let Jesus heal all of their sicknesses, drive the demons from their lives, take away their poverty, and give them the wealth and prosperity that "children of the King of kings" have every right to ask for and expect to receive.

I listened about ten minutes until the program came to an end, but as I continued driving along the freeway, I felt unsettled by the preacher's message. As a Christian, I believe that Jesus Christ can and still does heal diseases. I believe as well that he is able to restrict the activities of Satan and his demonic forces, and that

God provides for our needs, often abundantly. But Jesus never promised that following him would mean a problem-free life of health, prosperity, and freedom from temptation's snares. He called his followers to obedience and commitment to a cause, promising that persecution and suffering would likely be part of the dedicated Christian's life. Jesus was no pie-in-the-sky philosopher; he talked about down-to-earth things, dealt with people in the midst of everyday struggles, and let the disciples see his periodic frustration, sorrow, and grief. He modeled and talked about a spirituality that would draw people into closer communion with God and would lead to abundant life. But he never implied what the radio preacher implied, that Christianity was all about getting free from pain and problems.

Probably that was not her intention, but the radio preacher had turned God into a genie, ever available to evaporate our difficulties and flood us with health, prosperity, and modern miracles. In that radio broadcast, the speaker was picturing God as a celestial David Copperfield, able to work magic to make things appear and disappear instantly and sometimes in spectacular ways before the eyes of wonder-filled people who "have faith to believe." Maybe the radio sermon bothered me because I sometimes think in ways that are like the preacher's. Maybe we have all become magical thinkers. And maybe this magical thinking has colored the ways in which we live our lives and view spirituality.

MAGICAL THINKING

More than thirty years ago, a relatively unknown psychiatrist named Eric Berne wrote *Games People Play*, a book that became an immediate best-seller.[1] It was followed a few years later by an even more popular publication that built on Berne's theory of Transactional Analysis and shouted from its bright orange cover that *I'm OK—You're OK*.[2] Both books were based on the idea that we all spend our lives playing mental games that help us cope with stress, hide from reality, deal with interpersonal tensions, and avoid responsibility. Berne listed thirty-six games with inter-est-catching titles such as "See what you made me do?"; "Ain't it awful?"; "Yes, but"; and "Wooden Leg: What can you expect from someone as disturbed as me?" The books became best-sellers, in part because they pinpointed ways of thinking about life that most of us could see in ourselves and that most of us use all the time to deal with our frustrations and problems.

The writings of Berne and Harris have long faded in popular-ity, but people still play mental games, often with the encourage-ment of friends, seminar leaders, spiritual gurus, and even radio preachers. The mental games are based on partial truths, on ideas that have little basis in reality, or on the beliefs and enthusiastic testimonies from people we admire. These mental assumptions are less like games in the mind and more like fantasy-filled, mag-ical thoughts. They are called magical because they assume, often without much evidence, that if we act or think in a certain way, a desired result will follow. The popular possibility thinking is an example. If you think positively about something you want or visualize its coming into being, you can expect that your will to believe will bring the very thing you want. That's magical think-ing.

At times we all think magically—assuming, without much thought, that our ideas are valid. Magical thinking permeates the whole culture, but we see it with special clarity in Christians and in other people who are concerned about spirituality. Like the audience at a magician's performance, we pretend that we are seeing the real thing, and we don't spend much time thinking about how we are being deceived. In similar ways, magical thinkers rarely consider that their thinking may be unfounded in reality, often illogical, possibly even self-destructive and danger-ous. Some Christians and followers of the new spirituality ignore this lack of logic by convincing themselves that rational thought doesn't matter. Others look for personal experiences or selected Bible verses to back up the magic and squelch the voices of reason. Critics of the magic are dismissed as people who are ill-informed, spiritually deceived, lacking in faith, or out of touch with reality.

145

Probably my list is incomplete, but at least nine examples of magical thinking appear frequently.

NINE TYPES OF MAGICAL THINKING

1. I deserve it.
2. I've earned it.
3. I can have it.
4. I can handle it.
5. I can't help it.
6. I didn't do it.
7. I feel good about it.
8. I know it's right because it works.
9. I've never given much thought to it.

---

1. "I Deserve It"

Entitlement has become a controversial and much-discussed word, especially in American society. This is the idea that certain people are entitled to special benefits, rights, privileges, and preferential treatments because they are female, gay, African-American, poor, immigrants, disabled, specially educated, or members of some other special group. Some people claim to be victims of sexual, racial, or other prejudice and claim special benefits because of past and present discrimination against the group to which they belong.

This "I deserve it" game guides many of our day-by-day activities. "I know I shouldn't have this dessert, but I deserve it after such a hard day at work," concludes the overweight businessman trying to justify what he is eating. "I can't afford it and I shouldn't put another charge on my credit card," concludes another individual, "but I deserve what I plan to buy after all the pressure I've been under." This mentality is typical of people trying to justify stealing or taking supplies home from their offices. They rationalize that "I deserve what I am taking when I have so little and the owners have so much."

That radio preacher exposed this kind of thinking. She didn't use these words, but her message said, "You are a Christian, so you deserve to have your problems solved and your poverty gone. As a Christian, you have a right to be rich and healthy."

2. "I've Earned It"

This bargaining mentality is very close to entitlement thinking. Instead of concluding, "I deserve it because of my gender, sexual orientation, skin color, or prominence," this second type of magical thinking concludes, "I've earned it because of what I have done or have promised to do." This is the view that "I will get what I want by striking a bargain with God. If I hold up my side of the deal, I will earn the blessings that I want from God whom I expect to hold up his side of the deal." The thinking is magical because "the deal" is often one-sided, dreamed up in a human mind, but with no biblical or other evidence that God feels obligated to be part of the bargain.

Some people expect special privileges because of their accomplishments or status. I know a psychologist who rose to some prominence as a seminar speaker in churches and on college campuses around the country. His lectures were well received, and before long he began to think that he was somebody special, entitled to special perks like fancier hotel rooms and VIP treatment at conferences. When he didn't receive what he expected, he responded with indignation and sometimes a lack of cooperation. My friend based his "I deserve it" thinking on the views that he had of himself as an important speaker, entitled to preferential perks and recognition.

This thinking permeates the whole spirituality movement, especially in people who believe they can earn their way to a better life, to a better reincarnation, to favor with God, or to heaven. The so-called health-and-wealth or seed-faith gospel that is common in many churches and preached by some television and radio evangelists proclaims, "If I give, I will get—and the more I give, the more I can expect to get." In other church circles there is a tranquillity-and-stability gospel that assumes, "If I am a good Christian who prays regularly and serves in the church, I can expect God to protect me from mental illness, suffering, worry, or other problems."

Is this magic? God promises to provide for our needs, to bless those who give abundantly, to flood our lives with inner peace, deep joy, and spiritual strength. For centuries, believers have seen that he is faithful to fulfill what he has promised. But God gives out of his grace and love. He isn't into bargaining, holding on to things that could enrich our lives until we earn enough points to redeem the divinely held prize. We benefit spiritually when we discipline ourselves to worship, pray, serve, give, and meditate. But God gives because he loves us and wants to bestow good things on us, not because we dream up fantasies about our abilities to earn his favor.

3. "I Can Have It"

This possibility thinking view of life dreams about possibilities but often ignores realities. This magical thinking is encouraged by the media with the glitzy portrayals of life, by the lotteries and casinos with their visions of instant wealth, and by motivational speakers who don't even have *failure* or *lack of success* in their vocabularies. It is thinking popular with potential athletes, people climbing career ladders, spirituality seekers visualizing world peace or harmony, and Christians who determine to "see things with the eyes of faith" and expect God to act.

I try to be a possibility thinker. I work to shake off negative, cynical, or pessimistic perspectives in my life, and I like to imagine and dream about things that could become reality. I get enthusiastic about encouraging young visionaries (most of the visionaries I know are young) to pursue their dreams and to keep trying even when they encounter setbacks or obstacles. I am motivated by thinking about career goals, ministry possibilities, books that need to be written, and the potential open to all of us for maturing into greater spiritual intimacy with God. Possibility thinking is not bad or wrong—except when it ignores reality.

Buoyed by the possibilities of riches and success, people can disregard reality, make unwise financial decisions, move too quickly in making choices, and get themselves into disastrous financial and other problems as a result. These people assume, with little basis other than magical thinking—and the encouragement of some possibility preachers and motivational gurus—that God will rescue them and free them from entanglements that come when they don't count the cost or when they make decisions that don't make sense.

Like the entitlement and bargaining types of thinking, the "I can have it" magical thoughts bring confusion, anger, and disillusionment when the magic doesn't work and we don't get what we thought we deserved, earned, or expected. What does it do for our faith if we pray but things don't get better, if we give but we don't get rich, if we think positive thoughts about our careers but we don't get promoted? Sometimes the failures lead to self-blame or feelings of guilt, despair, and anger. When things don't turn out as expected, we often blame ourselves because we didn't have enough faith or didn't trust enough for God to provide. If a religious leader reinforces the idea that a lack of faith causes God to withhold what we want, then the weight of guilt becomes heavier. Often there are discouragement, anger with God, and a turning away from the divinity who failed to meet our expectations. Possibility thinking can be motivating and helpful. But without hard work and a dose of realism, possibility thinking can become magical thinking that leads to a mountain of disappointments and heartaches.

4. "I Can Handle It"

It's the macho way and maybe the American way to say, "I can handle things by myself"; "I don't need help"; or "We can do anything if we set our minds to it." My wife sometimes points out that I don't like to ask for directions. I know many men who are the same. We have great confidence that we can find where we are going without stopping, looking at a map, or asking for guidance. While we drive around hopelessly lost, we have an "I can take care of it" state of mind that gets us more confused and often more lost.

Unlike "I can have it" thinking, the magical assumption that "I can handle it" involves a belief in quick fixes. Accustomed to fast foods, instant pain medication, high-speed computers, and immediate credit approval, "I can handle it" thinking assumes that change can come quickly and that all is possible for those who make the effort or have the know-how. Closely connected with this is an "I can handle this," "I can kick this habit" type of thinking that looks for never-fail formulas for resolving problems without help from anybody. Life, of course, is rarely that simple, predictable, or controllable.

"I can handle it" thinking often is seen in the search for spirituality. Scores of seminar speakers and Sunday sermons give formulas for Christian growth, spiritual direction, better relationships, effective evangelism, and/or freedom from personal struggles—all of which we can handle ourselves (with a little help from God) quickly. Christian twelve-step programs sometimes reflect this thinking, and so do some new spirituality approaches that provide rules for finding enlightenment, aligning forces, or getting in touch with supernatural entities. More dramatic are some of the exorcisms that claim to take control of demons. Others assume that offering a "prayer of faith" or "taking dominion" over a situation will resolve problems quickly and efficiently.

5. "I Can't Help It"

This kind of magical thinking lets people think of themselves as victims of what somebody else has done. In turn, these self-proclaimed victims can have unrealistic, magical expectations about getting special treatment because of experiences, behaviors, and attitudes that they can't change or control. The "I can't help it" mind-set fuels the recovery movement, gives people excuses to avoid taking responsibility for their actions, and sends many to twelve-step groups where they recite their problems to one another and sometimes stay "in recovery" for years. Criticize this thinking and you might be accused of being unsympathetic and in denial about the victim's—or your—real problems.

The recovery movement has helped many people. The different twelve-step and other programs for recovery still enable people to get free from the entanglements of the past. Recovery groups provide a sense of community, a place to be with others who have similar struggles, an environment where people find support, and freedom to grapple with solutions. In the best programs, people are enabled to escape from the entanglements of "I'm a victim" thinking and take responsibility for shaping their lives and futures.

As we have seen in an earlier chapter, however, recovery programs with their "I can't help it" thinking have received much criticism. Under the heading "the spirituality of self-help," one book compares recovery and other self-help groups with cults: "Both systems promise an antidote to the general alienation and loneliness of our culture, a substitute for families and communities that have come unglued. Both demand substantial offerings of time and devotion to their respective programs, and encourage reliance on the group for social, emotional, and practical support."[3] The authors argue that, like cults, recovery and other self-help programs often are filled with religious jargon and view their methods as *the* source of truth and enlightenment.

Despite these similarities, and despite weaknesses in the recovery movement, it is unfair to assume that most or all recovery groups are cultlike. Many people really are victims of their dysfunctional families, held in the grip of their addictions, or immobilized by the traumas from their pasts. For them, "I can't help it" is a way of thinking that is both sincere and demoralizing. The thinking becomes destructive only when it holds people in bondage, robs them of hope, and keeps them tied to recovery groups, cults, unhealthy churches, or other spirituality groups that promise freedom but instead deliver endless reminders of their sinfulness, weaknesses, and victimization.

6. "I Didn't Do It"

A lot of people like to play the blame game. Feuding spouses blame each other. Politicians blame people in the opposing party. Corporations blame the unions, which blame the corporation management. Little kids get caught doing something wrong and blame their sisters or brothers. Everybody blames the media or the government for our problems, and when all else fails, we go outside the country and blame Japanese businesspeople, the countries who won't buy our products, or the foreign sweatshops that undercut our prices.

Blaming isn't always wrong. Other people *are* to blame for many of our problems, and we do need to hold people accountable for what they have done or failed to do. That is why we have laws and courts that set standards, determine responsibility, and issue fines or jail terms. *Arbitration* and *mediation* have become common words in our language as we seek ways to resolve differences and define where blame and responsibilities really lie.

But the blame game can become a habit that lets us push responsibility onto somebody else and avoid doing anything to change our attitudes or actions. If we can find somebody else to blame, we can play the "poor little me" game that evokes sympathy from others and lets us escape from facing our failures, incompetencies, sinfulness, or stupidities. Often people successfully get off the hook by claiming that somebody else is the culprit. "It has worked in the past and worked for others," one reasons, "so why shouldn't it work for me now?" Besides, in many instances others genuinely are to blame, so to say "it wasn't my fault" can be a believable and effective self-defense.

This blame-game mentality permeates a lot of religion. "The devil made me do it" is more than the humorous line of a television comedian. It is an often-accurate statement that can be used or abused by religious people. Sometimes we blame serious problems on dysfunctional churches, toxic faith, self-centered and manipulative religious leaders, or satanic ritual abuse that is hard to prove because there is so little convincing evidence. Followers of the new spirituality play similar games, blaming their past lives, their karma, their unconverging forces, or some other unprovable source. Some churches and Christian fiction writers take biblical statements about the demonic and weave them into fanciful stories or interest-riveting methods for battling the forces of hell and driving out demons. All problems are blamed on the demons; all solutions center on magiclike exorcisms and power encounters often built on the imaginations of the exorcists and their awestruck congregations.

As a Christian, I believe in the forces of evil. The Bible warns us repeatedly about the impact of Satan and the principalities and powers that can ruin our lives and prevent a healthy spirituality.[4] But spiritual growth and renewal are destroyed as well when we shun responsibility for our actions or sinfulness, cast blame onto other people or forces, and think of magical ways to keep from shouldering blame in ourselves.

7. "I Feel Good About It"

When I was growing up, we sang a wonderful hymn that I still like. The people in the church would raise their voices in unison and enthusiastically sing, "He lives, He lives, Christ Jesus lives today!" One line in that song has always bothered me, however. At the end of the chorus the lyrics ask, "You ask me how I know He lives? He lives within my heart." Probably the songwriter wasn't thinking like this when the hymn was written, but the words imply that there is no need to answer the question of why a Christian knows Christ lives; it is enough to feel his presence "within my heart."

There is nothing wrong with feeling good "in my heart" about God, a person, or a belief. We've all had the experience of making a decision and then moving forward because it "felt right" or not going ahead because we "just don't feel good about it." Sometimes the inner emotional sensations can be unconscious green lights or ominous warning signals. Christians might recognize inner sensations as the nonverbal tugging of the Holy Spirit who prompts and guides us, especially when we want his leading and direction.

But many spirituality seekers base most of their decisions on feelings and inner promptings. "Don't confuse me or try to persuade me with facts," these seekers might say. "I feel in my heart that what I have decided is right." This is building one's beliefs, spirituality, life, and eternal destiny on emotions and subjective experiences that resist arguments and have little concern about what is logical. Technically this is not magical thinking; it is nonthinking of the type that characterizes a lot of contemporary spirituality.

For many people today, including many Christians, spirituality is internal, experiential, deeply felt, and subjective. They have little interest in participating in institutional religion, finding a faith that can be defended with good arguments, building sound theologies, or looking to the Bible or any other sacred writing as words from God. Instead, they are fascinated with angels, out-of-body experiences, human encounters with aliens, energy transformations, and reported miracles. Some of the most popular churches bypass careful teaching, encourage people to "feel the Spirit's power," and move the masses with highly emotional testimonies, demonstrations of healing, and "signs and wonders" that defy rational analysis. For many people, outside the church and within, personal faith and spirituality are disconnected from critical thinking and from institutional religion.[5] Researcher Wade Clark Roof concludes that much of our population has "grown up in a post-sixties culture that emphasizes choice, knowing and understanding one's self, the importance of personal autonomy, and filling one's potential—all contributing to a highly subjective approach to religion" and spirituality.[6] Religion is dismissed as being too restrictive, but spirituality is embraced eagerly as a way of "plugging into" the supernatural using anything that feels right and "works" for us. The result is a spirituality that adopts any lifestyle that we find personally satisfying and follows any teaching that lines up with our personal experiences or intuitions. Even in mainstream Christianity there is a form of experience-dominated magic that talks about "plugging into" the "power" and "energy" of the spiritual world like turning on the electricity whenever we want.[7]

Roof calls this the mystical spirituality of people whose perspectives on life are "rooted more in their own biographies and experiences" than in any religious teaching that tries to "provide answers for all times and in all places."[8] Even evangelical churches emphasize our subjective walks with a God who meets our needs and doesn't ask for much in return. When experience is assumed to be most trustworthy, the intellectual aspect of religion has to be downplayed. What we believe will be less important than how we feel. Will anything, then, keep us from unrestrained superstition and moral chaos?[9] Will "I feel good about it" be the only basis on which we evaluate morals, make decisions, determine how to live, and make sense of suffering, death, and the mysteries of the universe? Raw subjectivism is a pretty shaky foundation on which to build our lives and spirituality.

8. "I Know It's Right Because It Works"

Philosophers call this *pragmatism*. It is the point of view of many churches and spirituality seekers that if something works, then it must be right. In religious circles it is the idea that apparent miracles, rapid church growth, big ministries, successful money-raising campaigns, effective therapies, and dramatic testimonies of healing show that "what we believe and are doing is right." This thinking can be seen in sincere people who proclaim their wonderful successes as evidence of God's blessings and Satan's defeat. It is thinking that denies that lots of people succeed very well without God.[10] It is thinking that forgets the biblical warnings that Satan and his forces can produce miracles.[11]

Pragmatic thinking forgets as well that many things "work" that are not beneficial, morally right, respectful of individual rights, or evidence of truth. Manipulation often works to change people, at least for a while, and so do the rhetoric of cult leaders, the persuasive techniques of clever advertising, the use of force or threats, the infliction of pain, the promise of rewards, the taking of drugs, the suggestions of therapists, and the power of an emotionally charged religious service.

Several years ago, somebody sent me an article written by a psychologist who had a problem with compulsive overeating and wanted to find a method that would work to remove his addiction. "I consider myself an intelligent, rational and well-educated person," the article began.

> I have a law degree and a master's degree in psychology and I have taught law and psychology at the graduate level. I have always been skeptical of formal religion. I do not believe in magic nor do I think that prayer can lead to an alteration of the laws of nature. In my early days in Overeaters Anonymous I had a very hard time with the God talk and the suggestion regarding prayer and powerlessness.

> However, I stayed on and struggled with the Steps as best I could. And over the years . . . I have been convinced that addictions and compulsive disorders are fundamentally spiritual problems and that deepest healing calls for addressing the underlying spiritual hungers that drive one to search in all the wrong places for satisfaction and relief.[12]

The writer never searched for help in the church or turned to the God of the Bible. Instead, he found relief in twelve-step groups and in a view of spirituality that "involves not simply changing thoughts, but changing levels of consciousness; opening to deep sources of intuitive wisdom and power hidden in the depths of human consciousness."[13] For him, this "opening" worked. To me, it is hard to grasp what he really is talking about, and I'm not inclined to jump to similar conclusions solely because of a convert's testimony that "it must be right because it worked." I would like more convincing evidence.

9. "I've Never Given Much Thought to It"

This may be the most honest of the nine forms of magical thinking that we have discussed. It admits that a lot of our conclusions about life and about spirituality result from beliefs and behaviors that we have accepted without much thought or questioning. I have some good friends who live in a western city that is a bastion of evangelical churches and Christian ministries. My friends belong to one of several community discussion groups that regularly meet over dinner and discuss a variety of subjects, often including religion. One night, somebody asked why more of the Christians in the community were not involved with the discussion groups. "They're scared of questions," one of my friends replied. "They are afraid that their own spiritual foundations will be weakened, and they fear that they won't have answers for the tough questions. It is easier and more comfortable to stay with other believers."

My friend's explanation may be a little strong. While some Christians might be afraid of tough questions, there may be others who don't enjoy the kind of give-and-take discussion that these dinner groups appreciate. Whether or not they participate in group discussions, nobody I know has answers to all of the difficult questions in life, and nobody is an expert on spirituality. But it is sad to think that millions of us blithely seem to accept our beliefs and pursue our spiritual journeys without giving much serious thought to why we believe and without challenging some of the questionable statements that are tossed about in religious circles. Periodically I get together with a man who has a sharp mind, a successful career, and advanced degrees, but he is so much influenced by his opinionated pastor that he never thinks to question what is said. Passively he concludes, "If my pastor says it's true, then it must be right."

Probably you've heard other conclusions that people accept without much thought or challenge:

- "If it isn't in the Bible, it probably isn't true."
- "Real Christians rejoice and refuse to grieve when a loved one dies."
- "Christians don't stay angry; they forgive and forget and get on with life."
- "If you were a good Christian, walking with God, you wouldn't need counseling."
- "If I really believe in my heart, I won't have to ask questions."

Father Andrew Greeley once described a few tense moments when he appeared as a guest on Phil Donahue's talk show. "Shouldn't all good Catholics agree in everything with the pope—birth control, celibacy, abortion, the ordination of women?" Donahue asked. He wasn't interested in discussion or answers, the priest wrote later. Donahue, "fangs bared ... had his own simplistic paradigm and he wanted an answer to fit it."

When he left the program, Father Greeley thought to himself that someday he would write a book to pry the talk-show host and others away from their "stone wall of ignorance." Even as he later wrote the book, the author knew that Donahue would never read it: "He already knew all there was to know about American Catholics."[14] There is a danger that any of us can be the same— convinced of our conclusions about spirituality or the church, caught in magical thinking, and unwilling to listen to any dissenting facts or voices.

MAGIC AND RELIGION

Somebody has said that *belief* in God is religion, and *using* God for our own ends is magic. If that distinction is valid, then a lot of contemporary spirituality, including some of the spirituality in the Christian church, is a brand of witchcraft, not much different from the crystal gazing, ritual sacrifices, channeling, astrology fascination, and Buddhalike meditation that so many of us reject. Faith becomes magic when it involves techniques for getting what we want by believing strongly enough and by knowing the rules for using God.[15]

Jesus once told a parable about house building. Some people build their lives on shaky foundations like the man who constructed his house on sand and watched helplessly as the rains came, the streams rose, the winds blew, and the house fell with a great crash. Others are like the man who built his house on the rock. The rains and streams and winds battered that house as well, but it stood firm because it had a solid foundation. Jesus didn't leave anybody to question the meaning of his story. The wise person who builds his or her spirituality on the rock is the one who hears the words of Christ and puts them into practice.[16]

Will an individual experience personal-spiritual benefits from that decision? Absolutely. But rock-solid spirituality is not based on intuitive meditation, magical thinking, or religious practices that are intended to move supernatural forces so we can get what we want. Rock-solid spirituality is built on clear thinking, solid evidence, involvement with community, and devoted willingness to understand the words of Jesus and put them into practice.

I have come to the conclusion that two powerful forces are at work in me, both vying for my attention, energy, and devotion. These forces first surfaced many years ago, and they still grapple for control of my life. Both have a powerful bearing on my spirituality. One force in me is named *Success*. It is the drive to "make it" in this life, to succeed in my field, to write books that will be lauded, and to give speeches that will be applauded. This is a dangerous force, one that can lead to the pride, arrogance, manipulation of others, and insensitivity that I have seen in many people who get to the top. I try to control the drive in me by resisting acclaim if it comes and downplaying my accomplishments. I say that power, recognition, and riches don't matter, but deep in my heart I know that they really do matter. In our society we believe that the successful person is the one who has worth and value. I suspect that my drive for success reveals a search for the self-acceptance and self-affirmation that I have always lacked.

I know two men, both Christian psychologists, who are near the end of their careers but consumed with the effort to prove— to others and to themselves—that they really did make a difference in this life and that their accomplishments amounted to something of value. I never want to be like that. And despite my fascination with success, I don't want to be like the prosperous and acclaimed superstars who have stress-filled marriages, strained relationships, inner turmoil, and empty lives along with all their trophies.

The other force in my life has the name *Service*. Jesus talked about it when the disciples had a dispute about who among them would be greatest—most successful—in God's kingdom. We live in a world where people want the power to lord it over others, Jesus said, but that should not characterize believers. "Instead, whoever wants to become great among you must be your servant, and whoever wants to be first must be your slave." Even Jesus came not to be served but to serve.[17] For him, service was the primary goal; success was unimportant. Whenever I think about this, I realize that Jesus was presenting radical thinking that goes against everything that most people in our society believe.

I know that my life and my spirituality will be more fulfilling, stable, and peaceful if I build on the solid-rock teachings of Jesus, who taught us to be servants. As I have grown older, with God's help I have been letting go of the drive for success and learning to be more content with being a servant. I know that some people are both successful and effective servants, but their numbers are few and I'm not among them. I know, too, that my spiritual growth will always be stunted if the success force in my life is allowed to override the servant force.

There may not be a success-service struggle in you as there is in me, but it is likely that you have similar inner turmoil. These internal struggles make us all more vulnerable to the magical thinking that promises to resolve turmoil, boost self-esteem, and give us our hearts' desires without much effort. When they are built on magical thinking and distorted values, our lives and our spiritualities are like the houses built on sand. They aren't built on solid foundations, and they don't stand firm.

WEIGHTY SPIRITUALITY

In a book that had a significant influence on me, Gordon MacDonald tells the story of a yachtsman named Michael Plant who set out alone to cross the Atlantic Ocean in a sailboat.[18] Plant was an expert, with superior seafaring skills, a state-of-the-art vessel, and experience in taking long solo trips. His friends and family gathered at the dock to give an enthusiastic send-off, not suspecting that they would never see their sailing friend again.

A few days into the voyage, storms rose in the North Atlantic. Radio contact with the respected yachtsman stopped. Days passed with no signals or sign of the boat. Then, one day, a freighter found the little vessel floating upside down not far from the Portuguese Azores. Plant was nowhere to be seen.

Sailboats apparently do not capsize easily. They are built to remain upright even when they are pounded by giant waves. Why, then, had Plant's boat tipped over? MacDonald gives the answer. In order for a sailboat to maintain a steady course and "in order for it not to capsize but to harness the tremendous power of the wind, *there must be more weight below the waterline than there is above it*. Any violation of that principle of weight distribution means disaster."[19] Plant knew that, of course, and his boat had an eight-thousand-pound weight bolted to the keel to assure stability. But for some reason, the ballast beneath the waterline broke away. When there was nothing to ensure stability, the boat capsized in the storm.

MacDonald applies this concept to life. The world today is filled with thousands of spiritual gurus and guidelines. Many are like the superstructure of an attractive yacht—pleasing to look at, admirable, promising comfort and pleasant journeys in the future. But without something underneath, something unseen but deeper, our lives and our spiritualities capsize when we encounter tragedy, suffering, or the storms of life and are "pressed or forced to look below the waterline for explanations, for stabilizing assistance, for significance, and for truth and wisdom."[20] Like a boat without ballast, there will be no ultimate stability to our spiritual lives if we build on magical thinking without solid intellectual and biblical weight underneath.

KEEPING FREE OF MAGICAL SELF-DECEPTION

Almost four hundred years ago, Galileo turned from his telescope and began writing his conclusions about the universe. In a treatise that was immediately banned by the church, the seventeenth-century astronomer argued that the sun, not the earth, was the center of the universe. The Vatican accused Galileo of teaching a theory that was "absurd, false in philosophy and formally heretical." It was a theory, said the church leaders, that "can in no way be probable, which has been already declared and finally determined contrary to the Divine Scripture."[21]

Years later, the church looked at the evidence, softened its hardline resistance, developed a better understanding of Scripture, and vindicated Galileo. But the famous astronomer was no longer alive. He had gone to his grave condemned by sincere believers who strongly clung to incorrect beliefs.

Today, we live in a highly sophisticated, technology-dominated age, but our world still is filled with sincere people who strongly cling to incorrect beliefs. Postmodern culture lets us avoid the necessity and hard work of evaluating our spiritual convictions. Instead, many people—including many followers of Christ— conclude that truth is subjective, that "if it feels good and if it works for you, it must be true." In such an environment, magical thinking is accepted without hesitation. The opinions of spiritual leaders are never questioned, even as the faithful believers in the days of Galileo never questioned the pronouncements of their church leaders. As a result, millions of spirituality searchers sail through life, basing their earthly journeys and eternal destinies on magical thinking and emotional spiritualities that have little depth beneath the waterlines of personal experience.

Entire books have been written about critical thinking, telling readers how to avoid logical fallacies, inaccurate conclusions, and magical fantasies.[22] Some of these books are hard to read, but they give principles of good thinking that can be grasped easily and applied to our spiritual searches. I can mention only a few.

Guilt by Association

What is wrong with the following statements?

Carl Jung was a psychologist who engaged in occult activities.

Gary Collins is also a psychologist.

Therefore, Gary Collins is engaged in occult activities.

I give this example because it is similar to a charge leveled against me by an author who was critical of psychology. Just because one psychologist participated in occult activities, it does not follow that all psychologists are occultists. Apply this to spirituality and you see the dangers of guilt by association. Just because a prominent television evangelist or two have widely reported moral problems, it does not follow that *all* television evangelists, Billy Graham included, are the same. Just because some Christians are hyperemotional, politically rigid, tenaciously intolerant, or afraid to talk with nonbelievers about their beliefs, it does not follow that all—or even a majority—are the same. Just because some followers of New Age spirituality appear to be flaky, out of contact with reality, or disinterested in anything Christian, it does not follow that all seekers are similar. We must be careful lest we see a few extremes and sweep aside whole groups of people, entire denominations, every member of a political party, or an entire profession.

Overgeneralization

This is the fallacy of building a whole way of thinking on one or a few examples. It is the common tendency to believe that what is true in one situation or for one person will be true in all situations. Before we developed more stringent testing methods, this used to happen often in medicine and psychology. Somebody would stumble onto a new procedure that cured a disease or solved a difficult problem. Armed with a few examples, the more dramatic, the more convincing, the "inventor" or "discoverer" would begin to proclaim his or her new cure.

Overgeneralization happens all the time in religious circles—and often in our minds. We hear a testimony about what God has done, see a demonstration that looks like a miracle, or learn that God apparently has spoken in a vision to one person, and we conclude that something similar is available to everybody. We hear about a young person who started taking drugs after listening to a particular type of music and conclude that all who listen to that music will fall by the wayside. A seeker is flooded with love and acceptance by a cult member and assumes that everybody in the cult is like this. Several years ago, on television and in the movies, the spiritual experience of Shirley MacLaine was so convincing that eight million people bought her book *Out on a Limb*. Could that many people be wrong? They could if they base their conclusions on the personal experience of one prominent leader and conclude, without carefully examining what she taught, that all people will have a similar experience.

Seeing What We Expect to See

What is your opinion of teenagers? If you think they are mostly impressionable kids with a lot of pressures but with potential to succeed in this life, you are likely to see what you look for. If you think all teens are irresponsible, sex-crazed, lazy, and constantly seeking ways to get high or drunk, you will find evidence to support your beliefs. Probably you also will see what you look for

164

and expect to see in "New Agers," "worldly people," "postmodernists," "the pope," "Jerry Falwell," "pentecostals," "Catholics," "fundamentalists," "Baptists," or "the Christian Right." It is an easy step for any of us to make up our minds, form an opinion, and then find the facts to fit. Armed with these biases, college professors, politicians, preachers, and authors, among others, proclaim messages that are based more on prejudgments and selected information than on fairness, balance, and carefully evaluated data.

This fallacy is hard to avoid. We all look for evidence to support our beliefs and reject or ignore data that go against our convictions. Sometimes we take this a step farther and bring about what social scientists call *self-fulfilling prophecies*. When we act in accordance with what we believe, our actions, in turn, often bring about the results that we expected. If a teacher expects a group of students to succeed academically, often they succeed above average—maybe because they were given extra attention and encouragement by the teacher who expected them to do well. Expect them to fail and often they fail. That is a self-fulfilling prophecy—bringing about what we expect. Mark McMinn and James Foster write,

> Self-fulfilling prophecy may also be used to explain Robert Schuller's and Norman Vincent Peale's results with positive mental attitude (PMA), which they advocate as a mental, emotional and spiritual tool. With egos bolstered by positive belief that something good will happen, positive thinkers may attempt ventures which they previously avoided. Since "nothing ventured is nothing gained," simply trying new things may produce increased success. The effectiveness of PMA need not be labeled satanic or interpreted in some mysterious fashion. For those expecting PMA to lead to success, it might actually work simply because it adds to their confidence.[23]

This helps explain why people in religious, political, or spirituality groups remain convinced of their beliefs. They do what they can to make happen what they expect to happen. In turn, their beliefs are reinforced. Couple this with a few prominent examples of success, a tendency to overgeneralization, or a postmodern mind-set that discounts rational analysis, and the believer is locked into his or her way of thinking, regardless of any evidence to the contrary.

Groupthink

Groupthink is a word that social scientists began using frequently after evaluating the decision of President Kennedy and his advisers to invade Cuba in the 1960s. A small brigade landed at the Bay of Pigs, expecting to overthrow Castro and his communist regime, but the troops were quickly surrounded and trapped. It was a foolish decision—even Kennedy admitted that later—but it was made by a group of people so eager to please one another and to reach a group consensus that they failed to evaluate the situation realistically. Many of the president's advisers had individual doubts about the success of the mission, but nobody said anything. Each person assumed that "everybody else is convinced, so I guess I am wrong in my doubts." This is the most prominent but probably not the only case of magical thinking in the White House.

Sometimes groupthink happens in churches when all the people think alike. It happens among the proponents of different kinds of alternative medicines, when the advocates all agree that the new method works and then look for evidence to prove what they have already concluded. We may see groupthink in possibility thinkers, crystal gazers, channelers, Bible study groups, twelve-step groups, or anyplace else where people gather together, talk about an issue, and never entertain the idea that their group consensus might be more magical than valid.

The Correlation Error

This is a misuse of statistics. It assumes incorrectly that when two events occur together, one must cause the other. It fails to recognize that other causes may create the similarities. Consider the now established fact that people who have clear religious beliefs also tend to have better health. Can we assume from this statistic that religion causes your health to be better? Might it be just as logical to assume that healthier people are more attracted to religion? More likely, the better health comes because religious people are less likely to smoke, drink, or take risks that could interfere with their physical well-being.

An interesting example of this correlation error appeared in a book written by a professor who should have known better. He saw that the number of psychological problems had increased and so had the number of psychologists. Maybe, because there were more problems, there was a greater need for helpers, but that was not what the professor concluded. He wrote, "It seems like there is a direct ratio between the increasing number of helpers and the increasing number of those who need help. The more psychologists we have, the more mental illnesses we get; the more social workers and probation officers, the more crime; the more teachers, the more ignorance."[24]

AVOIDING LOGICAL ERRORS

The correlation error and the others described are all logical mistakes that encourage people to think magically. By avoiding these errors and carefully considering our beliefs, we can avoid the magic and find deeper, more valid, and satisfying spiritual roots.

How does all of this apply to you? How might it apply to people like Rich and Karen, the spirituality seekers who have appeared periodically in the preceding pages? Might they see magical thinking in some of their searchings? Rich is the kind of person who wants community more than intellectual answers. He isn't comfortable accepting ideas that are more magical than logical, but he is less interested in examining his thinking than in finding a group of spiritually sensitive people who know about forgiveness, who are willing to talk honestly about suffering, who are concerned about social action, who worship together, and who give mutual support and encouragement. Rich spent his early years hearing about God and about theology. Like others of his generation, he now wants to experience God, to know what it is like to walk with God. Sooner or later, Rich is likely to return to the church, probably a church that is more loving, contemporary, and sensitive to his needs than the Christian community where he grew up.

Karen may never embrace traditional religion. But she is uncomfortable with the magical thinking in many of the spiritualities that she pursues. She harbors many pictures of the church that she recognizes as distortions. Even so, she will continue on her current path at least until she sees authentic spirituality in Christians who are not afraid to talk about their struggles and searching. Like Rich, she wants deeper spiritual roots than what she now experiences. We turn to these deeper roots in the next chapter.

— 8 —

Solving the Spirituality Puzzle:

How Do We Put the Pieces Together?

Back in the early 1960s, when the cars were big and hair was short and families that prayed together stayed together, the Walceks said grace before meals and went to Mass every single morning. Emil and Kathleen sent their nine children to the local parochial schools in Placentia, California, and on Sunday mornings at St. Joseph's the family took up two pews. Then, one by one, the children set off on their spiritual travels, and in the process perfectly charted the journey of their generation.

With this introduction, the religion editor of *Time* magazine began an article that he titled "The Church Search."[1] Two of the Walcek children didn't bother to search. They dropped out of the church and have never come back. Another member of the family rejected the idea of a church wedding, was married on a cliff overlooking the Pacific, later got a divorce, and eventually returned to the Catholic church, concluding that "maybe the traditional way of doing things isn't so bad." Another came back

169

after marrying a Ukrainian Catholic. Daughter Mary Walcek married a "lapsed Methodist" and now worships "God's creation" in her own unstructured way. Another daughter drifted into the Hindu-influenced Self-Realization Fellowship. Her younger brother became a Unitarian because he wants morality but without dogma. One of the Walceks has spent the past few years exploring the "Higher Power" in twelve-step recovery programs, while the youngest member of the family is still searching. She called off the wedding when her nonpracticing Jewish fiancé embraced orthodoxy and "sparked a whole new journey" of spirituality in the woman that he had expected to marry.

The story of the Walcek family is like a summary of the preceding pages of this book. People are searching in various places, looking for something that will meet their spiritual needs and fill their spiritual emptiness. "Increasing numbers of baby Boomers who left the fold years ago are turning religious again," the *Time* writer observed, "but many are traveling from church to church or from faith to faith, sampling creeds, shopping for a custom-made God."[2] Critics contend that churches are doing whatever they can to lure and keep these fickle customers, even to the point of watering down the Christian message, replacing the old hymns with lively syrupy choruses, and entertaining the audiences with skits, music, or self-help talks that will keep the crowds coming. Catholic theologian Avery Dulles complains that just about everything in America, religion included, "succeeds to the extent that it can arouse interest and provide entertainment."[3] But will spirituality searchers stay and be satisfied with a revitalized religion that subtly shifts from a focus on the glory of God to an emphasis on the gratification of human desires? Ask that question about yourself.

With all of this in mind, I called a man who has spent a lot of time studying spirituality from a Christian perspective. Dr. Gary Moon is a psychologist and a creative writer whose passion is to stimulate spiritual growth through an institute that he runs in Georgia. "Tell me," I asked my friend, "how would you distinguish between authentic Christian spirituality and all of the other approaches to spirituality on the market?"

The answer I heard surprised me because it was so short and so simple: "Genuine spirituality—the kind that will last, bring ultimate fulfillment, and survive in the crises of life—is a spirituality that never forgets two crosses: the cross of Christ and the cross of suffering." Most of the new spiritualities ignore both, although a few may say something about suffering. Many of the Christian spiritualities give a nod, at least, to the cross of Christ, but they dismiss suffering as evidence of a lack of faith. Instead, they emphasize the healing and health, possessions and problem relief, miracles and magical thinking that are supposed to characterize true faith.

TWO CROSSES

The cross of Christ is at the core of Christian spirituality. There are varied individual and denominational perspectives on the Cross, but there is widespread agreement on the basics. God created the human race in his own image. We were not made to act like robots. Instead, we have some God-given freedom, including the freedom to turn away from God and to sin. That is what we have all done repeatedly. Because God is just, he cannot let sin pass unnoticed. But God is also loving, so he sent his Son, Jesus Christ, to die on the cross to atone for our sins. Jesus died and was buried in a tomb, but then he rose to life again and gives eternal life to all who believe in him. Today, God is willing to pardon us if we want to admit our sinfulness and accept his offer of forgiveness.

This core message is stated with brevity and clarity in the New Testament book of Romans:

For all have sinned; all fall short of God's glorious standard. Yet now God in his gracious kindness declares us not guilty. He has done this through Christ Jesus, who has freed us by taking away our sins. For God sent Jesus to take the punishment for our sins and to satisfy God's anger against us. We are made right with God when we believe that Jesus shed his blood, sacrificing his life for us. . . . [God] is entirely fair and just in this present time when he declares sinners to be right in his sight because they believe in Jesus.[4]

The biblical writer noted that "since we have been made right in God's sight by faith, we have peace with God because of what Jesus Christ our Lord has done for us."[5] Throughout the Bible, we are given many promises of the personal peace, inner joy, emotional strength, abundant living, new perspective on life, and numerous other benefits that come to yielded followers of Christ.

But the Bible admits that we also will have problems and trials that will stretch us and teach important lessons.[6] Christian spirituality is not a blissful withdrawal from the pressures of life into a self-centered nirvana. If anybody, including you or me, is serious about following Jesus and experiencing his spirituality, "you must put aside your selfish ambition, shoulder your cross, and follow" him.[7] This is not a call to pathological masochism; it is recognition that true believers are likely to have difficulties, to bear crosses of suffering. The serious Christ-follower and seeker after true Christian spirituality must be willing to follow with total commitment, even to the point of being persecuted or put to death. Few approaches to spirituality are that demanding. Few are as realistic.

Christian spirituality is unique because of its God, its views of the universe, its outlook on evil, its emphasis on grace, and its focus on people. Christian spirituality also involves worship, guidelines for daily living, perspectives on suffering, and spiritual practices that bring ongoing and growing intimacy with God. We will discuss each of these pieces of the Christian spirituality puzzle in this chapter and the next.

SEEING GOD

The question surprised the young man sitting in the psychiatrist's office. The doctor was well respected as a former missionary, medical school lecturer, and distinguished psychiatric practitioner. But the meeting that day was not a professional consultation. The two men had known each other for a long time. They were friends and companions on the spiritual journey. Both knew the pain and injustice of apartheid in their native South Africa, but as they met, their minds were far from politics. The doctor was listening as his friend freely shared some struggles that were leaving him bedraggled in spirit, weary in body, and withdrawn in his relationships. The mentor listened attentively and then was silent for a long time before raising his question.

"What is your picture of God?" he asked quietly.

Writing about the meeting later, Trevor Hudson described how the question seemed so unrelated and irrelevant to his concerns at the time. What did the question have to do with crowded days, a packed schedule, and strenuous efforts to achieve and accomplish? But the question communicated something deeper, that the way we live is profoundly influenced by the picture we have of God. Hudson had built a picture of God as a passive, generally disinterested spectator, sitting on the edge of our lives, perusing what we do without much concern or involvement. He perceived God as a benign dispenser of occasional favors, expecting perfection and withholding his blessing or approval from all who did not meet the impossible standards.

When such distortions creep into our pictures of God, "their negative effects reverberate throughout our lives," Hudson wrote.[8] Too many of us have a God who is too small, too distant, too disinterested, too demanding, too harsh, or too much like our earthly fathers. Even in our churches, God is increasingly trivialized and brought down to our level: "In the end, God seems more user-friendly, more approachable, more like us, but less worth worshiping or entrusting with our eternal destinies."[9] Look at the new spiritualities, the magical thinking, the miracle-worker perspectives, the God-is-my-buddy mentality, and we see a God who is not worth following, trusting, or honoring. It is not surprising that many people prefer to create a god in their own image, to conclude that god is within, or to decide that "god is me."

Christian spirituality regards God as a friend, somebody whom we can call Father with affection and gentleness. He is also an awesome Being who is holy, sovereign, just, loving, and worthy of our praise and adoration. Nobody has ever seen God, and we who are frail and imperfect creatures cannot look on his face. But if you want to know what God is like, read the Psalms. Read the Gospels to know the Jesus who said that anyone who had seen him had seen the Father.[10]

The God of Christianity is not attractive to many followers of the new spiritualities. In an era when we try to make God into our own image, he refuses to be restricted and recast into something created by human imagination. In a time when people want to worship God in their own ways, he shuns false adoration and calls for obedience. People who want to set their own standards and create their own moral values aren't interested in a God who insists on holiness and calls for obedience to his standards. When we create rituals intended to manipulate God so we can have what we want, he complains about our religiosity and shows that he wants a relationship.

I have a friend who is like Karen. He has no interest in "Western religions" and prefers to build his spirituality on various forms of Buddhism. But my friend admits that he is challenged by the idea of a relationship with God. A daily walk with God seems far different from and more attractive than the pursuit of peaceful consciousness.

Wherever you are on the spiritual journey, stringently challenge your pictures of God. Recognize that all of us tend to make God in our own image. Most often we form a human image that is greatly removed from what the sovereign God is like. The God of the Christian is far greater and far more loving than any of our little minds can imagine. He is a God in three persons: Father, Son, and Holy Spirit. We do him a great disservice and we create distorted pictures in our minds if we stress one of the three and ignore the others.

Consider the Holy Spirit, for example. For many years, it seems, churches proclaimed unbalanced views of God because they paid little attention to the Holy Spirit. Now some believers so emphasize the Holy Spirit that God the Father and Jesus Christ the Son are lost in the Spirit enthusiasm. The Holy Spirit lives within believers, not as an internal force or an energy but as a person. He guides us, convicts us of sin, strengthens, comforts, counsels, and points us to truth. But he also points us to the Father and to the Son.

Many spirituality seekers have turned away from their distorted views of God, abandoned any search for truth, and built spiritualities based on their creative minds and self-preoccupations. "It is always true to some extent that we make our images of God," suggests Brennan Manning. "It is even truer that *our image of God makes us. Eventually we become like the God we imagine.*"[11] When we stop thinking of God as vindictive and mean, or as a distracted, disinterested grandfather, then we can see God for what he is really like. We can move forth confidently with a spirituality that fills our souls and sustains us through the pace, pressures, problems, and possibilities of life.

We cannot know God completely, but we can get closer and closer to knowing him better. To have a more accurate understanding of what God is like, read about him in the Bible, at least briefly and on a regular basis, if possible. In the Bible, the book that Christians call the Word of God, we get the only authentic picture of God and his message to human beings.

Many years ago I started a practice that has become a treasured part of my spirituality. Almost every day I go for a two-mile walk, often in the early morning when the world is quiet and I have not yet become distracted by the cares of the day. As I walk, I meditate on God's nature. In my mind, I run through the alphabet, and for each letter (with the exception of a few like *q* and *z*), I remind myself of the characteristics—theologians call them attributes—of God. I try to thank him for what he is like—not for what he is doing for me or for what I want, even though these are important to me and, I am sure, to God. By going through this list, I get a clearer view of God in all his wonder and diversity. God is:

A — almighty, awesome, able, admirable

B — bountiful, beautiful, beneficent, boundless

C — caring, compassionate, comforting, creative, the Creator who still holds the world together

D — dependable

E — eternal, everlasting, ever-present

F — forgiving, faithful

G — good, great, gracious, giving, the God of grace

H — holy, high and lifted up, honorable

I — immutable (never-changing), incomprehensible, immortal

J — just, the justifier, joy-giving

K — knowledgeable, kind

L — Lord, love, loving, life-sustaining

M — majestic, marvelous, mighty, merciful

N — near, never-failing

O — omnipotent (all-powerful), omniscient (all-knowing), omnipresent (present in every place)

P — pure, powerful, perfect, peace-giving, praiseworthy

R — redeemer, righteous, reigning as King

S — sovereign, supreme, sensitive, sustaining, strong, strength-giving

T — tender, trustworthy, true

U — unfailing, unchanging

W — worthy, wonderful, wise, wisdom-giving, worthy of worship

If these reminders of God's character are built mostly on my creative mind, then sooner or later my picture will get distorted. That is why I often look to see how God is described in the Bible. I want my picture of God to be accurate and never far from my conscious awareness.

In a book about God the Father, novelist Michael Phillips asked a question far different from the query that Trevor Hudson heard in South Africa, but equally provoking: Can you live on the basis of what you believe (including what you believe about God), no matter where you take those beliefs and no matter what you come up against?[12] Think about this: Does your spirituality help you make sense of life, cope with tragedy, find hope in times of suffering, and guide your lifestyle? A belief about God that is weak and distorted may be little better than no belief at all.

WHAT ABOUT THE UNIVERSE?

There is a true story about a young Christian in Tanzania who was given a plot of land on which to build a home where he would live with his new wife and eventually raise a family. "You must not build on this land," the young man's uncle protested when he learned about the construction plans. "Our ancestors are buried there and if a house is built, they will do bad things to the family."

Encouraged by his family, the Christian, whose name was John, replied that they all respected the ancestors but had no fear of anything happening if the house was built. The uncle became increasingly distressed and consulted the village shaman who provided a charm to put on the land. "It's magic and will make the foundation crack," the shaman predicted.

But the foundation stayed strong, and the house kept being built, so the uncle went back to the shaman. He bought a more powerful charm and put it near the building, but still nothing happened. Increasingly frantic, the uncle went to a famous shaman and purchased what was described as a very powerful charm, one that would make the house walls fall down. The uncle waited, but the house stood firm and John and his wife moved in.

The uncle was confused. Why had the charms not worked? He knew that John's family was known in the village for the seemingly strange practice of praying out loud and singing hymns every night. When the house remained standing, the uncle concluded that the songs probably had something to do with the stability of the house. He pondered this for a long time but decided eventually to become a Christian—much to the delight of John and his family.

Two Views of the World

Former missionary Bryant Myers told this story to introduce an idea about the universe that originated with a seminary professor named Paul Hiebert.[13] According to Heibert, people in the West look at the universe as having two separate and unrelated parts: the spiritual or supernatural world of God and angels, and the physical-observable world with its germs and business decisions. In contrast to this two-tier universe, many people around the world see the universe as having three parts—the supernatural and observable worlds, plus a middle part involving shamans, witch doctors, astrology, magic, curses, and charms.

Western View		Traditional View
• God • Allah • Angels	**Truth**	• God • Allah • Angels
Excluded Middle	**Power**	• Witches • Curses • Charms
• Germs • Business Decisions	**Does It Work?**	• Herbs • Food • Clan

As shown in the diagram, at the top level we ask, "What is true?" or "Whose God is really the true god?" At the lower level we ask what works. This is where most people in the West live and think. The middle level is all about power. It asks, "Whose god or what god is most powerful?" Professor Hiebert calls this the excluded middle that most Westerners tend to ignore. It is the point where the spiritual (upper level) and the material (lower level) interact. It is a level where a lot of contemporary spiritual searching appears to take place. This is where some Christians look for miracles, signs, visions, and what they call power encounters. New spiritualities are at this level as well, not interested in truth (the top level) but not content, either, to stay at the lower level of wondering what works.

The Rest of the Story

For months after his apparent conversion, John's uncle came to church where he felt welcomed and accepted. When his son got sick, the uncle found a doctor and also asked the Christians to pray. But the son died. Shortly thereafter the uncle went back to his traditional practices, visiting the shamans and declaring that he was no longer a Christian.

This story and the two worldviews can shed helpful light on spiritual searches. The uncle was interested in power. He wanted a spirituality that would give him the power to control and give protection against the forces, sicknesses, and disappointments of life. When the Christian powers didn't seem to work, he went back to the charms and curses of the medicine man.

Some modern spirituality seekers wear Western clothes and search the World Wide Web, but they are very much like John's uncle in rural Tanzania. They are looking for a spirituality that will give them power over the forces of the universe or knowledge about how to cure their diseases, tap into life energies, control their destinies, or slow the aging of their bodies. Other people care less about power but look (as on the lower level of the diagram) for something or someone that works to bring change, inner transformation, or other evidence of an impact on life. Still others are more like the seminary students that I used to teach, concerned about truth (that's the upper level), knowing who and what is right.

The Christian message meets each of us at our point of need—experiencing God's power, seeing God's work in our lives, or knowing God's truth. When we stay at one of these levels and ignore the other two, our spirituality is incomplete and distorted. Evidences of God's power can lead some people to Christ, but an apparent lack of power can lead these same people away from the faith if they are like John's uncle who apparently had little understanding of the truth or little awareness of God's work in his life. It may not fit the postmodern way of thinking, but Christian spirituality is holistic. It involves the truth of God, the power of God, and the action of God—all three working in the universe and in individual lives.

WHAT WILL WE DO ABOUT EVIL?

It is no secret that we live in a world of violence, rampant crime, drug smuggling, political turmoil, bloody wars, emotionally and physically destructive abuse, and vicious battles between gang members in our streets. It would be self-deceptive and out of contact with reality to assume blithely that evil is nonexistent or not pervasive in our world. We can withdraw into a variety of spiritual experiences, some of which are genuine times of closeness to God, but as long as we live on this earth, the evidence and impact of evil are never far away.

Despite all the news reports that bring real-life stories about conflict and crime, the people in our culture seem to have an ongoing fascination with evil. We don't have to be crusaders against Hollywood or television to know that much of the media seems obsessed with portraying violence, depravity, and debauchery in the most graphic ways. Fascination with the occult has permeated the entertainment industry and affected many games, books, songs, and movies.

The same fascination has appeared repeatedly both in the new spiritualities and in Christian spirituality. Jung, for example, struggled to account for evil. He took part in séances, recounted "uncanny" experiences with what he thought might be demons, and wondered whether spirit beings might be "out there." Even some of his admirers have questioned Jung's attempts to account for evil by looking to the shadow side of the collective unconscious.

Within recent years, many Christians have developed an increased interest in demonic agents and evil influences. As David Powlison notes, however, "a great deal of fiction, superstition, fantasy, nonsense, nuttiness, and downright heresy flourishes in the church under the guise of 'spiritual warfare' in our time."[14] Without giving much thought to the Bible's teachings about evil, Christians in churches around the world have succumbed to a growing obsession with the unseen world of evil, an infatuation with superstition, and a gospel that has less to do with Christ and more concern about Satan, demonic forces, devil chasing, demon binding, and deliverance—all presented under the name of spiritual warfare.

Spiritual Warfare and Spirituality

Despite the extremes and excesses that dominate much of the spiritual warfare movement, Christian spirituality gives serious consideration to the power of evil and the impact of Satan. It is naive and simplistic to assume that we can have an authentic and fulfilling spirituality if we ignore evil and overlook the demonic.

Psychiatrist and popular writer M. Scott Peck reached this conclusion in his spellbinding best-seller *People of the Lie*.[15] Peck boldly wrote about evil, sin, and the demonic. He gave graphic descriptions of exorcisms with which he was involved, and discussed how evil relates to mental illness. Many of his conclusions were at odds with traditional Christian doctrine, but his book opened a fresh discussion of evil that many spirituality seekers had not considered seriously before the book appeared.[16]

The Bible describes Christian spirituality as a struggle, "not against flesh and blood, but against the rulers, against the authorities, against the powers of this dark world and against the spiritual forces of evil."[17] Often this is a battle with an unseen enemy who is subtle and deceptive, a master tempter intent on creating divisions and arousing accusations. The biblical picture of the prince of evil is not that of a Halloween character with horns, pitchfork, red suit, and tail. Instead, Satan masquerades as an attractive angel of light who controls demonic forces that make themselves look like "servants of righteousness," prophets, and ministers of Christ.[18]

Behind this pretty-picture facade is a demonic host with a divide-and-conquer strategy that slowly leads people to believe that they are better off divided. It is a strategy that pulls husbands from wives, sex from marriage, children from parents, business partners from each other, people with one skin color from those whose skin color is different, nations from peaceful coexistence, individuals from belief in God, spirituality from the Holy Spirit, and Christians from their biblical roots. The result is a culture of divorce, abuse, litigation, violence, social confusion, distorted values, spiritual emptiness, and hypocrisy.

The Bible, the guidebook of Christian spirituality, doesn't instruct us to learn the names of demons, talk to them, shout for them to leave, and stage spectacular confrontations with satanic forces. We are urged to keep alert to Satan's tactics and to stand firm against evil.[19] We resist the demonic in the same ways that we stimulate our spirituality—by taking effort to avoid temptation, repenting, maintaining self-control, growing in our understanding of biblical truth, obeying, serving, and praying for protection. When Jesus taught his followers to pray, he urged them to ask God to "deliver us from the evil one."[20] The devil is pictured as an enemy who prowls around looking for somebody to devour, but an enemy that can be resisted by those who stand firm in the faith, humble, and strengthened by God's mighty hand.[21] Christians believe that God ultimately is sovereign. The biblical message from beginning to end is an account of the all-powerful God constraining demons—a God who in the end will defeat the forces of evil decisively and forever. That core feature of Christian spirituality leads us to the topic of grace.

AMAZING GRACE

Several years ago I had a wonderful experience that I had not planned and never anticipated. Early one Saturday morning I aroused my tired family so we could grab a quick breakfast and take the subway from our London hotel to a spot on the Mall, about half a block from Buckingham Palace. For years I had known about the annual celebration of the queen's birthday known as the trooping of the color. On the day of our arrival for a brief visit to England, we realized for the first time that we had come to London on the weekend of the parade. We would be able to stand with the crowd and watch the procession to and from the place where the royal ceremony would take place. We watched as each member of the British royal family passed, back in the days before so many had discredited themselves with their soap opera–style antics. But the part of that sunny June morning that I liked best was the parade of the massed pipe bands, marching in precision down the Mall, with the steady beat of their drums and the swirl of the pipes filling the air with music.

Bagpipe music is not heard often, at least on the side of the Atlantic where I live, and rarely do we hear the bagpipes played solo. When that happens, it seems that the most popular tune is the old hymn "Amazing Grace." I remember attending a funeral service that closed with everybody standing and listening to a taped version of "Amazing Grace" played by a solo piper. The man who had died showed little interest in anything spiritual during his lifetime. As I stood with the other mourners listening to the music, I wondered if he ever understood what grace is all about and why it is amazing and so important in Christian spirituality.

Grace is an expression of goodness, given without strings attached, to people who don't deserve what they receive. God's grace is the goodness of God shown to people who don't deserve it.[22] We become Christians and begin to experience authentic spirituality when we reach out and accept the gift of salvation, offered by God because of his grace. All of us have sinned, according to the Bible, but we are "justified freely by his [God's] grace through the redemption that came by Christ Jesus."[23] God sent his Son to earth "in order that . . . he might show the incomparable riches of his grace, expressed in his kindness to us in Christ Jesus. For it is by grace you have been saved, through faith . . . not by works."[24] We have nothing to boast about as Christians. We do not do anything to deserve God's gift of salvation. He offers it because of his grace, because of his unmerited favor toward us.

Christians like me are sad when we look around at the spirituality searches that are common today. So many people go through life picking and choosing from the cafeteria of spiritual alternatives, never finding satisfaction because they know nothing about God's grace. It is sad that "Amazing Grace" becomes a popular tune in the culture—a tune familiar to many people, sometimes even played on bagpipes, but a melody with lyrics that many people never understand. It was written two centuries ago by a hardened slave trader and self-described infidel who encountered the transforming power and grace of God. In words that he wrote for engraving on his tombstone, John Newton described himself as a man who, "by the rich mercy of our Lord and Savior Jesus Christ," was "preserved, restored, pardoned, and appointed to preach the faith he had so long labored to destroy."[25] John Newton's spirituality was solid and lasting because of God's amazing grace to a slave trader who didn't deserve what he was given.

Because grace is given by God, it is not something that we can pay back. We express our gratitude by being thankful, obedient, faithful, loving, and humble; trusting in God; taking refuge in him; and getting to know him better. In turn, God keeps extending his grace, through the present and into the future.[26] He doesn't ask us to strike a bargain—promising to work a deal where he will give more grace if we pay something in return, like a debtor pays part of the credit card bill each month to avoid being hounded by a bill collector. Grace is not a loan from the past. It is a gift that extends through all eternity. It is a gift that helps to mold our lives so that our spirituality is God-centered, Christ-honoring, Spirit-guided, life-influencing, and ultimately fulfilling. The divine gift of grace reminds us that God is concerned about people.

KEEPING PEOPLE IN FOCUS

When I first visited the Vietnam Memorial in Washington, D.C., I was surprised at how deeply I was moved. As my wife and I walked past the granite slabs listing the names of the thousands who died in that fateful conflict, we were too choked with emotion to speak. We didn't know any of the people whose names are carved on that memorial, but the sheer magnitude of the loss of life hit me as it never had before. In addition to thousands of Vietnamese civilians and military personnel, fifty-eight thousand Americans in the military died as a result of that war.

The Vietnam conflict has been described in many books, including one by Robert McNamara, who headed the Department of Defense and years later wrote *In Retrospect* about his mistakes as a leader. At the time of the war, most of us knew McNamara only through what appeared in the newspapers or on television. Paul Hendrickson studied the man and the era in much more depth, however, painfully concluding that the American defense secretary had deceived the nation and contributed indirectly to the loss of many men and women whose names now appear on the memorial in Washington.[27]

Apparently McNamara reached the conclusion, early in the conflict, that the war could not be won. He expressed his doubts privately to a few people in the government, but instead of stating his conclusions honestly and publicly, he soldiered on, supporting a war that he knew would fail and that even today evokes controversy and fury. In Hendrickson's opinion, if McNamara had resigned in 1965 (he left office in 1968) and told the world his real thoughts, there might be a McNamara Prize today for moral courage. Instead, the nation continued with a war that influenced millions and still tears at the fabric of American society in a way that people from other countries rarely comprehend.

All wars involve individuals, including the wars that rage today as I write and the wars being fought on the day that you read these words. We may read the news about military decisions, see the casualty statistics, watch the pictures on television, and stand before impressive war monuments dotting the land. But the conflicts of war are less about leadership, statistics, television images, or memorials, and more about individuals and their families who are impacted and changed, often permanently.

A similar focus on individuals must apply to discussions about spirituality. We have looked at new spirituality movements, alternative healings, cult groups, churches, and changing social conditions that have stimulated a spiritual search in millions of baby boomers and their Generation X followers. In these pages you have read about God, forces in the universe, the impact of demons, and the meaning of grace. Eventually, however, all of this must be brought down to a focus on individual people, like Rich and Karen, like you and me.

Christian spirituality is sensitive to individuals. It is concerned with how each person relates to God. All Christ-followers need the quietness of solitude and periods alone with God. On a regular basis we need to pray, read and think about the Scriptures, meditate on the nature of God, and sense the leading of the Holy Spirit in our lives. For many people in this hyperactive age of incessant busyness, squeezing out time to be alone with God can be a major challenge. But without taking the effort and making the time to get away, however brief, we lose contact with the ultimate Source of spiritual and psychological stability.

This crucial need for time alone with God should be balanced with the idea that Christian spirituality is much more than a Lone Ranger activity. We read little in the New Testament about individual spirituality, observes Trevor Hudson. "The biblical language for growing in Christ is *inter*dependent language, " not the language of *in*dependence.[28] Christ-following is anchored in community seen in four parts: the community of believers throughout history, the community of the local church, the community of one-to-one relationships, and the community of people outside the Christian fold.[29]

People from the Past

I grew up in Canada and now make my home in the United States, but I have traveled in many countries and lived for a while in England and in Switzerland. Each one of these countries, I have noticed, has its founding fathers and national heroes—people from the past who are acclaimed on special days and remembered for their courage, convictions, and contributions. In every nation, heroes from the past are revered as unseen companions who encourage modern citizens along the way. These heroic men and women give us a greater pride, a deeper heritage on which to build for the future, and a richer appreciation for the principles that led determined people to take risks and pay the price of sacrifice.

With refreshing honesty, the Bible describes people who failed in the spiritual quest, but we read as well about many others who endured and became our spiritual heroes. The New Testament book of Hebrews, for example, has a moving summary of the giants of the faith who walked with God and developed a rich spirituality.[30] We are the most recent additions to that great crowd, and we can learn from the example of their lives, their thoughts, their struggles, and their visions. Inspired by them, we are better able to cast off some of the self-centered sinful entanglements that so easily trip us up, and we can move forward, looking at Christ, without growing weary and downhearted.[31] Each of us is an individual wanting to grow spiritually, but we are not alone in the journey; we have a bond of kinship with those spiritual giants and strugglers who walked the spiritual road before us.

The Church in the Present

Several years ago, the cover of *Time* pictured a young woman wearing a T-shirt that proclaimed: "Jesus yes, the church no." I have mentioned this modern distrust of the church in earlier pages. Weakened by hypocrisy, pathology, irrelevance, magical thinking, self-aggrandizing leaders, and a few prominent sin-tasting preachers, the church as a whole has lost credibility with many like the grown-up children of the Walceks, whose family story began this chapter. No institution that includes people will ever be faultless, however, and the honest listing of church weaknesses and failures should not blind us to the genuine strengths that churches have shown since the time of Christ.

The New Testament describes the church as a *koinonia*, a community of Christ-followers who meet together on a regular basis for worship, prayer, encouragement, learning, sharing, and caregiving. The biblical writer pictures the church as a body with many parts. Like hands and feet and eyes that are needed for a body to function in a healthy, normal way, so the church consists of individuals with different abilities and God-given gifts, all intended to work together, "so that there should be no division in the body, but that its parts should have equal concern for each other. If one part suffers, every part suffers with it; if one part is honored, every part rejoices with it."[32]

Of course it doesn't always work that way. There are minimally active, nominal members in every congregation, there are stonewallers who resist change, and there are members who delight in creating division. Some churches stimulate the toxic faith that we have discussed. Others are oppressively hierarchical, demanding, and coercive. But millions of believers in church communities give support, encouragement in times of need, a place to be known and accepted, and opportunities to focus on something and someone who is bigger than themselves. I don't agree with the message on that T-shirt. If we say yes to Jesus, we cannot be Christ-followers and say no to the church that he created. "Let us not give up meeting together, as some are in the habit of doing," we read in the New Testament.[33] Instead, let us encourage one another and spur one another on to love and good deeds. Spirituality without community will never be satisfying or fulfilling. Christian spirituality without the church will never be strong, vibrant, and life-transforming.

Faithful Friendships

I wonder how many people, especially men, have lives that are flooded with acquaintances but empty of friends. Most of us know a lot of people, but we don't know many people well. We hide from our loneliness by delving farther into our work or by forming fantasy friendships with sports heroes, people on television, or strangers on the Internet. We fill our worlds not with one-to-one support, encouragement, and sharing, but with what Henri Nouwen called "empty chatter, easy confessions, hollow talk, senseless compliments, poor praise, and boring confidentialities. Not a few magazines become wealthy by suggesting that they are able to furnish us with the most secret and intimate details of the lives of people we always wanted to know more about. In fact, they present us with the most boring trivialities and the most supercilious idiosyncrasies of people whose lives are already flattened out by morbid exhibitionism."[34]

The majority of us want and need our lives to be deeper than this. When he started his ministry, Jesus pulled together a group of friends who hung out with him, prayed with him, learned from him, and grew spiritually together in communion with him. When he sent his followers out for on-the-job training, he sent them in pairs.[35] When the early Christians gathered, they met in homes, perhaps similar to the small groups that are at the basis of almost every growing and healthy church.

As I have grown older, one-to-one friendships have become an increasing part of my life. Every week, I meet individually with others on the spiritual journey, often over breakfast or lunch, frequently with younger journeyers who want to walk for a while with someone who has been on the spiritual path a little longer. Rarely do we have set agendas. Rarely am I seen as a counselor or spiritual guide. Instead, we hang out together, sharing our lives: expressing our care and support; encouraging one another toward greater commitment, better marriages, more balanced lifestyles, healthy self-control, more realistic career goals, greater visionary perspectives, growth in prayer and in the knowledge of God and his Word. Invariably I come away from these meetings enriched, invigorated, and often overflowing with praise to God, who has allowed me to participate, for a while, in the life of another journeyer.[36]

Compassionate Community

Christian spirituality is compassion oriented. It reaches out to the poor, the hungry, the needy, the sick, the victims of violence and their perpetrators, the down-and-outers in poverty-entrenched neighborhoods, and the up-and-outer suburbanites who often are too proud or self-sufficient to admit their neediness. Christ modeled concern for the needy, care for those in distress, and a willingness to come alongside people in their times of pain and confusion. He was deeply concerned as well for people who didn't know him, and he instructed his followers, as a last word of admonition, to go into the world and make disciples. This is the Great Commandment that motivates Christians to spread the good news about Christ and to penetrate the world, urging others to follow Jesus.

Someplace I read that Gandhi once told some believers, "I like your Christ, but I don't like your Christians." Who among us can deny that Christians have been insensitive in their evangelistic efforts, uncaring in the light of social adversity, unconcerned about the state of the planet where we live, self-centered in the face of needs in our communities or other parts of the world? Of course we have failed, and we will fail again. But we also will keep striving, reaching out to a needy world with Christ-motivated love.

It can be spiritually healthy to focus on the inner spiritual life and to grow into greater intimacy with Christ. But like Jesus and the biblical writers, we need an outward perspective, moving from the strength-building communion with God in the solitary place to the often draining service for others in the evil-infested marketplace. If I am overly involved with my personal pilgrimage and closeness to Christ, then I fail to show the compassion that he demonstrated and commanded. In contrast, if I focus on social service and reaching out but ignore the need for inner refreshment and communication with Christ, then the inner spiritual core dries up, and I cease to be an ambassador who brings Christ's message of healing and hope to people in need. Christian spirituality demands balance between solitude and service.

Apparently a lot of those grown children in the Walcek family missed the balance. They're still looking for lasting spirituality, unwilling or unable to see that it is found in Christ.

— 9 —

Completing the
Spirituality Puzzle:
How Do We Find Intimacy with God?

Many years ago, several centuries before the time of Christ, an astute man lived in the ancient city of Babylon. He was born in Jerusalem, but when that city fell to the armies of King Nebuchadnezzar, the man was brought to Babylon as an exile, along with about ten thousand of his fellow countrymen and women. Far from home, the man lived in a house with his family and apparently learned a lot about his new culture. A powerful intellect, he was acquainted with international affairs and history, familiar with the literature of his day, and he seemed to have impressive speaking abilities.

One day the man had a prophetic vision about the future—one of several in his life—and soon he sensed a calling to communicate special encouragement to his fellow Jewish exiles who must have felt cut off from God. In one of the visions, this man named Ezekiel was taken to a valley filled with dry human bones. "Talk to these bones," Ezekiel was told, and that's what he did, apparently oblivious or unconcerned about the fact that pass-ersby would have thought he was crazy.

Ezekiel's eyes must have bulged when he beheld the remark-able sight that came next. There was a rattling of the bones, then they came together. Tendons and flesh appeared and the bodies were covered with skin, but they must have looked like corpses. There was no life in them until Ezekiel spoke again. Instantly the motionless bodies came to life, and the man was standing in the presence of a vast army, strong and ready to do battle.[1]

This vision of the dry bones (made popular in the old spiritual about "dem bones, dem bones, dem dry bones") was intended as a message of hope about the future restoration of Israel. The story was never intended to say anything about contemporary Amer-ican spirituality, but it presents a picture that portrays a lot about what is happening today. Many people are spiritually dead, as lifeless as those old bones, and without any interest in anything spiritual. Others look like spiritual beings and want to be alive, but they are corpselike searchers who have no heartbeat or breath. Many are looking to find life within themselves or intent on following the latest life-promising spiritual gurus. Some may even think they have found life and convince themselves that their dead bodies have a vitality that isn't there. Only when God the Creator gives them life do they spring into spiritual exuber-ance and vigor that none of us can find on our own.

I admit that this picture is inconsistent with the contemporary worship of tolerance. Genuine Christian spirituality respects peo-ple whose seeking takes them in directions away from Christ. Jesus never forced anybody to follow him unwillingly. But the God of the Bible will not be merged into the sea of spiritual alter-natives, becoming one wave of spirituality equal to all the others. Jesus called himself *the* way, the truth, and the life. He made the bold proclamation that only through him could anybody come to God.[2] He pointed that out at the tomb of an old friend who had died. "I am the resurrection and the life," Jesus said.[3] The person who believes in him will live eternally, even though he or she dies

194

and becomes for a time like the bones that Ezekiel saw in the valley.

Jesus reemphasized the point at another time during his life on earth: "For my Father's will is that everyone who looks to the Son and believes in him shall have eternal life, and I will raise him up at the last day."[4] It isn't surprising that the people who listened to Jesus were divided when they heard his message.[5] Things are no different today. Spirituality seekers turn away from him in droves because they are unwilling to accept the exclusive nature of his teachings. They resist the idea that spiritual life is found only in him.

We have seen that Christian spirituality begins with a clear view of God. It is aware of his impact on the universe that he created. It has an appreciation for the alluring reality of evil, an emphasis on grace, and a focus on people. It also involves the four issues that we will consider in this chapter. Christian spirituality includes worship, gives guidelines for daily living, has a unique perspective on suffering, and calls believers to discipline themselves so that they can grow into a vibrant spirituality.

WORTHWHILE WORSHIP

It was intended to be the best birthday party ever. Invitations were mailed in advance. The enthusiastic ten-year-olds came directly from school. There were football and basketball, hot dogs and hamburgers, birthday cake and lots of ice cream, presents and laughter. But the wonderful part came when the ten-year-old host announced that everybody was going to the most exciting event in their little town—the high school basketball game.

"I can still see us spilling out of my parents' station wagon with laughter on that cool evening and running up to the gymnasium," recalls Donald Whitney in telling this story from his childhood. The young boy bristled with anticipation as he thought of the game to come, sitting on a bench with his best friends, cheering for their high school heroes. But the golden moment was shattered when the kids scattered. Nobody said "thank you" or "happy birthday." Without even a "good-bye" or a "thanks for the party," the guests went through the turnstiles and spread out to different parts of the gym, leaving the miserable ten-year-old to spend his birthday night sitting by himself in the bleachers.[6]

Too many people approach worship this way. They rush to the church from a life of frenzied activity, give the Guest of Honor a token gift, and sing him a few songs, then forget about him while they watch the performance, let their minds drift to other things, and focus on their friends. At the end they leave, happy to have fulfilled their weekly obligation, never thinking that they went to a worship service where they never worshiped.

Over my life, this description has been typical of me more often than I care to admit. For many years I have gone to church faithfully, sometimes out of habit or obligation, often as an opportunity to meet my friends, frequently without much thought of worship. The word *worship* comes from a Saxon term that means "worth-ship." True worship involves focusing totally on God and expressing our adoration and thanksgiving for his worth. It involves approaching and addressing God as worthy.

Until very recently I have struggled with this part of my spiritual life. For me, it has always been hard to worship when the worship leader or leaders steal the show and draw attention to themselves. It is hard to worship when the room is filled with distractions, sometimes made more intense by people on the platform who pop up and down, tell their jokes, recite their announcements, and lead us through an hour-long "worship service" that has little to do with sincere adoration of God or acknowledgment of his worth. I'm still learning to worship— probably I always will be—but at this stage in my life some things have become clear to me.

Worship Is Essential for Spiritual Growth

My marriage would not be in very good shape if I neglected my wife, never paid much attention to her, rarely talked to her, or didn't bother to tell her or show her my love. The same applies to one's walk with God. Worship is not an optional part of Christian spirituality. In the Bible, Christians are both commanded to worship God and warned about mindless worship that goes through the actions but means nothing.[7] Christian spirituality without worship is impossible.

I don't know who originated this little statement, but I've seen it in several books: modern people worship their work, work at their play, and play at their worship. That is not the way things will be for anybody who is serious about Christian spirituality.

Worship Must Focus on God

I like contemporary Christian music, much of it more than I like old hymns that have grown stale by endless repetition. But some of the modern lyrics seem to focus more on us than on God. Even when Scripture is set to music or the words are expressions of our honor and praise to God, it is too easy for me to sing along with a catchy tune and miss the whole message. Worship—which includes but is not limited to singing—must focus on God, must steer our thinking away from ourselves or from people who lead the worship, and must concentrate on what God is like as well as on what he does. Christian worship must be based on and include reference to the Bible because the Bible shows us what God is like. The more we know what he is like, the better we can worship him.

Worship Is Both Public and Private

If we look carefully at the life of Jesus, we see that he regularly went to the synagogue for the public worship of God, and he withdrew often to lonely places where he could pray in solitude. Some contemporary Christians never reach this balance. They get so involved with "personal devotions" that they practically isolate themselves from other believers. According to one pastoral writer, these people believe their personal devotional life is superior to anything they experience in corporate worship, so they disregard the public ministry of God's Word. We should be alert to the danger of becoming unbalanced in that direction. In my pastoral ministry, however, I have encountered many more professing Christians who go to the opposite extreme. They faithfully discipline themselves to attend corporate worship, but they neglect the regular practice of privately worshiping God. There is hardly a more common pitfall on the path to Godliness. Many progress little in Christlikeness simply because they fail to discipline themselves at this very point. Don't let this happen to you.[8]

The author's tone in this paragraph is a little preachy, but his conclusions are on target for anybody interested in authentic spirituality. Balanced Christian spirituality involves worship that is both public and private.

Worship Should Involve Expectation, Preparation, and Effort

What do you expect when you worship? If the answer is "not much," then you aren't likely to get much. The biblical worshipers expected to meet God in their worship—and they did. I've discovered that worship times are more meaningful and uplifting when I approach them with the expectation and the prayer that I will sense God's presence.

I've learned, too, that worship is better when we prepare by calming ourselves beforehand, by asking God to eliminate the interferences from our minds, by seeking his guidance and impact as we worship, by asking him to guide the leaders of public worship. It helps as well if worship is approached as something in which we are involved actively rather than as something we watch. We worship in singing, praying, listening carefully to the Scripture, seeking to apply what we learn, asking God to help us worship despite the distractions and without being annoyed by them.

Recognize, too, that there will be times—sometimes long periods of time—when we don't feel like preparing for worship, getting involved, or expecting anything to happen. Those times of spiritual dryness come into every life and sometimes last for months or even years. But we don't give up when we are in a spiritual desert. Sometimes we may be in the wilderness for a divine purpose that we may never understand, but eventually we will get to the refreshing streams of more fulfilling spirituality. Until then, we press on.

Worship Can Involve Different Forms

When we travel overseas, my wife and I like to visit cathedrals. They are places rich in history, often filled with art, and sometimes reverberating with music. I don't think I would worship very well in one of those places, however. I'm not much into icons and incense, robes and rituals, liturgy and language from another century. Nevertheless, a writer named Gary Thomas has helped me to see why some people worship best in more formal settings with symbols, rituals, and tradition.

Thomas believes that genuine spirituality, including genuine worship, always must be Bible based and characterized by adoration, willful submission, intellectual involvement, and body postures that express our praise.[9] But there are different "pathways" to worship, depending in part on our personalities, past experiences, and cultures. In addition to the traditionalist approach that points people to God through worship involving liturgy, rituals, and symbols, there is

- the naturalist approach that worships God out of doors.
- the sensate approach that worships God through the senses, including hearing great music and viewing works of art.
- the ascetic approach that worships God in solitude and simplicity.
- the activist approach that worships God by confrontation—standing against evil and calling sinners to repentance.

- the caregiver approach that worships God by loving and serving others.
- the enthusiastic approach that worships God through joyful celebration.
- the contemplative approach that worships God by loving him in deep adoration.
- the intellectual approach that worships God with the mind. People who worship this way feel closest to God when they grasp new understandings about him.

Most of us use more than one of these approaches, but for each of us, some approaches feel more comfortable and "right for me" than others. Probably God does not expect all of us to worship in the same way. Neither does he expect us to gather in groups of like-minded worshipers and condemn those whose style is different.

SPIRITUAL LIFESTYLES

Christian spirituality is not something pushed to the corner of our busy schedules and forgotten as we go about our hectic activities. Authentic spirituality should permeate every nook and cranny of our lives, transforming us to be more like the One we follow.

I have friends whose lives have been interrupted at times by what appear to be clarion calls from God to move in a new direction or to serve in a significant way. Some of these have been life-disrupting experiences involving changed lifestyles and separation from cherished friendships. I've not had these experiences. For me, and maybe for most people, spirituality is a day-to-day commitment, a slow journey on a long road, measured more by inches than by leaps and bounds. I've read in the Psalms that "no one on earth—from east or west,/or even from the wilderness—/can raise another person up./It is God alone who judges;/he decides who will rise and who will fall."[10] It is easy for any of us to complain because we have not risen to success or stardom like somebody else. We compare ourselves with superstar believers who seem to be soaring ahead of us, and even "lift [our] fists in defiance at the heavens" because of our frustrations and feelings of failure.[11] Instead, God calls us to be faithful and to keep moving into greater closeness with him. Eventually we will be able to look back, to see how far we have come in the journey. Then we can keep our successes and failures in healthier perspective.

The Life God Masters

Much of this was on my mind twenty-five years ago when our family lived in Geneva. I was there to write a book about a well-known Swiss counselor named Paul Tournier. Sometimes on a Sunday afternoon, our little family would wander around the old part of the city, and occasionally we would find ourselves in the cathedral that stands on a hill and remains the only Protestant church of its type in Europe. John Calvin lived, preached, and wrote in Geneva more than four centuries ago. I knew nothing about him at the time, so I went to a bookstore and purchased a little volume titled *Calvin: L'homme que Dieu a dompté*. The book was an interesting account of Calvin's life, but I was most impressed by the title on an English translation that I found later. Calvin was called *The Man God Mastered*.[12]

Isn't this what Christian spirituality is all about, being mastered by God so we become more like him? Writing to the persecuted church in the first century, the apostle Peter gave some guidelines for spiritual living. The words ring with special clarity in a modern translation:

> *As we know Jesus better, his divine power gives us everything we need for living a godly life. . . . And by that same mighty power, he has given us all of his rich and wonderful promises. He has promised that you will escape the decadence all around you caused by evil desires and that you will share in his divine nature. So make every effort to apply the benefits of these promises to your life. Then your faith will*

produce a life of moral excellence. A life of moral excellence leads to
knowing God better. Knowing God leads to self-control. Self-control
leads to patient endurance, and patient endurance leads to godliness.
Godliness leads to love for other Christians, and finally you will grow
to have genuine love for everyone. The more you grow like this, the
more you will become productive and useful in your knowledge of our
Lord Jesus Christ.[13]

The writer of this Bible quotation told us to accept God's power and the promises for living a godly life. Then he urged us to make every effort to apply these benefits to our lives. That is what spiritual living is all about. Guided and strengthened by the Holy Spirit, we as Christians openly accept what God has for us, but we also work diligently to build these characteristics into our lives so they can permeate all that we are and do.

Spiritual Wellness

A few years after our family had come home from Switzerland, I began hearing some of my psychologist friends talk about something called *spiritual wellness* or *spiritual well-being*. These are vague terms, rarely defined concisely, but often having something to do with spiritual health, mental stability, and maturity.[14] *Spiritual wellness* is a sense of personal completeness and peace with God. It is an awareness that God is present in our daily lives, that we are in communion with him, accepted and forgiven, growing in love, joy, peace, patience, kindness, goodness, faithfulness, gentleness, and self-control.[15]

Unlike many pieces of the spirituality puzzle, *spiritual well-being* has been studied scientifically through the use of a questionnaire known as the Spiritual Well-Being Scale. It's a test that tries to assess a person's relationship to God and satisfaction with life. More than five hundred research studies have used the scale, often comparing those having high spiritual wellness scores to those whose scores are lower. Among the conclusions is evidence that people with high levels of spiritual well-being have lower blood pressure, lower anxiety, greater self-esteem, higher levels of self-confidence, more hope, and lower levels of dependency, depression, stress, and aggressiveness. Spiritual well-being also is associated with health and how people react to illness. For example, cancer patients with higher levels of spiritual well-being have less pain and a lower degree of impairment, feel less isolated socially, and are less likely to despair or be anxious. People chronically ill with diabetes, emphysema, hypertension, or heart disease feel less hopeless about their conditions if they have higher spiritual well-being.[16]

What does this have to do with you? It is a little piece that helps complete the spirituality puzzle by reminding you that genuine spirituality can make a difference in how you live. You may have no visions or unusual calls to change the direction of your career. You may not notice that God is doing much to master your compulsions, your harmful habits, or your life. You may not sense a special level of spiritual well-being or growth in the traits that characterize outstanding Christians. But you can move ahead, knowing that God *is* at work in any person who wants a Christ-honoring spirituality. He has given you all that you need to grow spiritually, and he works from the inside out to transform you and bring you into greater Christlikeness. That is the essence of Christian spirituality. It isn't pushed to the corners of your life. Instead, it molds, masters, renovates, and revitalizes you, flowing into every part of your life. It impacts your lifestyle, helps you formulate your values, influences your mental and physical health, and gives a peace of mind that people all around you are seeking.

GROWTH THROUGH SUFFERING

Between the time that I wrote the three-word heading of this section and the day that I began this sentence, a major disruption came into my life. I got up early on a day set aside for writing and drove in the rain to meet a young seminary student for breakfast. Jon and I get together on a regular basis for an hour and a half of conversation, sometimes about psychology or spirituality, more often about life. He is a visionary, filled with youthful creativity and enthusiasm, genuinely committed to serving God, and filled with a genuine love for people—especially the people of Africa. But Jon and his wife are struggling with the diagnosis, confirmed a few weeks after their wedding, that she has multiple sclerosis. On the morning of our recent meeting he handed me a copy of a book on suffering that they had been reading together.[17]

It was raining hard when I left our breakfast meeting and drove home. About the time of my departure from the restaurant, Julie discovered that the little pond on our property had suddenly risen again and was pouring floodwaters into the lower level of the house, inundating the new carpet that we had installed after an earlier flood last year. Weeks ago, the village engineer had assured us that action had been taken to ensure that another flood wouldn't occur. Clearly the man was wrong. While I rushed to rescue the few things that we had put back into the rooms downstairs following our other flood, my wife got on the phone, making calls for help and trying to locate sandbags. The hours that followed were a blur of pumping water, emptying water-filled boots, and stacking sandbags in a cold, driving rainfall that set one-day records and later turned into snow.

I know now that many people had worse flooding than we did—far worse. I ended the day tired, thankful for friends, grateful to God that a bad situation and significant disruption had not been a tragedy. We knew that a few hours of mopping up, pulling water from the carpet, and blowing the room dry would take care of the problem and bring us back to normal. Dealing with the village that created the pond in the first place might be a tougher task. Julie made some coffee in the evening, and I sank into a chair and started reading the book that Jon had given me in the morning.

It was written by one of Jon's professors, a man whose wife had been diagnosed with an inherited neurological disease that would cause slow deterioration of a part of her brain, lead to an inability to control body movements, and bring psychological symptoms including memory loss, depression, hallucinations, and paranoid schizophrenia. The professor and his wife had seen the disease in her mother, and the doctors indicated that there was a fifty-fifty chance for each of the couple's three children to develop the disease as well.

The professor, theologian John S. Feinberg, had written his doctoral dissertation on the impact of evil and had lectured often on the topic of suffering. Now his theological theories were being put to the test. He was learning that suffering is more than an intellectual problem; it is an emotional problem as well. The professor wondered if God could be trusted. Had God been deceptive by letting him marry a woman with a genetically transmitted disease? Was God being unfair? Why had such tragedy come rushing into their lives while other equally committed Christians had been spared? In the face of suffering, how do Christians deal with feelings of confusion, discouragement, helplessness, and anger with God for not stopping the tragedy? How do we live with a God who allows suffering and doesn't always stop it?

"The truth is, I couldn't figure it out," Feinberg wrote. "I had all those intellectual answers, but none of them made any difference in how I felt at the personal level. As a professor of theology, surely I should understand what God was doing in this situation. On the contrary, I began wondering if in fact I really understood anything at all about God. The emotional and psychological pain were unrelenting, and even devastating physical pain resulted from the stress."[18]

A Suffering Spirituality

I cannot begin to comprehend the struggles that my friend Jon and his professor are going through, along with their wives. Our little flooding problem that seemed so disruptive and overwhelming when the waters were pouring in is nothing in comparison to the far more intense suffering that people experience around the world every day. Nobody understands suffering, and often we don't handle it well. It can be hard to be with suffering people, hard to know what to say. Wouldn't it be easier and more comfortable to have a "me and my own personal happiness" form of spirituality that brushes aside the perplexities of life, brashly proclaims that God will magically deliver us from all suffering, and arms us with a boatload of clichés to bestow on people who grieve or suffer? Most of us are realistic enough to know that such a view is neither helpful nor practical. It isn't biblical, either.

Christian spirituality faces suffering squarely; Christian spirituality doesn't try to hide it, gloss over it, or explain it away. We don't stop asking questions, but we know that some of the questions about suffering have no satisfactory answers. We don't know why the God whom we call sovereign lets some experience great suffering and others experience little. We are uncomfortable—at least I am—when we hear about God's taming the soul and bringing spiritual wholeness through the process of breaking us.[19] No human mind can comprehend why God showed us suffering so dramatically on the cross and calls us to share with Christ in his suffering.

We do know, however, that God often reveals himself more clearly in our greatest times of weakness and need. Suffering shapes us spiritually, like strong winds and pounding waves shape a rocky coastline. When we suffer with grief and go through trials, our faith and our lives are refined like gold in fire. The biblical writer even told us to rejoice in our suffering because it produces perseverance, character, hope, and a fresh awareness of God's love.[20] Suffering, writes Michael Horton, "strips us of our pride, self-sufficiency, complacency, and our oblivion to the things to come. Eternity is more deeply engraved on the rough palms of God's suffering children."[21] Suffering also gets our attention and pulls us from the self-focused, God-ignoring lives that most of us live on a daily basis. When we suffer, we discover that others care, and we are motivated, in turn, to reach out with comfort and compassion.[22]

I spent an afternoon with the head of a large Christian relief organization, discussing the needs of suffering people around the world and talking about ways to bring hope and compassion. As we talked, he told me that the word *compassion* comes from words that mean "with" and "suffering." Our lives would be easier without suffering, but "with suffering" we can better know a joy in caring that would not come otherwise. "As with many people, my feelings of self-worth are tied in large part to my work and productivity," Feinberg wrote as hopelessness and illness engulfed his life. "In the midst of this dilemma, the Lord gave me opportunities to do things to help others. This was just what I needed, because it gave me a chance to get my focus off our problems and onto somebody else's needs."[23] The Feinbergs learned that compassion brought benefits to themselves even as they brought comfort to others.

Recently I pulled out a copy of *The Wounded Healer*, one of the first books written by Henri Nouwen and probably the first that I read.[24] Nouwen emerged as one of the giant spiritual leaders of the past few decades so I looked with interest to see what he had said about suffering. The next to last sentence in his book summarized the message: "What we can know . . . is that man suffers and that a sharing of suffering can make us move forward."[25] That's it; nothing more profound. But maybe that cogently summarizes the role of suffering in our spiritual lives.

Most of us expect to go through life relatively free of troubles. When I was in graduate school, they used to call this the "thee, thee, but never me" way of thinking. When tribulations come into our lives, we are crushed, deeply disappointed, angry, and shocked because we expected to be spared. These reactions are natural, but the Bible gives us a different perspective. It tells us to expect persecution and suffering, gives us partial insights into why suffering happens, calls us to persevere, and urges us to move forward in the midst of our pain.

DISCIPLINED SPIRITUALITY

The founder of the Salvation Army, General William Booth, knew about suffering; he encountered it among poor people every day. Once a reporter asked General Booth to tell the secret of his success. He hesitated as he thought of an answer, then replied, "I will tell you a secret. God has had all there was of me to have. There may have been men with greater opportunities; but from the day I got the poor of London on my heart, and a vision of what Jesus Christ could do, I made up my mind that God would have all there was of William Booth."[26]

General Booth was serious about his spirituality. He didn't keep it in the closet of his mind, to be pulled out on Sunday and sometimes during the week, but otherwise left hanging while he went about his other activities. Booth determined to give everything to God. As a result, his life showed a growing spiritual depth and a compassionate outreach that ignited a spiritual passion around the world that continues to this day.

It is easy for me to dismiss this as an inspiring, irrelevant story about a man in another century, on another continent, who wouldn't be able to let God have all of him if he expected to survive in the power-driven, technological world where we live. But I can't dismiss Booth's story too quickly. There always have been fully dedicated Christ-followers who were touched by God and committed to making a difference. Maybe their numbers have been small, but as he did when he walked on the earth as Jesus and built a kingdom with a handful of disciples, God still moves in a few dedicated people, deepening their spiritual lives, and using them to reach out to others. I want to be that kind of man— even though I have a long way to go. If you have read this far, you may want to be that kind of person as well.

But wanting spiritual depth and becoming deeply spiritual are two different things. The world is filled with people who want to be successful, want to participate in the Olympics, want to write a book, want to get a degree, want to know God intimately, but who never come anywhere near their goals. Sometimes, of course, they are impeded by circumstances and a lack of opportunities. But often the failure to achieve is a problem of discipline and determination. Without discipline, you can want to lose weight, but you won't stick to a diet. Without discipline, you can want to succeed in athletics, but you will never make the team. You may want to be an accomplished musician and may have genuine musical talent, but without disciplined practice, you won't achieve musical excellence. Without spiritual disciplines, you will never come to spiritual maturity. Godliness without discipline is impossible.

This is a conclusion that many spiritual seekers, including those who have no interest in following Christ, would accept. People of the world's religions and followers of the new spiritualities pray to their gods, read their holy books, faithfully attend their spirituality groups, chant their incantations, give to their priests, reach out to others with evangelistic zeal, listen to their spiritual leaders, and worship at their shrines. Some spirituality seekers are as devoted as any General Booth, any Olympic athlete, or any corporate ladder climber worshiping the god of success. Christian spirituality, however, is unique in its purpose, some of its practices, and all of its focus.

The Purpose of Christian Spirituality

The musician who spends hours practicing scales on a piano or refining skills as a violinist has one ultimate purpose: to play music. And the person who is committed to the spiritual disciplines has one purpose as well: to become more godly. "Train yourself [or discipline yourself] to be godly," Paul wrote in 1 Timothy 4:7 (NIV).

Don Whitney, the man who had that disappointing childhood birthday party, suggests that we think of the disciplines as spiritual exercises intended to promote godliness. God uses three primary ways to build Christlikeness, Whitney writes. One is the impact of other *people* who sharpen our lives, challenge our thinking, and file away our rough, ungodly edges. The second is *circumstances,* such as financial pressures, physical conditions, open opportunities, closed doors, and the suffering that we have been discussing. The third influence is the *spiritual disciplines.*[27] Unlike people and circumstances that come to our lives from the outside in, the disciplines are used by God to change us from the inside out. And in contrast to people and events that may come without our choice or invitation, each of us can decide whether we want to pursue the disciplines and how seriously we treat them. When we engage in the spiritual disciplines willingly and expectantly, we place ourselves before God, allowing him to work within to bring a spiritual transformation. It is a transformation into greater and deeper godliness.

It is true that disciplines are not uniquely Christian. Muslims pray consistently, and they fast. Hindus eat a healthy diet. Buddhists meditate. Modern seekers channel, concentrate on angels, participate in séances, or meditate in front of self-created altars. Researchers like Harvard's Herbert Benson tell us that prayer and meditation improve our health and coping skills, regardless of what we believe or what deity we think about (if any) when we pray.[28] But Christian spirituality differs from these others in terms of its ultimate purposes. Its goals go beyond improving health, changing lifestyles, finding enlightenment, or bringing relaxation—important as these are. The Christian disciplines seek to build intimate relationships with a personal God, to enhance our service to others, to develop character so that we can better love others, to know God better, to appreciate suffering, and to find hope, especially in times of difficulty.

The Practices of Christian Spirituality

I was first introduced to the concept of spiritual disciplines by Quaker writer Richard Foster, whose *Celebration of Discipline* became a best-selling book among Christian spirituality seekers.[29] Foster wrote about twelve disciplines that he grouped into three categories: the inward disciplines (meditation, prayer, fasting, and study); the outward disciplines (simplicity, solitude, submission, and service); and the corporate disciplines (confession, worship, guidance, and celebration). Whitney adds Bible intake, evangelism, journaling, learning, and stewardship to the Foster list. A slightly different grouping, suggested in a recent book by Siang-Yang Tan and Douglas H. Gregg, is shown in the table "Spiritual Disciplines."[30]

SPIRITUAL DISCIPLINES

Drawing Near to God: *Disciplines of Solitude*
- Solitude and silence
- Listening and guidance
- Prayer and intercession
- Study and meditation

Yielding to God: *Disciplines of Surrender*
- Repentance and confession
- Yielding and submission
- Fasting
- Worship

Reaching Out to Others: *Disciplines of Service*
- Fellowship
- Simplicity
- Service
- Witness

Like the practice of an athletic or musical skill, these disciplines are things we do and habits that we cultivate over time, often with many distractions that can pull us off schedule. But when discipline has direction, there are fewer distractions, and there is less drudgery. According to Whitney, "If your picture of a disciplined Christian is one of a grim, tight-lipped, joyless half-robot, then you've missed the point. Jesus was the most disciplined Man who ever lived and yet the most joyful and passionately alive."[31] He is our example of one who was disciplined for godliness.

As we have seen, there is no set list of spiritual disciplines. Some disciplines—such as prayer, meditation on the Bible, confession, worship, submission, and involvement with other believers—are key, rock-bottom requirements for all Christian spirituality. Other practices—such as journaling, spiritual direction (from a more experienced believer), accountability, or giving affirmation—don't appear on all the lists and might not be right for everybody. Since most of the disciplines are described in detail elsewhere, we have no need (or space) to discuss them in depth here. In all of our consideration of disciplines, however, two themes are crucial and necessary for genuine Christian spirituality. Spiritual disciplines that bring us into godliness must involve a greater knowledge of God as revealed in the Bible. And true spiritual growth must point us to Christ and be guided by the Holy Spirit.

The Focus of Christian Spirituality

In this chapter and the one before, we have looked at nine unique characteristics of Christian spirituality, characteristics that set the Christian approach to spirituality apart from all the rest. These nine are at the core of our finding growing intimacy with God. Authentic and growing spirituality has a unique view of God, perspective on the universe, understanding of evil, emphasis on grace, concern for people and community, stress on worship, outlook on living, appreciation for suffering, and commitment to spiritual disciplines. And it is all focused on knowing God better, loving his Son, Jesus Christ, and being sensitive to the guidance of the Holy Spirit.

Not long ago, I heard a thought-provoking talk about the life of the apostle Peter. If you are familiar with New Testament history, you know that Peter was impulsive, maybe a little brash, and sometimes arrogant. When Jesus predicted that he would be denied by Peter, the reaction was immediate. Peter stated firmly that he would never do what he did a few hours later—deny that he even knew Jesus.

After the Resurrection, Jesus and Peter were standing together on a beach following breakfast. The disciple must have felt guilty and maybe afraid of how Jesus would react to the three denials. But there was no stern lecture, no demand for an apology, no call for penance. Instead, Jesus asked the same question three times: "Do you love me?" The question was not "Have you worked for me?" or "What have you done for me?" or "How much have you sacrificed for me?" or "What are you going to do for me now?" Jesus wanted to know if Peter loved him.

I have thought a lot about that as I have looked at my spirituality. I think God is pleased with my efforts to serve him, my desire to know him better, my wanting to please him. But I wonder if he is most interested in whether I love him. If I love him, I will show it in my attitudes and actions, whether anybody notices or not.

Christian spirituality moves us from dead, dry-bones religion to the vibrancy that Ezekiel saw in his army, who had life breathed into them by God. This God-breathed spirituality quickly moves us past the obstacles of magical thinking, pathological churches, or critical Christians, and brings us into growing intimacy with God. The result is a greater Christlikeness within and without. That growth in Christlikeness is what Christian spirituality is all about.

— 10 —

Moving Beyond the Spirituality Puzzle:

What Keeps the Spiritual Journey Alive?

Not long ago, I was looking again at some of those brochures described in an earlier chapter of this book. One of the flyers invited participants to come for a gathering of "kindred spirits, guided by leading edge visionaries on the edge of new discoveries." I wonder how the conference went? Did the people who attended get the spiritual nourishment that the brochure promised? Did they go from the conference with the promised "power that will reshape the world we'll be returning to, into places of greater nurturance for the human spirit"? Did their interaction with kindred spirits on the leading edge of spirituality equip them to grow spiritually as they move into the next millennium? I wonder.

More than that I am sad. Throughout this book, I have tried to paint a picture of contemporary spirituality searchers, treating them—maybe you're among them—as people worthy of respect. I never want to put down a genuine spirituality seeker, and I never want to condemn people outside the church or within it who have reached conclusions and taken directions that I consider futile and even wrong. We are all on a spiritual journey through life, but as I have reconsidered the spirituality that Christ offers, I am saddened to watch so many people looking in so many directions and finding nothing other than kindred spirits on the leading edge of spiritual confusion.

There are four reasons for this confusion, according to a religion professor.[1] First is a declining trust in religious leaders. *Jonestown, Waco,* and *Heaven's Gate* have become household words, symbolizing the impact of dangerous cult leaders. The media have filled us with reports of television preachers who paid for sex and mismanaged money, pastors who have had affairs and abandoned their wives, priests who have been homosexuals or molesters of children in their congregations. Second, there is a disenchantment with organized religion. As we have seen, many people prefer to forget the church or synagogue and make up a religion all their own. Third, there is a religious pluralism that sends a din of messages from different spirituality groups, each claiming to have the truth, each vying for attention and devotion. Fourth, there is the widespread belief in intellectual autonomy. That is, each person should make his or her decisions, apart from other people, especially people connected with organized religion.

Steeped in these attitudes, people continue the search for a satisfying spirituality. Living in a fast-paced society, most of us want to find and embrace a credible life-philosophy or spirituality that is able to bring balance and greater stability into our busy lives. We want something that fits our schedules and relates to our daily concerns, something that can be trusted. This search is not new.

THE *AFFECTIONS* OF JONATHAN EDWARDS

More than two centuries ago (in 1746), an American revivalist preacher named Jonathan Edwards wrote *Religious Affections*, a book that one Harvard historian has called the greatest work of religious psychology ever written on American soil.[2] Edwards wanted to draw a line between genuine Christian spiritual experience and forms of spirituality that he considered counterfeit.

I've never read Edwards's book, but Roanoke College professor Gerald McDermott read *Religious Affections* in graduate school and was profoundly influenced. Later he wrote that Edwards's book helped "make sense of the confused tangle of spiritualities on the American scene. It dispelled much of the bewilderment I felt when trying to understand why so many people who seemed to be Christians had lost their faith or horribly compromised their testimonies."[3] Using *Religious Affections* as a skeleton, McDermott wrote "a manual of discernment for the twenty-first century—a blueprint for spirituality in today's confusing world."[4]

It would be unfair and impossible to summarize McDermott's book in a few paragraphs, but many of his conclusions are relevant as we move beyond the spirituality puzzle and grow into closer intimacy with God. Both Edwards and his modern interpreter identify some "unreliable signs of true spirituality" and describe a dozen reliable signs that we at least can list and translate into more modern terminology.

We will begin with some of the unreliable signs.[5] If you have been around churches, you probably have seen them. You may have noticed them in your life and assumed that they reflected a genuine walk with God. Not necessarily.

Intense religious feelings, for example, can be exciting. They can give a warm inner glow of joyfulness, especially if we have been in an emotionally charged religious meeting. In themselves, emotions can be pleasurable, enriching, and good, but they don't necessarily indicate that one is a genuine Christ-follower or that the feelings come from a religious source. Even the people who shouted "Hosanna" on Palm Sunday were excited, but they were also fickle and maybe not true believers. Maybe they were swept along by crowd enthusiasm and political expectation, with little personal spiritual involvement at all.

JONATHAN EDWARDS'S SIGNS OF

1. *Supernatural impact.* There is evidence that the Holy Spirit lives within us, giving guidance, a new perspective on the world and on God, along with Spirit-stimulated character change. As a result, we show more love, joy, peace, self-control, and other fruit of the Spirit.

2. *Attraction to God and his ways for their own sake.* The emphasis is not on ourselves, on what God will give us, on our feelings, or on religious experiences. The emphasis is on knowing God, pleasing him, and loving him.

3. *Seeing beauty in God's holiness.* This may be the most distinguishing sign of true Christian spirituality. It involves a deepening appreciation for God's innate goodness, perfection, justice, mercy, and love. Because we so value his moral nature, we are filled with praise. We want to steer away from viewing, thinking about, or experiencing evil because it is so distasteful to God. In time, we become more godlike, beautiful people.

4. *A new kind of knowing.* This is not so much intellectual decision making as it is discernment: sensing what is right or true or the best direction to take. It is a sense of God's approval or leading, a new way of seeing facts or the world that often cannot be explained or justified intellectually.

5. *Deep-seated conviction.* This is a strong inner conviction that what we believe is valid. The biblical writer of Hebrews called faith *"being sure* of what we hope for and *certain* of what we do not see."[6]

6. *Humility.* True religion involves walking humbly with God, according to the prophet Micah.[7] This is not a false piety that denies the strengths God has given. It does not involve putting ourselves down and wallowing in insecurity or self-pity. Humility is a quiet recognition that all we have and are comes from God. It is an

TRUE (CHRISTIAN) SPIRITUALITY

attitude that is open to new insights and has little concern about inflating our ego or enhancing our image.

7. *A change in nature.* Rather than a self-directed change in lifestyle or habits, this is a gradual inner transformation. It is not a change of basic personality so much as a greater Christlikeness that others begin to notice in our attitudes, outlook, and behaviors.

8. *A Christlike spirit.* This is difficult to define but involves the emergence of Christlike characteristics such as meekness, courage, a willingness to forgive, love, and a genuine concern for poor and unfortunate people. The Bible knows nothing of true Christians who are miserly, spiteful, habitually unforgiving, self-righteous, or arrogant. Nobody is perfect and we all are tempted to sin, but the true Christ-follower shows signs of becoming more like the Master.

9. *An awesome awareness of God.* The Bible tends to use the phrase "fear of God" to imply deep respect and adoration, an intense determination to please God.

10. *Integrity.* This involves a balance between what we say we believe and what we show with our lifestyles. This is a consistency of our talk with our walk.

11. *Hunger for God.* This is an insatiable desire to know him better and a refusal to stick with the religious status quo.

12. *Christian practice.* Probably the most observable sign, this also is the most imitated. The hypocrites that Jesus vehemently condemned had outwardly pious behavior, but behind the facade they were self-centered and not very spiritual. Christian practice involves surrender, perseverance, Christian zeal, and a willingness to serve even if it involves suffering.

Eloquent and frequent talk about God and religion can be suspect. Genuine believers like to talk about their beliefs, but people with false religions are eager to talk as well. There is nothing innately wrong with frequent and passionate praise for God, but praise-talk doesn't necessarily flow from spiritual depth or obedient commitment to Christ.

Appearances of love and humility can be deceptive. Edwards wrote that these are imitated more than any other Christian virtues because they are the easiest to turn on.

Zealous, time-consuming devotion to religious activities may be seen as an indicator of spirituality, but such activities could reflect compulsivity, guilt-motivated actions spurred on by a manipulative religious leader, efforts by insecure people to find acceptance, or the evidence of pressure from one's religious group. "A true saint and a hypocrite . . . may be similar in outward appearance," McDermott concludes. "Outward devotion to God is no guarantee of inner spirituality."[8]

The so-called reliable signs of true spirituality don't guarantee anything, either. No person can look on another and conclude that somebody is genuinely spiritual, although the reliable signs can give clues. Some of the characteristics of spirituality listed in the table "Jonathan Edwards's Signs of True (Christian) Spirituality," are difficult to see—especially in people you don't know well.

This impressive list can be very intimidating. I don't know how Jonathan Edwards's readers felt, but most of us today would likely feel that the twelve reliable signs are harder to attain than the twelve steps in a multitude of recovery groups. Recognize, however, that these are ideals that emerge over time, not instantaneous traits that spiritual giants have and the rest of us don't. Even the greatest saints lived with spiritual failure, but they found forgiveness and continued to grow. Nobody ever becomes morally perfect in this world, and nobody always feels spiritual. Sometimes we feel defeated, overwhelmed, cut off from God, or that we are in the spiritual wilderness mentioned earlier. God doesn't call his followers to be successful, emotionally charged, or never tempted, but he does call us to be faithful. He understands our weaknesses and struggles, knows about our persecutions and pressures, and promises to always stay with us, even when he seems far away.

LIFE ON A TIGHTROPE?

David Hazard was a teenager back in the days when talking about God wasn't banned in the public schools and when teachers and students had freedom of speech so they could discuss their spiritual journeys and questions. It was a time when the Jesus movement was still new and a lot of kids were curious.

One of the teachers talked openly about being "born again," so the students decided to ask about it. "What is it like—what does it *feel* like—to know God?" somebody inquired. The teacher stumbled a little in his answer, turning to the clichés that he probably heard in his church, talking about "being saved," "accepting Christ," and "knowing your sins are forgiven because of the shed blood of Jesus."

But the students pushed him to know what it really is like. The teacher's answer made a great impact on young David Hazard as he listened: "For me, knowing God is like walking on a tightly stretched rope, high over a bottomless chasm of blackness. Below me, I hear screams of torment. Up ahead of me, somewhere, I know I'll walk out into the light someday. For now, I pray and read God's Word, and carefully put one foot in front of the other to keep from sinning again."[9] The students sat in silence. The teacher's picture was nothing that any of them wanted. Nobody asked any more questions.

Before the end of the year, however, the teacher changed. He appeared more self-assured in class, less inclined to stutter and fumble with his notes. Something had happened to bring his frightening image of the spiritual walk down to earth. "Knowing God is not a tightrope to me anymore," he told the class a few days before they left on summer vacation. "Knowing God is like resting in an open field."

In these pages I have tried to show that knowing God is even more than that. It is walking through life with an awesome, almighty, holy Being who is acquainted with all our ways, tender, forgiving, guiding, compassionate. He understands people who search for the sacred and try to put together the spirituality puzzle. He calls himself the truth, the way, and the life, and he proclaims that all who seek him will find him. Living on this earth will never be problem-free, but Christ-followers can experience an inner peace that no psychiatrist can stimulate, and an in-depth spiritual satisfaction that no spirituality guru can duplicate. Christ-followers can know the joy of community and the inner experience of stability, whatever the storms of life.

THE ULTIMATE SPIRITUALITY—
GLORIFYING GOD

It must have been a festive occasion, a few days before the Crucifixion, when Jesus entered Jerusalem riding on a donkey before palm-waving crowds of enthusiasts. It seemed to the religious leaders that the whole world had gone after him.[10] Later, in meeting with his disciples, Jesus used a word that appears in our English translations of the Bible but doesn't come into our language much today.

"The hour has come for the Son of Man to be *glorified*," he said. "Father, *glorify* your name!" he prayed, and a voice came from heaven, saying, "I have *glorified* it, and will *glorify* it again."[11]

I have read these words often but didn't think much about them until recently when I was in a worship service, singing, "Father, I love you, I worship, I adore you, *glorify* your name in all the earth." I stopped and asked myself what I was singing about. What does it mean to *glorify* God? What does it mean when Christians sing, "I will *glorify* the King of kings, I will *glorify* the Lamb, I will *glorify* the Lord of lords"? How does anybody glorify God, and what does that have to do with spirituality in the information age?

To glorify God is to acknowledge his majesty, sovereignty, purity, holiness, and other attributes. To glorify God is to express our praise and adoration. Doing these things doesn't sound very contemporary—in an era fascinated with angels, aliens, near death experiences, mantras, karma, channeling, alternative healings, shamans, and leading edge experiences with kindred spirits. But Christian spirituality never attempts to be faddish, and it never aims to merge with the other spirituality cafeteria items. Its greatest uniqueness is its undeviating focus on the supreme God of the ages.

As a believer and a pilgrim who wants to know God more intimately, I need to focus my entire life in the direction of glorifying God, bringing him honor. In the process, I bring benefits to myself and grow into greater spiritual depth, but for the Christian, these are secondary goals. How, then, do we glorify God?

To glorify God, *we need to know the Father*. We need to know what he is like and know him experientially. The Word of God helps us to know the Father. The Son of God allows us to approach the Father. The Holy Spirit of God guides and points us both to the Father and to the Son. God's Son, Jesus Christ, once walked the earth in visible form and taught that anyone who had seen him had seen the Father.[12]

To glorify God, *we need to be like the Father*. To be like him totally is impossible, but Christian spirituality seekers are called to be holy, as God is holy.[13] We'll never reach this goal completely because there can be only one God. But we are to move in the direction of godlikeness. Because Jesus died and atoned for our sin, we can be forgiven and made righteous in God's sight. The Holy Spirit then guides and empowers believers on the Christian spiritual pilgrimage as we move to increasing godlikeness.

To glorify God, *we need to communicate with the Father*. We don't show him any honor or respect when we ignore him. He has communicated to us through his Word and sent his Son to restore the broken relationship that would have prevented communication. It seems amazing, but God wants two-way communication with us. Like all communication, that takes time, energy, and determination.

To glorify God, *we need to obey the Father*. In the Garden of Gethsemane, Jesus told the Father, "I have brought you glory on earth by completing the work you gave me to do."[14] Earlier he told the disciples, "I love the Father and . . . do exactly what my Father has commanded me."[15] This is complete obedience, the kind that imperfect people like us can be challenged to move toward even though we will never reach the level of perfection that is the goal. God expects obedience, not because he wants to enslave us, but because he knows what is best for us. Whenever we obey the Father's will as revealed in the Bible, honor comes to his name. Ultimately that has secondary benefits for us.

To glorify God, *we need to submit*. Is this the same as obedience? They go together, but sometimes submission is more of an attitude than an action. It pleases God and honors him when we yield everything to him—family, career, life, health, circumstances, possessions—all with an attitude of trust that says, "Here it all is, Lord. Your will be done!"

To glorify God, *we need to praise the Father*. Maybe as much as anything else this is how we bring honor to God. Hebrews 13:15–16 describes what pleases God: offering praise from our lips and doing good to others. God must like to hear us sing, even if we sing off-key, because music is so common in the Bible, especially in the Psalms. "I will sing to the LORD as long as I live;/I will sing praise to my God while I have my being," the Old Testament writer said, maybe in the words of a song.[16]

To glorify God, *we need to show care*. God is pleased and honored when we show acts of caring and goodness to all people, including other believers.[17] He is honored as well when we follow his mandate to care for the earth, his creation, as an act of obedience and dedication. Part of that creation includes you and me. We honor God when we take care of ourselves, keeping our bodies pure and healthy, offering them as living sacrifices to God.[18]

To glorify God, *we need to serve*. As we have seen, Christian spirituality reaches out to others in acts of kindness, compassion, and service. Even when we do our jobs, we can bring glory to God by working diligently, knowing that ultimately we are serving the Lord.[19] When we serve him gladly and bear fruit, we bring glory to the Father.[20]

To glorify God, *we need to love.* Sometimes people work compulsively and diligently, accomplishing the mission of the church, sometimes building their own self-images, or maybe attempting in vain to earn God's favor. God is honored by service, but he is honored more when we show love. Jesus quietly gave that message to Peter when they talked together on the beach after the disciple had denied Christ and Jesus asked, "Do you love me?"

Sometimes loving is very difficult. Loving Christ is hard enough when we are caught up in pressure-filled days and hyperactive lifestyles. Loving others is even tougher. On the Christian spiritual journey, therefore, we have to rely on the Holy Spirit working in our lives to give us the love that we wouldn't have otherwise.[21] We don't just show loving acts of service by doing things for others. We love.

To glorify God, *we need to unite with other Christians.* We can learn a lot about what is important to a person by listening to what he or she says when the end of life is near. In the hours before his death, Jesus prayed for the unity of his followers, present and future, asking that they would be one. The prayer strongly implies that this unity brings glory to God.[22] Unity demonstrates God's love. The world sees this and the Father gets the glory.

To glorify God, *we need to be willing to suffer.* The Bible never tells us to seek out suffering, but when it comes, we allow it to bring honor to God. The early church endured suffering, so the apostle Peter sent a letter of encouragement. You are likely to have all kinds of grief and trials, he told the believers. We aren't likely to understand it and we surely won't like it, but we accept the conclusion that suffering leads to a more purified faith and that, in turn, brings honor to God.[23]

To glorify God, *we need to resist Satan and his forces.* Submit yourselves to God and resist the devil, we are told in James 4:7, "and he will flee from you" (NKJV). God is not glorified when we are swept along by our lusts, evil desires, cultural enticements, and self-centered behaviors. The devil seeks to undermine our lives and lead us into ways that do not glorify God. We need divine help in resisting these forces. God is honored—glorified—when that happens.

To glorify God, *we need to proclaim God's glory*. Psalm 19:1 tells us that the heavens declare the glory of God, but he also gets honor when people proclaim his glory in unison and among the nations.[24] The proclamation can be sung in worship services, whispered in quiet prayers, or stated more openly in conversation. Christians also seek to live in ways that let others see God being honored in our actions, attitudes, and daily lifestyles.

Rich and Karen

I wonder how Rich and Karen would respond to all of this? I wonder how you respond?

As you will remember, Karen has had no contact with Christian spirituality. She might reach this part of the book and wonder why anybody would try to distinguish reliable from unreliable signs of spirituality. For Karen, anything is reliable if it works for her. Even so, she might be attracted to the idea that it is possible to have an intimate relationship with God. She would admire people who are gentle and loving, who have deep-seated convictions, who believe in a God that they can trust and hold in awe. She is likely to appreciate the determination of sincere Christians to keep their talk consistent with their walk. Even people who are open to all spiritualities, like Karen, are not very tolerant of hypocrisy. She might not be into glorifying God—that seems very Christian, very Western—but she might resonate with the ideas of being able to communicate with God, to experience divine love, to serve and care for people, to find communion with other spiritually alert individuals. Karen would appreciate a spirituality that does not ignore suffering, that takes evil seriously, that is honest about our struggles, that gives people a greater peace of mind, and that makes forgiveness a central part of spiritual maturation. She might even respond positively to the fact that Christians find security, stability, and ultimate peace in their relationship with the God who has clear standards and who calls his people to obedience. When they look openly at Christian spirituality, searchers like Karen often get past their preconceived ideas and see that Christian spirituality really does have something to offer.

Rich already knows that there is good in the Christian perspective. He needs to look honestly at his legitimate criticisms about the religious environment where he grew up. He can acknowledge that Christian spirituality seekers are not perfect, but he would benefit from thinking seriously about what the Christian approach to spirituality has to offer. Probably Rich needs to find a group of believers whose worship styles are closer to his personality and preferences. He doesn't need to be hurried, but in time—maybe even in time of crisis—he will see that the alternatives to Christian spirituality may not be as alluring or fulfilling as he thought originally.

A HEAVY ENDING, A HOPEFUL BEGINNING

James Newsome still can't get free of his past.

Around midnight on October 31, 1979, Newsome was driving on the south side of Chicago in the green Ford that he had borrowed from his brother. When a police car approached him from behind and the officers signaled him to pull over, the driver remembered thinking, *I wasn't violating any traffic laws.* But the officers took the man to the police station and began questioning him about a robbery and murder that had occurred in the neighborhood on the previous night. The murderer had used a getaway car like the one Newsome was driving, and before long the police began building a case against the man who claimed to know nothing about the incident. During the trial, the attorneys discounted the testimony of Newsome's girlfriend and two sisters who said they had been with him watching television at the time of the crime. The state's attorney downplayed the fact that fingerprints taken from store items and handled by the murderer did not match Newsome's. On September 26, 1980, he was found guilty and sentenced to life in prison.

He stayed there for fifteen years, living in violent, gang-controlled jails and working tirelessly in the prison law libraries preparing appeals and other documents to get his conviction overturned. He had help from some legal experts who were able to demonstrate that the fingerprints at the murder scene matched those of a death-row inmate who, at the time of the murder, was out on parole after serving three years in prison for armed robbery. In January of 1995, the state dropped its case against Newsome, the governor granted a pardon, and James Newsome became a free man.

To the surprise of his friends, he doesn't appear to be bitter or seething in anger despite the injustice that he encountered. But wherever he goes today, people still treat him as though he were guilty and permanently tarnished by his prison experience. "Now I have to deal with this stigma, this social scar," the ex-prisoner told a reporter a few months after his release. But James Newsome has always been ambitious, determined to beat the odds, and intent on reaching his goals. He wants to become a successful lawyer. Many of us hope he succeeds.

I don't know if James Newsome had any interest in spirituality, so his story may seem to be a strange choice to conclude this book. But the man's determination and struggle to get free of his unjust incarceration are not far removed from the spiritual struggles that many are facing today on the edge of the twenty-first century. Many will seek for a lifetime and never find anything that satisfies or gives them freedom. Many will join with the modern multitudes who drift from one spirituality to another, picking and choosing, trying a few and bypassing others. Some people will consider Christ and decide that following him is too old-fashioned, too demanding, too traditional. Like the rich young ruler who came to Jesus, they will hear his message and walk away.

But there are others, I hope you are included, who will survey the spirituality landscape, read about heavy things—such as the things we have discussed in this chapter—and commit or recommit to following Christ. It will be a spiritual journey that probably will involve pain and frustration, but a journey that moves us beyond the spirituality puzzle, satisfies like no other, and brings us to a bright eternal future.

Are you willing to step out, yield yourself to Christ, and travel this spiritual road along with the rest of us?

Notes

Chapter 1

1. Barbara Kantrowitz, "The Search for the Sacred: Americans' Quest for Spiritual Meaning," *Newsweek,* 28 November 1994, 53.
2. Ibid., italics added.
3. C. S. Lewis, *A Grief Observed* (New York: Bantam Books, 1961).
4. Ibid., 4–5.
5. Alan E. Nelson, *Broken in the Right Place: How God Tames the Soul* (Nashville: Thomas Nelson, 1994), 17.
6. Thomas Moore, *Care of the Soul: A Guide for Cultivating Depth and Sacredness in Everyduy Life* (New York: HarperCollins, 1992).
7. Ibid., xi.
8. Quoted by Connie Lauerman, "Soul Food: Thomas Moore and a Host of Authors Tell Us Why We're Unhappy," *Chicago Tribune,* 25 June 1996.
9. L. Gregory Jones, "Spirituality Lite: Thomas Moore's Misguided Care of the Soul," *Christian Century,* 6 November 1996, 1072–74. This article is a review of Thomas Moore's *The Re-Enchantment of Everyday Life* (San Francisco: HarperCollins, 1996).
10. The magazine is *Christian Counseling Today.* Some of the following paragraphs are adapted from a lead article that I wrote for the soul care issue. Gary R. Collins, "What in the World Is Soul Care?" *Christian Counseling Today* 3, no. 4 (fall 1995): 8–12.
11. Arthur A. Dole, Michael D. Langone, and Steve Dubrow-Eichel, "Viewing the 'New Age' Phenomenon," *The Cult Observer* 12, no. 4 (1995): 10.
12. Moore, *Care of the Soul,* xi.
13. The following paragraphs are adapted from an entry on *soul* in the *New Illustrated Bible Dictionary* (Nashville: Thomas Nelson, 1995), 1195–96.
14. Stephen Arterburn and Jack Felton, *Toxic Faith: Understanding and Overcoming Religious Addiction* (Nashville: Thomas Nelson, 1991).
15. See, for example, Psalms 38 and 51.
16. Matthew 23:27 NKJV.
17. Acts 8:27–31.
18. Luke 10:38–42 NKJV.
19. I am grateful to John Ortberg for this example.
20. Henri J. M. Nouwen, *The Genesee Diary: Report from a Trappist Monastery* (Garden City, NY: Image Books/Doubleday, 1981), 139, 122.

21. Deuteronomy 18:10–12.
22. Ron Grossman and Charles Leroux, "America, the Rootless: Nation of Strangers," *Chicago Tribune*, 25 December 1995.
23. Robert L. Wise, *Quest for the Soul: Our Search for Deeper Meaning— Humanity's Loss, Pursuit, and Recovery of the Fingerprint of God* (Nashville: Thomas Nelson, 1996), 27.
24. Philip Cushman, "Why the Self Is Empty: Toward a Historically Situated Psychology," *American Psychologist* 45, no. 5 (May 1990): 599–611.

Chapter 2

1. Dorothy S. Becvar, *Soul Healing: A Spiritual Orientation in Counseling and Therapy* (New York: Basic Books, 1997).
2. John A. Saliba, *Understanding New Religious Movements* (Grand Rapids: Eerdmans, 1995), 24.
3. Ibid.
4. This departure is documented and discussed by Thomas C. Reeves, *The Empty Church: The Suicide of Liberal Christianity* (New York: Free Press, 1996). See also Jim Naughton, *Catholics in Crisis: An American Parish Fights for Its Soul* (New York: Addison-Wesley, 1996).
5. Jill Neimark, "Shaman in Chicago," *Psychology Today*, September-October 1993, 46–50, 70, 72, 74–77.
6. Charles Strohmer, *The Gospel and the New Spirituality: Communicating the Truth in a World of Spiritual Seekers* (Nashville: Thomas Nelson, 1996), xiii.
7. Betty Eadie, *Embraced By the Light* (Placerville, CA: Gold Leaf Press, 1992).
8. Elliot Miller, as quoted by Richard Abanes, *Embraced By the Light and the Bible* (Camp Hill, PA: Horizon Books, 1995), 19.
9. Eadie, *Embraced*, 112–13, 70, 41–42.
10. Gordon J. Melton, Jerome Clark, and Aidan A. Kelly, *New Age Almanac* (Detroit: Gale Research, 1991), 304.
11. Eadie, *Embraced*, 55, 57.
12. James Redfield, *The Tenth Insight: Holding the Vision* (New York: Warner Books, 1996), 60.
13. Russell Chandler, *Understanding the New Age* (Grand Rapids: Zondervan, 1993), 218–19.
14. Katrina Raphaell, *Crystal Enlightenment*, vol. 1 (Santa Fe, NM: Aurora Press, 1985), 32.
15. Strohmer, *The Gospel and the New Spirituality*, 97.
16. Marty Kaplan, "Ambushed by Spirituality," *Time*, 24 June 1996, 62.
17. Ibid.
18. Chandler, *Understanding the New Age*, 85.
19. Eugene Taylor, "Desperately Seeking Spirituality," *Psychology Today*, November-December 1994, 62.

20. Rich and Karen are fictional characters, each with a combination of attitudes, values, and perspectives that are seen frequently in the groups they are intended to represent.

21. Kenneth L. Woodward, "On the Road Again," *Newsweek*, 28 November 1994, 61.

Chapter 3

1. Russell Chandler, *Understanding the New Age* (Grand Rapids: Zondervan, 1993), 16.

2. In an article dealing with the popular books on personal and spiritual growth, a University of Dayton professor concluded that "the primary discipline underlying most of their books is psychology," not theology. See Dennis M. Doyle, "Traffic Jam on the Spiritual Highway," *Commonweal*, 9 September 1994, 18–22.

3. Viktor E. Frankl, *Man's Search for Meaning: An Introduction to Logotherapy* (New York: Washington Square Press, 1963).

4. Ibid., 104.

5. Ibid., 117.

6. Abraham H. Maslow, *Religions, Values, and Peak-Experiences* (New York: Penguin Books, 1976).

7. Ibid., 4.

8. Martin L. Gross, *The Psychological Society* (New York: Touchstone/Simon & Schuster, 1978), 4.

9. Ibid., 9.

10. Laura Markowitz, "Culture Healers," *Utne Reader* 79 (January-February 1997): 57.

11. This is the description given by Dr. Nate Booth, head corporate trainer for the Anthony Robbins Companies. The description is taken from a page on the World Wide Web titled "Working with Anthony Robbins Is Like . . . !"

12. Anthony Robbins, *Awaken the Giant Within: How to Take Immediate Control of Your Mental, Emotional, Physical & Financial Destiny!* (New York: Summit Books, 1991).

13. More recent approaches to alcoholic addiction have challenged the higher power concept and even the assumed effectiveness of AA. See, for example, Connie Lauerman, "Is AA Still the Best Way?" *Chicago Tribune*, 2 January 1997. The article begins, "Those who find the 12 steps of Alcoholics Anonymous too tall an order may find those alternatives more to their liking."

14. M. Scott Peck, *The Road Less Traveled* (New York: Simon & Schuster, 1978). The Abanes quote is taken from a book by H. Wayne House and Richard Abanes, *The Less Traveled Road and the Bible* (Camp Hill, PA: Horizon Books, 1995), 2.

15. Warren Smith, "M. Scott Peck: Community and the Cosmic Christ," *SCP Journal*, 2/3 (1995), 21.

16. M. Scott Peck, *The Different Drum: Community Making and Peace* (New York: Simon & Schuster, 1987), 192.

17. This quotation is from a book that I have leaned on heavily in writing this section: Stanley J. Grenz, *A Primer on Postmodernism* (Grand Rapids: Eerdmans, 1996), 3. See also Thomas C. Oden, *Between Two Worlds: Notes on the Death of Modernity in America and Russia* (Downers Grove, IL: InterVarsity, 1992).

18. Grenz, *Postmodernism*, 4.

19. Ibid., 11.

20. Ibid., 16.

21. Ibid., 13.

22. William Dyrness, "Can Americans Still Hear the Good News?" *Christianity Today* 41, no. 4 (7 April 1997): 32–35.

23. Grenz, *Postmodernism*, 15.

24. Jim Leffel and Dennis McCallum, "The Postmodern Challenge: Facing the Spirit of the Age," *Christian Research Journal* 19, no. 2 (fall 1996): 38. For a more detailed discussion of the impact of postmodernism, see Jim Leffel and Dennis McCallum, *The Death of Truth* (Minneapolis: Bethany House, 1996).

25. Leffel and McCallum, "The Postmodern Challenge," 37.

Chapter 4

1. Jill Neimark, "On the Front Lines of Alternative Medicine," *Psychology Today*, January-February 1997, 52–57, 67–68.

2. Isadore Rosenfeld, *Dr. Rosenfeld's Guide to Alternative Medicine: What Works, What Doesn't—And What's Right for You* (New York: Random House, 1996).

3. The details of Chopra's life in this section are adapted from David Van Biema, "Deepak Chopra: Emperor of the Soul," *Time*, 24 June 1996, 64–68.

4. Deepak Chopra, *Ageless Body, Timeless Mind: The Quantum Alternative to Growing Old* (New York: Harmony Books, 1993).

5 Biema, "Emperor of the Soul," 67–68.

6. Chopra, *Ageless Body*, 19.

7. Biema, "Emperor of the Soul," 66–67.

8. Quoted by Neimark, "Alternative Medicine," 68.

9. If you want to read more about new spirituality approaches to healing, consider the following books: Marc Ian Barasch, *The Healing Path: A Soul Approach to Illness* (New York: Putnam, 1993); Herbert Benson with Marg Stark, *Timeless Healing: The Power and Biology of Belief* (New York: Scribner's, 1996); Bill Moyers, *Healing and the Mind* (New York: Doubleday, 1993); and Stanley Krippner and Patrick Welch, *Spiritual Dimensions of Healing: From Native Shamanism to Contemporary Health Care* (New York: Irvington Publishers, 1992).

10. Randolph C. Byrd, "Positive Therapeutic Effects of Intercessory Prayer in a Coronary Care Unit," *Southern Medical Journal* 81, no. 7 (July 1988): 826–29.

11. Kimberly A. Sherrill and David B. Larson, "Adult Burn Patients: The Role of Religion in Recovery," *Southern Medical Journal* 81, no. 7 (July 1988): 821–25.

12. The following examples are adapted from Claudia Wallis, "Faith and Healing," *Time*, 24 June 1996, 58–64, and from Bob Condor, "Can Faith Heal?" *Chicago Tribune*, 4 December 1996.

13. Larry Dossey, "Can Prayer Harm?" *Psychology Today*, March-April 1997, 49. Dossey's book is *Prayer Is Good Medicine* (San Francisco: HarperCollins, 1996).

14. Dossey, "Can Prayer Harm?" 50.

15. Ibid., 76.

16. Gary Thomas, "Doctors Who Pray: How the Medical Community Is Discovering the Healing Power of Prayer," *Christianity Today*, 6 January 1997, 20–30.

17. Figures are from a February 1996 *USA Weekend* poll, cited by Gary Thomas, ibid., 24.

18. Reported by Wallis, "Faith and Healing," 62.

19. This story was reported by Nancy Gibbs, "Angels Among Us," *Time*, 27 December 1993, 56–65.

20. Ibid., 56.

21. Ibid.

22. See, for example, the John Travolta movie *Michael* where the chief character is portrayed as "an angel with a devilish side."

23. Terry Lynn Taylor, *Messengers of Light: The Angels' Guide to Spiritual Growth* (Tiburon, CA: H. J. Kramer, 1990), 34.

24. My conclusions about the popularity of angels are adapted from an excellent book by Ron Rhodes, *Angels Among Us: Separating Truth from Fiction* (Eugene, OR: Harvest House, 1994), 29–34.

25. Ibid., 33.

26. Taylor, *Messengers of Light*, 19.

27. Rhodes, *Angels*, 35. See 2 Corinthians 11:14–15.

28. Celia Coates, "Plugging In," *Common Boundary* 14, no. 5 (September-October 1996): 24.

29. Kathleen F. Phalen, "In Search of Goddess: Brush with Death Opens a Channel to the Divinity Within," *Chicago Tribune*, 28 July 1996.

30. Leslie Miller, "Getting in Sync with 'Indian Time,'" *USA Today*, 13 October 1993.

31. For more information, please write to Andrew Counts, The Eighth Day Life Center, St. Luke's Episcopal Church, 821 Edgewood Dr., Charleston, WV 25302.

32. J. Marshall Jenkins, "Practical Concerns About the Definition of Spirituality," *Interaction* (a publication of the Association for Spiritual, Ethical and Religious Values in Counseling; winter 1997): 2.

33. Kevin Giles, "The Quest for Spirituality?" *Grid* (a publication of World Vision Australia; winter 1996): 1. The definition is from a report of the Christian Research Association titled *Believe It or Not: Australian Spirituality and the Churches in the 90s.*

34. M. Robert Mulholland Jr., *Invitation to a Journey: A Road Map for Spiritual Formation* (Downers Grove, IL: InterVarsity, 1993), 16.

35. Rowland Croucher, "Sprititual Formation," *Grid* (a publication of World Vision Australia; winter 1991): 1–2, italics added.

Chapter 5

1. *Chicago Tribune,* 28 March 1997.

2. Jef Zeleny and Susan Kuczka, "Those Who Said No Shudder with Relief," *Chicago Tribune,* 30 March 1997.

3. Tricia's story was adapted from Margaret Thaler Singer with Janja Lalich, *Cults in Our Midst: The Hidden Menace in Our Everyday Lives* (San Francisco: Jossey-Bass, 1995), 46–47.

4. See, for example, Ron Rhodes, *The Culting of America* (Eugene, OR: Harvest House, 1994).

5. James W. Pennebaker and Amina Memon, "Recovered Memories in Context: Thoughts and Elaborations on Bowers and Farvolden (1996)," *Psychological Bulletin* 119, no. 3 (1996): 381–85.

6. According to a fascinating and carefully documented discussion of abuse, written by an expert who also is familiar with suggestibility and hypnosis, "there is a well-considered basis for concluding that not every allegation of abuse can be believed. . . . In almost all the cases in which I have been involved over the past decade, repressed memories of abuse were 'discovered' only after . . . the therapist first introduced it as a possibility," and used a number of suggestive methods to "uncover" the memory. See Michael D. Yapko, *Suggestions of Abuse: True and False Memories of Childhood Sexual Trauma* (New York: Simon & Schuster, 1994), 29, 126. For a frightening tale of repressed memory that destroyed a family, see Lawrence Wright, *Remembering Satan: A Case of Recovered Memory and the Shattering of an American Family* (New York: Knopf, 1994). See also Lenore Terr, *Unchained Memories: True Stories of Traumatic Memories, Lost and Found* (New York: Basic Books, 1994).

7. This oft-quoted sentence is from Ellen Bass and Laura Davis, *The Courage to Heal: Women Healing from Sexual Abuse* (New York: Harper & Row, 1988).

8. This fictional story is adapted from Yapko, *Suggestions,* 132, 134.

9. John A. Saliba, *Understanding New Religious Movements* (Grand Rapids: Eerdmans, 1995), 67.

10. Ibid., 55–56.

11. Mollie Stone was interviewed by researchers whose findings formed the basis of an influential book by Wade Clark Roof, *A Generation of Seekers: The Spiritual Journeys of the Baby Boom Generation* (San Francisco: HarperCollins, 1993), 63–88.

12. Ibid., 64.

13. Saliba, *New Religious Movements*, 40.

14. This is the conclusion of Michael Horton, *In the Face of God: The Dangers and Delights of Spiritual Intimacy* (Dallas: Word, 1996).

15. Psychology students know that explanations built on psychological needs really don't tell us anything. To say I am spiritual because I have a need for God only answers one question by raising another: Why do I have a need for God? I might believe that God has given us a need to believe, but I can't prove that. Needs cannot be proven or measured scientifically, except for physiological needs, like the need for food or water. In this chapter I use the word *needs* as a convenient term to refer to some of the motives and desires that may or may not be inborn but that seem to guide human behavior nevertheless.

16. Linda's story is told by Roof, *A Generation of Seekers*, 89–99.

17. Ibid., 80.

18. Yapko, *Suggestions*, 94–95.

19. One survey asked baby boomers, "Is it good to explore many differing religious teachings and learn from them, or should one stick to a particular faith?" Sixty percent said they would prefer to explore, 28 percent said stick to a faith, 11 percent couldn't choose or said to do both. Roof, *A Generation of Seekers*, 71.

20. See, for example, 1 Samuel 13:7–14.

21. Michael F. Brown, *The Channeling Zone: American Spirituality in an Anxious Age* (Cambridge, MA: Harvard University Press, 1997).

22. This discussion of channeling, including the quotations, is adapted from an article by Christopher Shea, "A Serious Look at New Age Spirituality: An Anthropologist Examines How Channeling Has Filtered down to Middle-of-the-Road America," *Chronicle of Higher Education*, 28 March 1997, A16–A18.

Chapter 6

1. I missed the shuttle launch and many spiritual searchers miss the "real thing" because of ignorance. This should not imply, however, that lack of information is the only or the major cause of spiritual emptiness. The Christian believes that the root cause is rebellion: an unwillingness to submit to a sovereign God who demands obedience.

2. A good example of intellectually based spirituality that deals with a personal walk with God is Sproul's *The Soul's Quest for God: Satisfying the Hunger for Spiritual Communion with God* (Wheaton, IL: Tyndale, 1992).

3. Guenter Lewy, *Why America Needs Religion: Secular Modernity and Its Discontents* (Grand Rapids: Eerdmans, 1996).

4. Genesis 11:3–9.

5. Michael Horton, *In the Face of God: The Dangers and Delights of Spiritual Intimacy* (Dallas: Word, 1996).

6. The parable of the sower is recorded in Matthew 13:1–9. Later, Jesus interpreted its meaning to his disciples; see Matthew 13:18–23.

7. Stephen Arterburn and Jack Felton, *Toxic Faith: Understanding and Overcoming Religious Addiction* (Nashville: Thomas Nelson, 1991).

8. Ibid., 29.

9. Ronald Enroth, *Churches That Abuse* (Grand Rapids: Zondervan, 1992). For other treatments of abusive churches and toxic religion, see David Johnson and Jeff Van Vonderen, *The Subtle Power of Spiritual Abuse* (Minneapolis: Bethany House, 1991); Ken Blue, *Healing Spiritual Abuse: How to Break Free from Bad Church Experiences* (Downers Grove, IL: InterVarsity, 1993); and C. Peter Wagner, *The Healthy Church: Avoiding and Curing the 9 Diseases That Can Afflict Any Church* (Ventura, CA: Regal, 1996). For a somewhat different perspective, see Donald E. Sloat, *The Dangers of Growing Up in a Christian Home* (Nashville: Thomas Nelson, 1986).

10. Arterburn and Felton, *Toxic Faith*, 44.

11. From James Patterson and Peter Kim, *The Day America Told the Truth* (New York: Prentice-Hall, 1991).

12. Deuteronomy 18:9–14. Several times, magic arts are criticized in Revelation (9:21; 18:23; 21:8; 22:15).

13. Matthew 7:1; 1 Peter 2:17.

14. Jesus discussed forgiveness in Matthew 6:14–15 and 18:21–35.

15. Acts 2:44–47; Hebrews 10:24–25.

16. Peter L. Benson and Carolyn H. Elkin, "Effective Christian Education: A National Study of Protestant Congregations," a research project of Search Institute, Minneapolis, March 1990, 10.

17. Jennifer Ferranti, "In Memory of Richard C. Halverson: He Lived What He Preached," *World Vision*, April-May 1996, 21.

18. Wade Clark Roof, *A Generation of Seekers: The Spiritual Journeys of the Baby Boom Generation* (San Francisco: HarperCollins, 1993), 155.

19. Ibid., 119–22.

20. Ibid., 129.

21. Ibid., 131–32.

22. John 14:6.

23. M. Robert Mulholland Jr., *Invitation to a Journey: A Road Map for Spiritual Formation* (Downers Grove, IL: InterVarsity, 1993), 12.

Chapter 7

1. Eric Berne, *Games People Play* (New York: Garden Press, 1964).
2. Thomas A. Harris, *I'm OK—You're OK: A Practical Guide to Transactional Analysis* (New York: Harper & Row, 1967).
3. Stan J. Katz and Aimee E. Liu, *The Codependency Conspiracy* (New York: Warner, 1991), 21.
4. Ephesians 6:10–18.
5. Wade Clark Roof, *A Generation of Seekers: The Spiritual Journeys of the Baby Boom Generation* (San Francisco: HarperCollins, 1993), 30.
6. Ibid.
7. Michael Horton, *In the Face of God: The Dangers and Delights of Spiritual Intimacy* (Dallas: Word, 1996), 39.
8. Roof, *A Generation of Seekers*, 85.
9. A variation of his question has been asked by Horton, *In the Face of God*, 41.
10. Psalm 73 gives an interesting account of a believer who watches unscrupulous, God-rejecting people succeed very well, at least temporarily.
11. 2 Thessalonians 2:9–10. See also Deuteronomy 13:1–3 and Revelation 13:13.
12. Phillip Z., "Does Power of Rational Thinking Connect with Your Inner Core?" *Sober Times*, August 1991, 5.
13. Ibid. The author presents his conclusions with more detail in his book, Phillip Z., *A Skeptic's Guide to 12 Steps* (San Francisco: Harper/Hazelton, 1991).
14. Andrew M. Greeley, *The Catholic Myth: The Behavior and Beliefs of American Catholics* (New York: Scribner's, 1990), 2.
15. Horton, *In the Face of God*, 3, 37.
16. Matthew 7:24–27
17. Matthew 20:26–28 NIV.
18. Gordon MacDonald, *The Life God Blesses: Weathering the Storms of Life That Threaten the Soul* (Nashville: Thomas Nelson, 1994).
19. Ibid., 4.
20. Ibid., 19.
21. This story is told in more detail by two psychologists whose excellent book on clear, nonmagical thinking elaborates the themes stated in the remainder of this chapter. Mark McMinn and James Foster, *Christians in the Crossfire: Guarding Your Mind Against Manipulation and Self-Deception* (Newberg, OR: Barclay Press, 1990), 19–22.
22. See, for example, Vincent E. Barry and Douglas J. Soccio, *Practical Logic*, 3d ed. (New York: Holt, Rinehart, and Winston, 1988), or S. Morris Engel, *With Good Reason: An Introduction to Informal Fallacies*,

2d ed. (New York: St. Martin's, 1982). For a Christian treatment of this subject, see McMinn and Foster, *Christians in the Crossfire,* and Henry A. Virkler, *A Christian's Guide to Critical Thinking* (Nashville: Thomas Nelson, 1993).

23. McMinn and Foster, *Christians in the Crossfire,* 46.
24. William Kirk Kilpatrick, *Psychological Seduction: The Failure of Modern Psychology* (Nashville: Thomas Nelson, 1983), 31.

Chapter 8

1. Richard N. Ostling, "The Church Search," *Time,* 5 April 1993, 44–51.
2. Ibid., 45.
3. Ibid., 48.
4. Romans 3:23–26 NLT.
5. Romans 5:1 NLT.
6. See, for example, Romans 5:3–4.
7. These are the words of Jesus, recorded in Mark 8:34 NLT. See also Matthew 10:38 and Luke 14:27. If you are not familiar with Christian spirituality or the Christian message, consider reading the New Testament book of Mark.
8. Trevor Hudson, *Christ Following: Ten Signposts to Spirituality* (Grand Rapids: Revell, 1996), 24. See Chapter 1 titled "Drawing a Picture of God."
9. Michael Horton, *In the Face of God: The Dangers and Delights of Spiritual Intimacy* (Dallas: Word, 1996), xvii.
10. John 14:9.
11. Brennan Manning, *Lion and Lamb: The Relentless Tenderness of Jesus* (Grand Rapids: Chosen Books, 1986), 24, italics added.
12. Michael Phillips, *A God to Call Father: Discovering Intimacy with God* (Wheaton, IL: Tyndale, 1994), 182. The exact wording of the question as asked by Phillips is, "Can you *live* on the basis of what you say you believe—no matter where you take those beliefs, no matter what they come up against?"
13. John's story and Dr. Hiebert's theory are summarized by Bryant Myers, "Signs and Wonders and the Whole Gospel," *MARC Newsletter,* 96–1 (March 1996): 3–4.
14. David Powlison, *Power Encounters: Reclaiming Spiritual Warfare* (Grand Rapids: Baker, 1995), 13.
15. M. Scott Peck, *People of the Lie* (New York: Simon & Schuster, 1983).
16. For an insightful Christian critique of Peck's writings, including his views of evil, see H. Wayne House and Richard Abanes, *The Less Traveled Road and the Bible: A Scriptural Critique of the Philosophy of M. Scott Peck* (Camp Hill, PA: Horizon Books, 1995).
17. Ephesians 6:12 NIV.
18. 2 Corinthians 11:13–15 NIV.

19. Ephesians 6:11, 13–14. In James 4:7, we are instructed to submit our-
    selves to God and to "resist the devil and he will flee from you"
    (NKJV). We all need to submit to God and then resist Satan. While I
    tend to be critical of flamboyant public confrontations with the devil
    and his forces, especially when they appear to focus more on the
    self-styled deliverer than on Christ, I agree that on occasion, the
    resistance to Satan may involve exorcisms.
20. Matthew 6:13 NKJV.
21. 1 Peter 5:6–9.
22. John Piper, *Future Grace* (Sisters, OR: Multnomah, 1995), 75.
23. Romans 3:23–24 NIV.
24. Ephesians 2:7–9 NIV.
25. Cited by William J. Petersen and Randy Petersen, *The One Year Book
    of Hymns* (Wheaton, IL: Tyndale, 1995), no page number given but
    cited in the daily reading for March 17.
26. This idea is discussed in detail by John Piper in his 448-page book
    Future Grace.
27. Paul Hendrickson, *The Living and the Dead: Robert McNamara and Five
    Lives of a Lost War* (New York: Knopf, 1996).
28. Hudson, *Christ Following*, 97.
29. Ibid., 98. Hudson reminds us of the first three of these.
30. Hebrews 11.
31. Hebrews 12:1–3.
32. 1 Corinthians 12:25–26 NIV.
33. Hebrews 10:25 NIV.
34. Henri J. M. Nouwen, *Reaching Out: The Three Movements of the Spiri-
    tual Life* (Garden City, NY: Doubleday, 1975), 21.
35. Luke 10:1.
36. I don't have any formal guidelines for building friendships like
    these. When I was a professor, I used to invite students to join me for
    coffee, and friendships often followed. Now I ask God to lead me to
    the people he wants me to meet with. I try to show interest in the
    people I encounter and often will suggest, "We ought to have break-
    fast together sometime." Usually this leads to a meeting that may
    lead to deeper relationships. Two additional observations: my wife
    is very supportive of these friendships because they help me grow
    spiritually and she sees that they encourage others. In this age of mis-
    trust, I am cautious that there be no misinterpretation of my motives,
    so I meet mostly with men, my wife meets one-to-one with women.
    Sometimes Julie and I meet together with an individual or another
    couple.

Chapter 9

1. The vision of the dry bones is told in the Old Testament book of
   Ezekiel, chapter 37.

2. John 14:6.
3. John 11:25–26 NKJV.
4. John 6:40 NIV.
5. John 7:43.
6. Donald S. Whitney, *Spiritual Disciplines for the Christian Life* (Colorado Springs, CO: NavPress, 1991), 79–80.
7. Psalm 95:6; Matthew 4:10; 15:8–9.
8. Whitney, *Spiritual Disciplines*, 89–90.
9. Gary Thomas, *Sacred Pathways: Discover Your Soul's Path to God* (Nashville: Thomas Nelson, 1966). "Four elements are essential to every true expression of faith," Thomas writes on page 34. "It is essential that we love God, according to Jesus' words in Mark 12:30, with all our heart (adoration), soul (will), mind (belief), and strength (body)."
10. Psalm 75:6–7 NLT.
11. Psalm 75:5 NLT.
12. The English translation of the book is by Jean Cadier, *The Man God Mastered: A Brief Biography of John Calvin* (London: Inter-Varsity Fellowship, 1960).
13. 2 Peter 1:3–8 NLT.
14. An entire issue of the *Journal of Social Issues* (vol. 51, no. 2, summer 1995) is devoted to articles around the theme "Religious Influences on Personal and Societal Well-Being," but without any efforts to define *wellness* or *well-being*.
15. These characteristics are listed in Galatians 5:22–23 and described as "fruit of the Spirit." They are the inner characteristics of genuine Christian spirituality that grow in the lives of believers who are filled with the Holy Spirit and open to the Spirit's guidance. Of course we don't know if spiritual well-being makes life and health better or, instead, if healthy people are more drawn to spiritual wellness. We do know, however, that spiritual wellness, life satisfaction, physical health, and mental health tend to go together.
16. This paragraph is adapted from Craig Ellison, *From Stress to Well-Being: Counseling to Overcome Stress* (Dallas: Word, 1994). The book contains the Spiritual Well-Being Scale and a test known as the Psychospiritual Needs Inventory.
17. Jon and his wife have given me permission to share their story. I respect their privacy and our relationship enough that I would not have mentioned their suffering without getting their approval of what I have written and their permission to use this story.
18. John S. Feinberg, *Deceived By God? A Journey Through Suffering* (Wheaton, IL: Crossway, 1997), 33. Feinberg's book is a well-written, exceptionally helpful guidebook for those who suffer (and their counselors).

19. This is the theme of a thoughtful book by Alan E. Nelson, *Broken in the Right Place: How God Tames the Soul* (Nashville: Thomas Nelson, 1994).
20. Romans 5:3–5.
21. Michael Horton, *In the Face of God: The Dangers and Delights of Spiritual Intimacy* (Dallas: Word, 1996), 176.
22. 2 Corinthians 1:3–5.
23. Feinberg, *Deceived By God*, 74.
24. Henri J. M. Nouwen, *The Wounded Healer: Ministry in Contemporary Society* (Garden City, NJ: Doubleday, 1972).
25. Ibid., 104.
26. Robert Coleman, *Songs of Heaven* (Old Tappan, NJ: Revell, 1980), 43.
27. Whitney, *Spiritual Disciplines*, 15–16.
28. Herbert Benson with Marg Stark, *Timeless Healing: The Power and Biology of Belief* (New York: Scribner's, 1996).
29. Richard J. Foster, *Celebration of Discipline: The Path to Spiritual Growth*, rev. ed. (San Francisco: Harper & Row, 1988). The first edition of Foster's book, the edition that I read, was published ten years earlier.
30. Siang-Yang Tan and Douglas H. Gregg, *Disciplines of the Holy Spirit: How to Connect with the Spirit's Power and Presence* (Grand Rapids: Zondervan, 1997).
31. Whitney, *Spiritual Disciplines*, 22.

Chapter 10

1. Gerald R. McDermott, *Seeing God: Twelve Reliable Signs of True Spirituality* (Downers Grove, IL: InterVarsity, 1995), 16–18.
2. Ibid., 22. Perry Miller is the historian.
3. Ibid., 11–12.
4. Ibid., 23.
5. I have not mentioned all of the signs described in McDermott's book. I have taken the liberty of combining several of the signs and rephrasing some to make a more concise (and surely less complete) list than Edwards and McDermott proposed.
6. Hebrews 11:1 NIV, italics added.
7. Micah 6:8.
8. McDermott, *Seeing God*, 74, 76.
9. David Hazard, "Seeing More of God," *Discipleship Journal* 15, no. 1 (January-February 1995): 46.
10. John 12:19.
11. John 12:23, 28 NIV, italics added.
12. John 14:9.
13. 1 Peter 1:15–16.
14. John 17:4 NIV.
15. John 14:31 NIV.
16. Psalm 104:33 NKJV.

17. Galatians 6:10; Hebrews 13:16.
18. Romans 12:1.
19. Colossians 3:23–24.
20. John 15:8.
21. Galatians 5:22.
22. John 17:20–25.
23. 1 Peter 1:6–7.
24. Isaiah 42:12.

Index